FROM EMPEROR TO CITIZEN

—The Autobiography of Aisin-Gioro Pu Yi

VOLUME ONE

FOREIGN LANGUAGES PRESS
PEKING

First Edition 1964
Second Printing 1983

Translated by
W. J. F. JENNER

ISBN 0-8351-1159-8

Published by the Foreign Languages Press
24 Paiwanchuang Road, Peking, China
Printed by the Foreign Languages Printing House
19 West Chekungchuang Road, Peking, China
Distributed by China Publications Centre (Guoji Shudian)
P.O. Box 399, Peking, China
Printed in the People's Republic of China

Contents

CHAPTER ONE

MY FAMILY

My Grandfather Prince Chun

I was born in Peking in the mansion of Prince Chun on February 7, 1906. My grandfather Yi Huan, the seventh son of Emperor Tao Kuang (reigned 1821-50), was the first Prince Chun. Although my father was only his fifth son he inherited the title as the eldest, third and fourth sons died in childhood and the second son was taken into the palace to become the emperor Kuang Hsu (reigned 1875-1908). I was the eldest son of the second Prince Chun. I was nearly three when on November 13, 1908 the empress dowager Tzu Hsi suddenly decided to make me the heir to the throne as she and the emperor Kuang Hsu lay seriously ill. I became the adopted son of Emperor Tung Chih (reigned 1862-74) and the ritual heir of his cousin Kuang Hsu. Within two days of my entering the palace both Kuang Hsu and the Empress Dowager were dead. On December 2 I ascended the imperial throne as the tenth ruler of the Ching Dynasty[1] and the last emperor of China. Before three years were out the 1911 Revolution against the Ching Dynasty broke out and I abdicated.

My earliest memories are of the time of my abdication, but to make things clearer it would be best to start with my grandfather and my family.

In that blackest of eras, the late Ching Dynasty, the family of Prince Chun were for half a century the faithful servants of the empress dowager Tzu Hsi, and my grandfather in particular devoted his life to her service.

My grandfather was born in 1842 and died in 1890. Looking through the records of the imperial family one can see that he received few honours during the eleven-year reign of his brother, Emperor

---

[1] (1644-1911), a dynasty set up by the Aisin-Gioro clan of the Manchus, a people who originated in the Northeast of China.

Hsien Feng (reigned 1851-61), but that in the six months or so after Hsien Feng's death, when Tzu Hsi had just been made Empress Dowager, he was suddenly loaded with titles and positions.

The obvious reason why a young man of twenty was able to attain such eminence was that his wife's sister had become an empress dowager; but it was not the only reason. I remember that when I was young I heard an anecdote about how during a theatrical performance at home an uncle of mine, then six years old, was so terrified by one scene that he started to cry. My grandfather shouted at him in front of everybody, "What disgraceful behaviour! When I was twenty I captured Su Shun with my own hands, but if you go on like that you'll never be able to handle affairs of state." The capture of Su Shun had been the real beginning of his meteoric rise.

The Su Shun affair took place in 1861. The Second Opium War[1] had ended with a series of humiliating treaties and the emperor Hsien Feng lay mortally ill in his refuge in Jehol. He summoned to his deathbed three Ministers of the Presence and five Grand Councillors who had accompanied him in his flight, and having made his six-year-old son Tsai Chun heir to the throne, he appointed them as a regency council. The next day Hsien Feng died, and in accordance with his wishes the eight princes and high officials put Tsai Chun on the throne with the reign title Chi Hsiang and took all power into their own hands.

The most important of the eight regents were two princes and Su Shun, an Assistant Grand Secretary and President of the Board of Revenue who had earned the hatred of the Manchu nobility by promoting many officials of Han nationality and had a reputation for ruthlessness. A more basic reason for Su Shun's later disastrous fall was that his group underestimated the strength of Prince Kung (Yi Hsin), who had made the most of the unpleasant assignment of negotiating peace after the Second Opium War: in concluding the

---

[1] From 1856 to 1860 Britain and France jointly carried on a war of aggression against China. The Ching government was then devoting all its energy to suppressing the peasant revolution of the Taiping Heavenly Kingdom and adopted a policy of passive resistance towards the foreign aggressors, with the result that China suffered a disastrous defeat.

unprecedentedly humiliating Treaty of Peking he had won the admiration of the foreigners. As an uncle of the emperor with foreign support he was not prepared to take second place to Su Shun and his party, and he was encouraged by the Manchu nobility and other high officials who had long been Su Shun's political enemies. Just at this moment an edict was brought in secret from the two dowagers in Jehol.

One of the dowagers was the lady Niuhulu, who had been the empress of Hsien Feng and was later given the title Empress Dowager Tzu An; she was also known as the Eastern Dowager. The other was Empress Dowager Tzu Hsi, or the Western Dowager. Tzu Hsi had originally been a palace concubine. When pregnant she had been promoted to be a Secondary Consort, and as her child Tsai Chun was the only son of Emperor Hsien Feng she became an empress dowager when he succeeded to his father's throne. I do not know how it was managed, but as soon as she was made an empress dowager one of the censors memorialized requesting that the two dowagers should act as joint regents. This proposal met with the fiercest opposition from Su Shun and his fellow-regents on the grounds that there was absolutely no precedent for anything of the kind in the history of the dynasty. This did not worry the dowager Tzu An, who was completely without ambition, but it aroused Tzu Hsi's bitter resentment. First she persuaded Tzu An that the eight regents were untrustworthy conspirators and then she got Tzu An's consent to a secret letter being sent to Prince Kung summoning him to the palace in Jehol to discuss how to deal with them. To consolidate their newly gained power the eight regents tried every method to keep Prince Kung in Peking and the dowagers in Jehol apart.

There are a number of different stories about how the dowagers managed to dodge Su Shun's agents and make contact with Prince Kung. Some say that the dowagers' decree was secretly carried by a cook to Peking, while others maintain that Tzu Hsi had a favourite eunuch, An Te-hai, given a public thrashing and then sent to Peking to be dealt with by the court, thus enabling him to take the edict to the capital. Anyhow, the edict reached Prince Kung, and as soon

5

as he received it he submitted a memorial asking for an audience with the emperor. Su Shun's party tried to block this with an "imperial edict" saying that it was "most important" that he should "stay in his post", but they did not succeed. Su Shun then attempted to prevent him from meeting the dowagers by invoking the old rule of behaviour that a man should not meet his sisters-in-law, but this too failed.

There are many different accounts of how Prince Kung and the dowagers met. One story is that Prince Kung disguised himself as a *shaman* (a kind of wizard) and another is that he checkmated Su Shun by saying to him that it would be proper for him to meet his sisters-in-law if Su Shun were present to supervise the occasion; Su Shun was completely nonplussed and had to abandon his attempts at obstruction. Yet another story is that when Prince Kung went to sacrifice to the memorial tablet of the late emperor the dowager Tzu Hsi had a trusted eunuch bring him a bowl of noodles in which was hidden an edict written by Tzu Hsi. Whatever method was in fact used, the result was that Prince Kung and the dowagers were able to discuss everything.

When the dowagers returned to the capital Prince Kung was given a new title and the eight regents were arrested. The two princes among them were allowed to commit suicide, Su Shun was decapitated, and the others among them were either sent into exile or imprisoned. The new emperor's reign title was changed to Tung Chih and the forty-seven years of rule by Tzu Hsi had begun. My grandfather's great achievement in this *coup* was to arrest Su Shun at Panpitien as he was escorting the coffin of the dead emperor back to the capital, and this was why he received so many honours.

During the reign of Emperor Tung Chih he was further elevated until, when Kuang Hsu came to the throne, he was given an additional honour by which his title of prince could be inherited by his successors in perpetuity when normally titles went down one grade with each generation. During the reign of Kuang Hsu, Prince Kung lost favour a number of times but my grandfather continued to be heaped with honours until he seemed to have reached the very pinnacle of human glory.

6

In the Chun mansion I saw many scrolls of moral maxims in my grandfather's own handwriting hanging in the rooms of each of his sons and grandsons. There was one pair of scrolls which read

Wealth and Fortune breed more Fortune
Royal Favours bring more Favours.

At the time I thought that my grandfather must have been a very contented man, but now I see things differently and even think that he meant something else when he scolded his son during the theatricals.

If the twenty-one-year-old Prince Chun had been rather raw and inexperienced the Prince Chun who had lived through the thirteen years of the Tung Chih reign should certainly have learnt enough. As a member of the royal family he must have known a lot more than outsiders did about the deaths of the emperor Tung Chih and his empress and must have been more deeply affected by it.

In popular romances it is said that Tung Chih died of venereal disease, but from what I have heard the cause of his death was smallpox, and the diary of an eminent official of the time confirms this. Smallpox is not an incurably fatal disease, but while he was suffering from it Tung Chih received a shock which "made the pustules burst inwards" so that his condition became hopeless and he died. One day Tung Chih's empress went to visit him on his sickbed and burst into tears as she asked him why her mother-in-law, the dowager Tzu Hsi, was always scolding her. Tung Chih begged her to put up with it patiently, saying that some time in the future she would have her day. Tzu Hsi, who had never liked this daughter-in-law of hers, had long ago set informers to watch over her son and her daughter-in-law, and when she heard that the empress had gone to visit Tung Chih she herself went and stood outside his room to eavesdrop on them. Unaware of the disaster their few words of private conversation had brought about, they saw Tzu Hsi rush into the room in a flaming temper. She grabbed the empress by the hair and started to beat her mercilessly, and shouted instructions for palace officials to prepare rods. Tung Chih fainted from horror, and so Tzu Hsi did not have to carry out the beating. Once Tung Chih was dead Tzu Hsi put all the blame for his decease onto the empress and gave orders that her consumption of food and drink should be restricted. Two months later the empress died of her privations.

During Tung Chih's life it was an open secret that he got on very badly with his mother, Tzu Hsi. When I lived in the palace an old eunuch told me that when Tung Chih went to pay his respects to the eastern dowager Tzu An he used to stay there and talk with her for a while, but that to his own mother he said nothing. Even during the period when Tung Chih was himself ruling the Eastern Dowager took little interest in affairs of state whereas Tzu Hsi had already built up her own group of trusted supporters at court; the emperor could get hardly anything done without first consulting her. This was the real reason for the bad relations between mother and son. Tzu Hsi had a very highly developed lust for power and was most unwilling to abandon any power that came into her hands. From her point of view the principles of moral conduct and the ancestral code existed to suit her needs, and she was certainly not prepared to let them inhibit her. Whether it was her own flesh and blood, her in-laws or palace officials, the same principle applied: those who obeyed her flourished and those who crossed her were doomed. After the death of the emperor Tung Chih she revealed her true nature even more clearly; and it was because my grandfather had understood her character well that he almost went out of his wits with terror at the news that his son was being summoned to the palace to be emperor. An official who was present at that imperial council meeting wrote in his diary that when Tzu Hsi proclaimed Tsai Tien as the future emperor Kuang Hsu, my grandfather "beat his head on the floor and wept bitterly before falling to the ground in a faint. He was unable to rise even with support. . . ."

According to the ancestral code, a close relation of the generation below Tung Chih's should have been his heir, but this would have ended Tzu Hsi's regency as she would no longer have been the emperor's mother, so she overruled all protests and appointed her

8

nephew Tsai Tien, although he was of the same generation as Tung Chih, adopting him as her son.

From then on my grandfather had the curious experience of having honours showered on him by Tzu Hsi while he declined them, and when his son the emperor Kuang Hsu entered the palace he resigned all his offices, though he was unable to renounce his rank of hereditary prince. For several years after that his only duty was to supervise the emperor's studies. After Prince Kung fell from favour he was entrusted with very important offices by Tzu Hsi, but he remained exceedingly cautious, filling his house with inscriptions, scrolls and other objects to remind himself and his family of the dangers of being too great. In 1876, the second year of the reign of his son Kuang Hsu, he submitted a memorial as a counterplea to a hypothetical proposal in which he said that someone might in the future cite precedents from history to suggest giving him very great honours as the father of the sovereign. He was afraid that such honours would arouse Tzu Hsi's jealousy and put him in a dangerous position. A few years later this did in fact happen, and the empress dowager Tzu Hsi was so angry that the proposer retired from politics for three years.

There can be no doubt that from the time Kuang Hsu entered the palace onwards my grandfather must have got to know the character of his sister-in-law Tzu Hsi even better. During Kuang Hsu's reign (1874-1908) her temper became even more unpredictable. Once a eunuch who was playing chess with her said, "Your slave is killing this knight of the venerable ancestor." At this she flew into a rage and, announcing that she would kill his whole family, she had him dragged out and beaten to death. She treasured her hair very greatly; one day a eunuch who was combing it for her found a strand of it in the comb. In his panic the eunuch tried to conceal it but she saw what he was doing in a mirror and he too was beaten. The eunuchs who used to serve Tzu Hsi told me that all of them except her favourite Li Lien-ying used to be frightened when their turn came to be in attendance on her. As Tzu Hsi grew older she developed a facial tic and she hated people to notice it. When one eunuch had been looking at it for a little too long she

9

asked him what he was staring at; he could find no answer and was given several scores of strokes of the heavy rod. Another eunuch who had heard about this did not dare so much as to look up when he went on duty but she flared up at this too: "Why are you keeping your head down?" He could not think of anything to say either and suffered a similar punishment. Apart from the eunuchs, the palace women were often beaten as well.

For eunuchs to be flogged and even to die of it was nothing unusual in Peking's princely households and affairs of this sort were quite possibly not very shocking to my grandfather, but the sudden death of the eastern dowager Tzu An in 1881 must have seemed certainly something out of the ordinary even to him. It is said that Emperor Hsien Feng was worried before he died that when his Secondary Consort Yi (the future Tzu Hsi) was made an empress dowager as the mother of the next emperor she would make the most of her position to wield power and that his empress, later the Eastern Dowager, would be no match for her. He therefore left a special edict written in vermilion ink giving his empress the authority to control Tzu Hsi when necessary. The inexperienced Eastern Dowager, who had been brought up in a noble family and lacked worldly wisdom, once casually revealed this to Tzu Hsi. From then on Tzu Hsi spent all her time making up to her until the Eastern Dowager finally burnt Hsien Feng's testament before her eyes.

Shortly after that the Eastern Dowager died a sudden death in the palace. Some say that she ate some cakes sent her by Tzu Hsi and others that she drank some soup that Tzu Hsi had prepared with her own hands. There can be no doubt but that it was a great shock to Prince Chun as after this he was even more cautious than ever, regarding winning the trust and favour of Tzu Hsi as his sole duty.

When he was made responsible for the founding of a navy my grandfather misappropriated a large part of the funds to build the Summer Palace as a pleasure park for the Empress Dowager. The busiest stage in the building of the Summer Palace coincided with exceptionally heavy floods around Peking and in what is now Hopei Province, but a censor who suggested that work should be temporarily

suspended to avoid provoking the flood victims into making trouble
was stripped of his office and handed over to the appropriate
authorities to be dealt with. Prince Chun, however, said nothing
and worked his hardest to get the job finished. When the Summer
Palace was completed in 1890 he died. Four years later the so-called
navy he had created came to a disastrous end in the Sino-Japanese
War, and the marble boat in the Summer Palace was the only one
left of all the vessels on which so many tens of millions of taels
(ounces of silver) had been spent.

My Maternal Grandfather Jung Lu

My paternal grandfather Prince Chun had four wives, who bore
him seven sons and three daughters. Three sons and one daughter
survived him, of whom the oldest was my father who inherited his
title at the age of eight. From then onwards my family received
new "fortune and favour", and these, like the hardships and hu-
miliations suffered by the Chinese people, were all connected with
Tzu Hsi.

One major event was the marriage that Tzu Hsi arranged for
my father, an event that could be regarded as a product of the *coup*
of 1898 and the Yi Ho Tuan[1] affair of 1900. In the first place, it
was an honour conferred on her loyal servant Jung Lu for the great
services he had done her in 1898, a year in which he played a large
part in defeating the attempts of a group of reformers to eliminate
the influence of Tzu Hsi and modernize the monarchy.

Jung Lu, my maternal grandfather, was a Manchu bannerman who
was an expert political climber who would use any means to win
the favour and confidence of Tzu Hsi. He was a close friend
of her favourite eunuch Li Lien-ying, and his wife ingratiated herself

---

[1] The Yi Ho Tuan (Righteous Harmony Corps) were generally known as "Boxers"
in the West.

with the dowager so successfully that she was often called to the palace to keep her company and chat with her; he was therefore able to get an even more expert knowledge of the workings of her mind. Aware as he was of the bad relations between Tzu Hsi and Kuang Hsu he fully understood how this could affect his own future and was naturally more willing than ever to advise Tzu Hsi.

When Emperor Kuang Hsu issued a series of edicts in 1898 ordering political reforms, others who had been dismissed from office or were afraid that they were going to be squeezed out were reduced to helpless tears, but Jung Lu had already worked out a plan for Tzu Hsi. Jung Lu was the head of the group known as the "dowager's party" that was in power while Weng Tung-ho, the emperor's former tutor, headed the "emperor's party" that had no real power. It was through Weng Tung-ho's privileged position as an imperial tutor that the reformers were able to make contact with the emperor. Tzu Hsi followed the pre-arranged plan and forced Kuang Hsu to send Weng Tung-ho into retirement, and within a few days of his departure from Peking Jung Lu was given a grand secretaryship and made Viceroy of the metropolitan province of Chihli with command over the armies round the capital.

With the Reform Movement of 1898 Jung Lu finally got the chance he had been waiting for to strip the emperor Kuang Hsu of his power and put the country back into the hands of Tzu Hsi. Previously he had made a plan to carry out a *coup* when Tzu Hsi and Kuang Hsu inspected the new Peiyang (Northern) Army at Tientsin. When Kuang Hsu learnt of this plot he sent a secret message to the reformers asking them to think of a way to save him.

The reformers and the emperor foolishly put their trust in a subordinate of Jung Lu's named Yuan Shih-kai, an official who was in control of the New Army, an up-to-date military force, and brought him into their plot to execute Jung Lu and imprison Tzu Hsi when they went to inspect his troops at Tientsin. Yuan Shih-kai agreed to co-operate with them and then betrayed them by going straight to Jung Lu and telling him the whole story. On hearing the news Jung Lu took a train back from Tientsin and hastened to the Summer Palace to report to Tzu Hsi. The result was that the emperor was imprisoned, Tan Sze-tung and five other reformers were executed, their leader Kang Yu-wei fled to Japan, and the brief hundred days of reform was over. As another of the reformers, Liang Chi-chao, wrote, my maternal grandfather Jung Lu "combined in his person the highest civil and military offices and his power was greater than that of the court itself." In the words of the *Draft History of the Ching Dynasty*, "he had won the Empress Dowager's trust and devotion and he had no peer at that time. Everything, whether great or small, was decided by his word."

In the calamitous year of 1900, when Tzu Hsi used the Yi Ho Tuan to kill the foreigners and then used the foreigners to kill the Yi Ho Tuan, Jung Lu went even further in showing his loyalty to her. After the 1898 *coup* Tzu Hsi wanted to be rid of Kuang Hsu, and when one attempt to kill him under pretext of an invented illness was uncovered she decided first to appoint a successor to the previous emperor, Tung Chih, before deposing Kuang Hsu. She invited all the foreign envoys to come and offer their congratulations and show their support. They refused to come, and it is now quite clear that this refusal was not based on any personal disapproval of Tzu Hsi's character; it was because the ministers of Britain, France, America and Japan did not want to see an inordinate growth in the power of the pro-Tsarist Russia "dowager's party". Before this Tzu Hsi had never dared to provoke the foreigners. When they had slaughtered the Chinese people or seized the country's wealth it had meant little to her, but now that they were protecting the leading reformer Kang Yu-wei and blocking her plans to depose the emperor and appoint a new heir to the throne they were directly opposing her rule. This was more than she could possibly tolerate. Jung Lu advised her not on any account to provoke the foreigners but rather to think things over very calmly: it would be best not to be too explicit about the new heir's title. She followed his suggestion and changed his title to "Ta-ah-ko". The heir's father, wanting to see his son become emperor, joined with some other princes and high officials to propose another plan to Tzu Hsi: to use the anti-foreign Yi Ho Tuan to crush the foreigners and thus kill two birds with one stone.

The Yi Ho Tuan were the Ching court's biggest headache. Mistreated and oppressed by the foreign churches, the common people had received no protection from the court, which even joined with the foreigners in repressing them. Armed struggle had therefore broken out and Yi Ho Tuan were formed in various parts of the country under the slogan of "Eliminate the foreigners". In the course of their struggles the Yi Ho Tuan became a powerful armed force which was able to rout all the troops which the court sent against them. The question facing Tzu Hsi was whether to "exterminate" or whether to "conciliate" them. One group at court, including the father of the heir, advocated conciliating them for a time so that they could be used to drive out the foreigners who were interfering in the question of the succession. Another group, completely opposed to this in the belief that it would be bound to have disastrous consequences, urged that the Yi Ho Tuan should be exterminated.

Just when the supporters of the two policies were deadlocked Tzu Hsi received an urgent but unconfirmed intelligence report that the violent actions of foreigners in different parts of the country were intended to force her to hand power back to the emperor. This put an end to her hesitations as in a terrible rage she ordered that the Yi Ho Tuan were to be "won over" and that the foreign legations in Peking were to be attacked. Money from the imperial privy purse was given to the Yi Ho Tuan and rewards were offered for the heads of foreigners. As an additional earnest of her determination she had the leading advocates of exterminating the Yi Ho Tuan decapitated.

When the attack on the legations had failed, the coastal defences at Taku and the city of Tientsin had fallen and the allied armies of the foreigners were approaching Peking, Tzu Hsi changed her tactics. She started communicating secretly with the foreigners and sent emissaries to make contact with the legations while the fighting was still going on. When Peking fell she fled to Sian, and in order to show that she had not been the one to initiate resistance to the foreigners she had some of the leading supporters of the policy of "conciliating" the Yi Ho Tuan beheaded.

Throughout these changes of policy Jung Lu did all he could to keep himself out of trouble. Taking his cue from Tzu Hsi's behaviour he never went against her wishes and at the same time he prepared a line of retreat for her. When obeying her command to send soldiers to attack the barracks of the foreign troops in the Legation Quarter he did not issue them with artillery shells and even discreetly sent fruit to the foreigners as a token of his concern. After the armies of the eight foreign powers had entered Peking and Tzu Hsi had fled, Jung Lu proposed the single principle to which the officials responsible for negotiating the peace were to hold: any conditions could be accepted provided that Tzu Hsi was not held responsible for the affair and the emperor was not returned to power. Thus a treaty was signed in 1901 by which China had to pay an indemnity of a billion taels (including interest) and the foreign powers were allowed to station troops in the capital. Jung Lu was rewarded for these services with many fresh honours among which was the marriage Tzu Hsi arranged between his daughter and the second Prince Chun.

I was told later by some older members of the household that the marriage between my parents was very deliberately planned by Tzu Hsi. She had been rather suspicious of the family of Prince Chun ever since the *coup* of 1898 and someone suggested to her that the growth of a tall gingko tree on the tomb of the first Prince Chun implied, through a kind of wordplay on the name of the tree and the Chinese word for "prince", that his family would produce an emperor. On hearing this Tzu Hsi at once gave orders for the tree to be felled. But the real reason for her suspicion of the family was the interest shown by the foreigners in Kuang Hsu and his brothers. Before the events of 1900 she felt that in being partial to Kuang Hsu the terrible foreigners were extremely impolite to her. After 1900 the commander of the allied armies asked the emperor's brother to go to Germany as representative to apologize for the killing of the German minister during the troubles. The splendid reception accorded my father by the German Kaiser caused the Empress Dowager considerable uneasiness and strengthened her suspicions. Connecting her faithful henchman Jung Lu with the family of Prince Chun through marriage was the solution she eventually found to this dangerous problem. Tzu Hsi was a person who would devote the greatest pains to dealing with any situation that posed the slightest threat to her security: she had Kuang Hsu's Pearl Consort drowned in a well before her flight in 1900 out of fear that she might cause trouble for her later. In any circumstances, her first consideration was always the protection of her own rule. Thus it was that my father received the edict arranging his marriage almost as soon as he came back from Germany and reported on the "courteous reception" he had received there.

Tzu Hsi's Decision

After 1900 the father of the heir to the throne was one of those held responsible for the troubles of that year and his son was therefore stripped of the title. The question of the succession was not openly raised for another seven years.

In November 1908 Tzu Hsi contracted dysentery while celebrating her seventy-third birthday at the Summer Palace. After lying ill for ten days she suddenly made the decision to appoint a new heir, and in the course of the next two days the emperor Kuang Hsu and she herself both died. The day before the emperor died my father was summoned to court and appointed Prince Regent and I was taken into the palace. The next day, November 14, I became emperor-designate, and Tzu Hsi announced in an edict that my father was to consult her in his administration of all state affairs.

In the previous few years Tzu Hsi had been putting ever increasing power into the hands of Yuan Shih-kai, the unscrupulous Han official who had played such a vital role in the defeat of the reformers in 1898, but at the same time his control of the modern Peiyang Army and his opportunism caused her a great deal of concern. She was also worried by the close relationship that existed between Yuan

Shih-kai and Prince Ching (Yi Kuang), an ambitious Manchu who had started as a low-ranking noble and become a prince of the first rank and the leading Grand Councillor. In an attempt to curb their power she tried unsuccessfully to dismiss Prince Ching and in 1907 gave Yuan Shih-kai a nominal promotion that made him give up his command over the Peiyang Army.

Tzu Hsi fully understood that she could not end Yuan Shih-kai's actual control over the Peiyang Army at once and that the relations between Yuan and Prince Ching could not be broken in a moment. She herself fell ill just when she was planning her next move, and on her sickbed she received a piece of shocking news: Yuan Shih-kai was planning to depose Kuang Hsu and install the son of Prince Ching in his place. Despite Prince Ching's skill in dealing with foreigners and in flattering her, despite all that Yuan Shih-kai had done for her, and despite the fact that the target of their plan was the emperor Kuang Hsu whom she hated so deeply, she was at once aware of the threat that this plot posed to the Aisin-Gioro dynasty and to herself. She made up her mind very quickly. She sent Prince Ching on a mission outside the capital and moved one unit of the Peiyang Army out of Peking, replacing it with a more reliable one. By the time Prince Ching came back to Peking I had already become heir to the throne and my father had been made Prince Regent. To keep the loyalty of Prince Ching, who had so many foreign friends, she made his title of prince hereditary in perpetuity.

I once heard from an old eunuch about the suspicious circumstances of Kuang Hsu's death. According to his story Kuang Hsu was fairly well on the day before his death and what made him seriously ill was a dose of medicine he took. Later it was discovered that this medicine had been sent by Yuan Shih-kai. The normal practice when an emperor was ill was for copies of the prescriptions and diagnoses of the Grand Physicians to be given to each of the senior officials of the Imperial Household Department or, in the case of a serious illness, to all the members of the Grand Council. I was later told by a descendant of one of the Household Department officials that before his death Kuang Hsu was only suffering from an ordinary case of flu; he had seen the diagnosis himself, and it had said that Kuang Hsu's pulse was normal. Moreover he had been seen in his room standing and talking as if he were healthy, so that people were very shocked to hear that he was seriously ill. What was even stranger was that within four hours of this came the news of his death. All in all, Kuang Hsu's death was very suspicious. If the eunuch's story is true it is further proof that there was a conspiracy, and a deep-laid one at that, between Yuan Shih-kai and Prince Ching.

Another tradition is that when Tzu Hsi realized that her illness was fatal she murdered Kuang Hsu rather than die before him. This is possible, but I do not believe that she thought herself fatally ill on the day she proclaimed me successor to the throne. Two hours after Kuang Hsu's death she commanded my father, the Prince Regent, "You shall administer all affairs of state in accordance with my instructions." It was not till the next day that she said, "Now my condition is critical and I fear that I may never recover. In future all affairs of state are to be decided by the Regent. When there are important matters on which he requires direction from the Empress Dowager [Kuang Hsu's empress, a niece of Tzu Hsi's], the Prince Regent shall appear before her and ask her instructions before dealing with them." The reason why she chose such a regent as my father and such a successor to the throne as myself was that she did not realize at the time that she was going to die as soon as she in fact did. As Grand Empress Dowager (the title given to the grandmother of an emperor) she would not have been able to rule on the emperor's behalf, but with a docile Prince Regent between herself and the child emperor she could still have had everything her own way.

Of course, she can have been under no illusions that she was going to live for ever, and she must have regarded making this choice as doing all she could to protect the throne of the Aisin-Gioro clan. She may even have thought that her choice was right because the regent she chose was a brother of Kuang Hsu. It would have been quite natural to think that only a man in his position would not be hoodwinked by Yuan Shih-kai.

My Father's Regency

It was only during the last of the three years during which I was emperor and my father was regent that I got to know him, when he came to inspect my lessons shortly after I had begun to study. When a eunuch came in to report that "His Royal Highness" was coming, my tutor became very tense and hastily tidied the desk while explaining to me how I should behave with him. Then he told me to stand up and wait. A moment later a beardless stranger wearing a peacock feather in his hat appeared in the doorway of the study and stood stiffly before me. This was my father. I greeted him in the standard way and we sat down together. I picked up my book and started to read aloud as my tutor had instructed me.

I got stuck after the first two sentences as I was feeling flustered, but fortunately my father was even more nervous than I was and he kept nodding his head and mumbling:

"Good, good, very good, Your Majesty. Study hard, study hard!" He nodded a few more times then got up and went. He had only spent two minutes with me.

So now I knew what my father looked like: unlike my teacher he had no beard, his face was unwrinkled and the peacock feather at the back of his head was always shaking. He used to make a visit every two months, but he never stayed longer than two minutes. I also discovered that he had something of a stutter and realized that the reason his peacock feather shook was that he was always nodding his head. He said very little, and apart from "good, good, good" it was very indistinct.

My brother once heard my mother say that when my father resigned his regency after the 1911 Revolution[1] he went straight home from the palace and said to her, "From today onwards I can

---

[1] On October 10 of that year, a section of the New Army, at the urging of the revolutionary societies of the bourgeoisie and petty bourgeoisie, staged an uprising in Wuchang. This was followed by uprisings in other provinces, and the Ching Dynasty soon collapsed.

stay at home and hug my children." My mother was so angry at his light-hearted mood that she was reduced to tears; later she said to my brother, "Don't be like your father when you grow up!" This story and a couplet that my father once wrote out — "To have books is real wealth, to be at leisure is half-way to being an immortal" — show that while he did not have any genuine wish to "withdraw from the world" he did find his three years as regent a great strain. Those three years could be regarded as the three most unsuccessful years of his life.

From his own point of view his most fundamental failure was that he was unable to do away with Yuan Shih-kai. There is a story that his brother Kuang Hsu told him of his heartfelt wish and gave him an edict with the four words "Kill Yuan Shih-kai" written in vermilion ink, but as far as I know this meeting never took place. Although the Prince Regent wanted to kill Yuan to avenge his brother, he was prevented from doing so by a group of Grand Councillors with Prince Ching at their head. There is no way of knowing the details about this, but there was one remark of Prince Ching's which discouraged my father: "There would be no problem about killing Yuan Shih-kai, but what would happen if the Peiyang Army mutinied?" The result was that the new empress dowager, Lung Yu, let Yuan off by sending him home to nurse his "foot ailment".

At that time many people offered my father conflicting advice on how to deal with Yuan Shih-kai, some doing their utmost to defend him and others trying to eliminate him. The question of whether to kill or to support Yuan was not a struggle between reformers and conservatives or between the former "emperor's party" and "dowager's party"; nor was it one between Manchus on the one side and Hans on the other it was rather a power struggle between two groups of nobility and senior officials. The cabinet of the time, which was composed mostly of the members of the royal family, was divided into one faction headed by Prince Ching and another headed by Tsai Tse, a duke. It was principally this latter group that suggested policies to my father and wanted to win power. Caught in the middle of the fighting my father would take the advice first of one side then of another, agree with both and do nothing, thus satisfying nobody.

The people he found it hardest to deal with were Prince Ching and Tsai Tse. Before Tzu Hsi's death Prince Ching had been the leading Grand Councillor and after her death he became premier of the newly organized cabinet to the great indignation of Tsai Tse, the President of the Board of Revenue and Finance, who took every opportunity to denigrate his rival before the regent. But if Tzu Hsi had been incapable of removing Prince Ching, what chance did the Prince Regent stand? So although my father often agreed with Tsai Tse's suggestions he was incapable of acting on them and Prince Ching always came out on top. Yet Tsai Tse's defeats were really defeats for himself while Prince Ching's victories were really triumphs for Yuan Shih-kai living in his hometown in mock retirement. Although my father was aware of this there was nothing he could do about it.

In 1911 the Wuchang rising[1] suddenly erupted and the armies under a Manchu commander sent to put it down were defeated. Under irresistible pressure from Prince Ching and his associates my father had to call Yuan Shih-kai back from his retirement and give him the supreme military command.

My father was not a complete fool. One lesson he had learnt from the Kaiser during his trip to Germany was that the royal family had to control the army and that its members had to become army officers. He accordingly put his brother in charge of the palace guard, founded a special army under the royal family, and put other relations in charge of the navy and the army general staff. It is said that my father intended to eliminate Yuan Shih-kai whether he succeeded in putting down the rising or not. Whatever happened, he was not going to leave the armed forces in Han hands, least of all those of Yuan Shih-kai. But my father's plans were too impractical, and even his own brothers shook their heads over his incompetence.

When my grandmother was suffering from an ulcer of the breast which Chinese traditional doctors had been unable to cure he called

---

[1] The rising that sparked off the 1911 Revolution.

in a French doctor on his brothers' advice. The doctor wanted to operate, but as this was opposed by the whole family the only thing he could do was to apply ointment. Before doing so he lit a spirit lamp to sterilize his instruments. This gave my father a terrible fright and he asked the interpreter:

"Wha . . . what's he doing? Is he going to burn the old lady?"

Seeing how ignorant he was an uncle of mine signalled to the interpreter not to translate this question.

The doctor left some medicine for her and went. He was surprised to discover on a later visit that the old lady's condition had not improved at all and asked to see the box of ointment that he had left the previous time. My father fetched it himself: the original seal was unbroken. Once again, my uncles could not help shaking their heads and sighing.

After the death of Tzu Hsi everyone in my father's household called themselves reformers. From the details of my father's daily life one can see how in some ways he opposed superstition and was if favour of modernization. He did not reject the things that the old officials regarded as strange and improper contraptions. He was the first of the princes to have a motor-car or to install a telephone in his house. His household were the first to have their queues cut off, and he was the first of the princes and the nobility to wear Western clothing. But how far his real understanding of things Western went can be illustrated by the way he wore Western clothes. When he had been wearing them for a number of days he asked a brother of mine sadly: "Why do your shirts fit so well while mine are always longer than my jacket?" When my brother had a look he found that he was wearing his shirt outside his trousers and that he had been putting up with this discomfort for days.

He drove out some witches who had come to cure an illness of my grandmother's, and once kicked a hedgehog, an animal which the servants held in superstitious awe, into the gutter — though after doing so his face went deathly pale. He was against worshipping the gods and Buddhist chanting, but every time a new year or a festival came round he would be very conscientious about burning incense and making offerings.

I looked through my father's diary in the hope of understanding more about his three years of regency. There was not much useful material in it, though there were two interesting types of entries. One referred to conventional behaviour; for example, every May it would always say "Had my hair cut short as usual" and every August "Started to let my hair grow as usual." There were also entries about the different kinds of clothes he wore at different times of year in accordance with custom and the kinds of fresh food he ate. The other interesting kind of entry was detailed records of the movements of the heavenly bodies and summaries of what the newspapers carried on astronomy. There was a strong contrast between his jejune daily life and the enthusiasm he had for astronomy. Had he been a man of the present age he might have become an astronomer; but as it was he lived in that family and in that society and became a prince of the royal clan at the age of nine.

A Prince's Household

I had four grandmothers altogether. The principal wife of the first Prince Chun, the lady Yehonala, who was not my real grandmother, died ten years before I was born. I was told that this old lady was not at all like her sister, the empress dowager Tzu Hsi; she adhered rigidly to the conventional morality. When Tzu Hsi continued to watch theatricals as usual after the death of the emperor Tung Chih she would have nothing to do with it. Although she obeyed the summons to go to the palace for the performances she kept both of her eyes shut tight as she sat in front of the stage. When Tzu Hsi asked her why, she replied without even opening her eyes, "This is a time of national mourning; I cannot watch drama." Tzu Hsi was nonplussed. Many words were taboo to her and the members of her household had to be very careful in their speech, particularly with such words as "finished" or "dead". Throughout her life she was a devout Buddhist and would not go into the garden in the summer, saying that she was afraid of trampling any ants to death. Yet although she was so benevolent towards ants she was merciless when it came to beating servants. It was said that the incurable facial tic of one of the family's eunuchs was the result of a flogging she once had him given.

She had five children altogether, of whom the only daughter and the eldest son died in childhood within twenty days of each other. Her second son was the emperor Kuang Hsu, and he was taken from her at the age of four. After he went into the palace she gave birth to another son who did not live two days. When her fourth son was born she fussed over him terribly, frightened that he was not wearing enough and would freeze or that he would eat too much and suffer from a surfeit. My grandmother believed in the practice of going without food for a whole day sometimes, and she never allowed her children to eat their fill, even cutting up a prawn into three pieces before giving it to them. The result was that this fourth son died of malnutrition before reaching the age of five. As one old eunuch remarked, if my grandmother had not killed her children with misplaced kindness my father would never have inherited my grandfather's title.

Although my father was not her own child, she was responsible for bringing him up. Although she did not control the diet of my father and his younger brothers, she dominated them psychologically. The eunuch I mentioned above said that they even had to be careful when smiling, because if their smiles turned into laughs the old lady would shout at them: "Why are you laughing? Have you no manners?"

My grandfather's first secondary wife died young and his second one was my real grandmother. After the death of my father's first wife she was in charge of the household, and although she was not as bigoted as her predecessor, she was mentally unstable, a condition that was brought on by the fate of her children and grandchildren. She lost a daughter at the age of two, but what first deranged her was having her young sons adopted. She bore three sons altogether, of whom my father was the oldest. Her third son, Tsai Tao, had been brought up very close to her and when he was

24

eleven she received an edict from the empress dowager Tzu Hsi ordering that he was to become the adopted son of Yi Mo, a cousin of my grandfather's. The receipt of this document made her weep till she was seriously ill, and the shock left her rather unbalanced.

The childless Yi Mo was naturally overjoyed at being given a son and he gave a great feast to celebrate the event, just as if a son had been born to him. He had not, to Tzu Hsi's displeasure, been much of a man for ingratiating himself with her, and when she learnt how overjoyed he was she was even more angry with him and determined that his good fortune would not be allowed to last. There was a famous saying of hers that "if anyone causes me a moment's sorrow I shall give him a lifetime's misery." After some injury he suffered from her Yi Mo vented his feelings by painting a picture which simply consisted of a foot. This foot implied by a play on words that Tzu Hsi specialized in making trouble and that she had got the affairs of both her family and the country into a mess. On the picture he had written a verse of doggerel:

> Poor me, I tried to dodge the foot's dread power,
> And so I built a foot-avoiding tower.
> But though I built the tower very high,
> The foot still chased me up into the sky.

Somehow Tzu Hsi got to hear of this, and so to spite him she issued without warning another decree ordering that the boy Tsai Tao, who had then been adopted by Yi Mo for over five years, should be adopted once again by yet another relation. The shock made both Yi Mo and his wife sick, and when Yi Mo died soon afterwards Tzu Hsi deliberately sent Tsai Tao, the son who had been snatched away from him, as her representative to offer sacrifices for him. Acting in this capacity my uncle could not kneel before his memorial tablet. Yi Mo's wife also died within the year.

When Tzu Hsi ordered Tsai Tao to be adopted for the second time she also arranged to have his brother Tsai Hsun adopted by another cousin of my father's. It was indeed a case of

> Although I built the tower very high,
> The foot still chased me up into the sky.

The sudden loss of yet another son was an unexpected shock to my grandmother.

It was not long before she received a third blow. Just when she had arranged a match for my father an edict came from Tzu Hsi ordaining that he should marry someone else. Of course, she did not bother about obtaining the consent of the couple concerned or of the heads of their families, and nobody dared to utter a word of comment on anything that she had arranged. My grandmother was terrified on the one hand of incurring the displeasure of the Empress Dowager and on the other of what her son's original fiancée might do to herself if the engagement were broken off. If anything did happen it would be tantamount to resisting an edict of the Empress Dowager and the girl's family and her own might be held responsible. Although people tried to calm her fears by explaining that there could be no difficulty about cancelling a betrothal on orders from the Empress Dowager, my grandmother would not be soothed and she became deranged again.

Six years later she had another breakdown when a Grand Councillor came with an edict ordering that I be sent into the palace. I had been brought up from my earliest days by my grandmother and she doted on me. According to my nurse, she used to get up once or twice every night to come over and look at me; she did not even put shoes on for fear that the noise of their wooden soles would disturb me. Having reared me like this for more than two years she fainted at the news that Tzu Hsi was taking me into the palace. For the rest of her life she was very liable to fits of insanity. She died in 1925 at the age of 58.

After losing his father when he was seven, the second Prince Chun was brought up by the two old ladies in accordance with the instructions left by the first Prince Chun, and he led a traditional noble's life. When he was Prince Regent he had an enormous income, his mother ran his household, there was a special office to look after his property and entertain visitors and he had a host of guardsmen, eunuchs and servants to wait on him, to say nothing of the body of retainers to advise and amuse him. Thus he did not have to worry about household affairs and had no need for any

The empress dowager Tzu Hsi (*centre*)

My paternal grandfather Yi Huan, the first Prince Chun

My father Tsai Feng, the second Prince Chun

The empress dowager Lung Yu

My father's household.
From   right   to   left:
my   father,   his   mother,
his   secondary   mother,
his   wife   (my   mother)

My nurse Mrs. Wang

Myself at the age of two

Myself with the empress dowager Lung Yu in 1911

Yuan Shih-kai's assurance written on the Articles of Favourable Treatment (see pp. 37-38)

先朝政權未能保全僅留
尊號至今耿〻所有優待
各節無論何時斷乎不
許變更容當列入憲法

袁世凱誌
乙邓孟冬

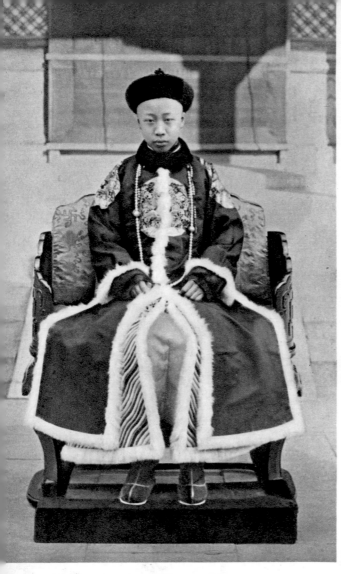

Myself in 1917

The monarchist
Chang   Hsun

Myself at the time
of my first wedding

Wan Jung

The procession to bring Wan
Jung to the palace about to
set out

Chen Pao-shen

Johnston in Ching robes

Cheng Hsiao-hsu

Lo Chen-yu

Tientsin life.
Above: With my brothers and sisters
Below: Golf

Birthday greetings at the Chang Garden from the Ching veterans

Birthday visitors. *Front row, third and fourth from left*: Wan Jung and myself. *Second row, far left*: Wan Jung's mother. *Second row, second from left*: Wan Jung's English teacher. *Fourth row, far left*: the Japanese staff officer Mino Tomoyoshi. *Fourth row, second from left*: the English journalist H. G. W. Woodhead

At a British military review, shaking hands with the British commander in Tientsin, R. M. Heath. Standing on the right of the picture is the Japanese garrison commander Takata Yutaki

useful knowledge. He had little contact with the outside world and had no social life apart from the exchange of formal visits.

My father had two wives, and they bore him four sons and seven daughters of whom all but two are alive today. My father died in 1951 and my own mother in 1921.

My father and my mother were completely different types. It is said that Manchu women are often far more capable than their husbands, and this may well be true. My wife Wan Jung and my mother were far more knowledgeable than myself or my father, particularly when it came to enjoying themselves or buying things. One explanation for the way in which Manchu girls were able to run their households and were treated with respect by their elders in their generation was that they all had the chance of being chosen for service in the palace and becoming imperial consorts; but my own opinion is that as the men were either idling or busy with official business, household management and financial affairs tended to fall on their sisters' shoulders so that the women naturally became rather more able. My mother was a favourite in her mother's home, and Tzu Hsi once said of her: "That girl isn't even afraid of me." Her extravagance was a big headache for my father and grandmother, but there was nothing they could do about it. Excluding his land-rents, prince's stipend and "Money for the Nurture of Incorruptibility" (a form of payment to officials that was supposed to prevent them from accepting bribes), my father had an income of 50,000 taels a year which was always paid in full even during the Republic, but it was never long after he received it before my mother spent it all. Later he tried all sorts of solutions including giving her a fixed allowance but none of them worked. He even tried smashing vases and other crockery to show his anger and determination. As he could not bear to lose all this porcelain he replaced it with unbreakable vessels of bronze and lead. My mother soon saw through his tricks and in the end my father would give her more spending money as usual. She spent so much that my grandmother would weep and sigh over the bills sent over by the counting house and my father had no option but to tell his stewards to sell more antiques and land.

My mother often used to sell on the sly the jewellery that she had brought with her at her marriage, and I later discovered that she secretly spent the money thus obtained on political activities as well as on her everyday luxuries. But the money that she and the other imperial consorts spent to try and realize their dreams of restoration was all pocketed by the eunuchs and others.

From earliest childhood my brothers and sisters were never frightened of my father and grandmother but were terrified of my mother. Of course, the servants were even more scared of her. One day my father came home to find that the doors and windows had not yet been shut, so he asked a eunuch why. The eunuch replied that as madam was not back there was no hurry. My father lost his temper and punished him by making him kneel on the ground. A maid remarked to him that "if it had been the master you would have been beaten black and blue." By "the master" she meant my mother who, like Tzu Hsi, loved being referred to as if she were a man.

I went into the palace when I was nearly three and did not meet my own mother and grandmother again till I was ten, when they were summoned to the palace. When I met them I felt a complete stranger and not at all close to them, but I do remember that my grandmother's eyes were fixed on me all the time and that they seemed to be glistening with tears. My mother left quite a different impression on me: I found her frightening as well as distant. Whenever she saw me she would say with a severe expression: "Your Majesty must study diligently the precepts of your ancestors," or "Your Majesty must not be greedy; Your Majesty's body is a sacred body, Your Majesty must get up early and go to bed early. . . ." I still have that very stiff impression of her when I think of her today. What a difference of character there was between my grandmother, who was of humble origin, and my mother, brought up as she was in a grand family.

CHAPTER TWO

CHILDHOOD

Accession and Abdication

On the evening of November 13, 1908 the mansion of Prince Chun was in chaos. My grandmother fainted before hearing the end of the Dowager's decree that had been brought back by the new Prince Regent. Eunuchs and serving women were pouring ginger tea and sending for doctors while on the other side of the room a child was crying and adults were trying to pacify it. My father, the regent, was rushing all over the place: entertaining the Grand Councillor and the eunuchs who had come with him from the palace; telling people to get the child dressed; forgetting that the old lady had fainted; being called in to see her; and then forgetting that the Grand Councillor and eunuchs were waiting to take the future emperor into the palace. During this confusion the old lady came round and was helped into an inner room where the future emperor was still "resisting the edict", howling and hitting the eunuchs as they tried to pick him up. The palace eunuchs were forcing themselves to smile as they waited for the Grand Councillor to tell them what to do next while the Councillor was helplessly waiting for the Prince Regent to deal with the situation. But all the regent could do was to nod. . . .

Some of the older members of the household described this scene to me later; my memory of it disappeared long ago. They said that the confusion was ended by my wet-nurse who gave me the breast and thus ended my cries. This action of hers brought my father and the Councillor to their senses: they decided that she should take me to the palace before handing me over to the eunuchs who would carry me in to see Tzu Hsi.

I still have a dim recollection of my meeting with Tzu Hsi, the shock of which left a deep impression on my memory. I remember suddenly finding myself surrounded by strangers, while before me was hung a drab curtain through which I could see an emaciated and terrifyingly hideous face. This was Tzu Hsi. It is said that I burst into loud howls at the sight and started to tremble uncontrollably. Tzu Hsi told someone to give me a string of candied haws, but I threw it on the floor and cried, "I want nanny, I want nanny", to Tzu Hsi's great displeasure. "What a naughty child," she said. "Take him away to play."

Two days after I entered the palace Tzu Hsi died, and on December 2, the "Great Ceremony of Enthronement" took place, a ceremony that I ruined with my crying.

The ceremony took place in the Hall of Supreme Harmony (Tai Ho Tien). Before it began I had to receive the obeisances of the commanders of the palace guard and ministers of the inner court in the Hall of Central Harmony (Chung Ho Tien) and the homage of the leading civilian and military officials. I found all this long and tiresome; it was moreover a very cold day, so when they carried me into the Hall of Supreme Harmony and put me up on the high and enormous throne I could bear it no longer. My father, who was kneeling below the throne and supporting me, told me not to fidget, but I struggled and cried, "I don't like it here. I want to go home. I don't like it here. I want to go home." My father grew so desperate that he was pouring with sweat. As the officials went on kotowing to me my cries grew louder and louder. My father tried to soothe me by saying, "Don't cry, don't cry; it'll soon be finished, it'll soon be finished."

When the ceremony was over the officials asked each other surreptitiously, "How could he say 'It'll soon be finished'? What does it mean, his saying he wanted to go home?" All these discussions took place in a very gloomy atmosphere as if these words had been a bad omen. Some books said that these words were prophetic as within three years the Ching Dynasty was in fact "finished" and the boy who wanted to "go home" did go home, and claimed that the officials had a presentiment of this.

What really gave them forebodings, of course, was much more than a couple of chance sentences. The records of the time show that the rising anti-Manchu storm, serious enough in the last years of

Kuang Hsu, became ever more menacing during my reign. Later, the increasing power of Yuan Shih-kai was another headache for some high officials and members of the royal clan who saw that outside the government they had to reckon with the revolutionaries while inside they had to reckon with Yuan Shih-kai; they regarded my reign as one of the most ill-omened in history.

After making a very poor show as emperor for three years I made a very poor show of abdicating. One incident of those last days stands out clearly in my memory. The empress dowager Lung Yu was sitting on a *kang*[1] in a side room of the Mind Nurture Palace (Yang Hsin Tien) wiping her eyes with a handkerchief while a fat old man knelt on a red cushion before her, tears rolling down his face. I was sitting to the right of the Dowager feeling rather bewildered and wondering why the two adults were crying. There was nobody in the room besides us three and it was very quiet; the fat man was sniffing loudly while he talked and I could not understand what he was saying. Later I learnt that this fat man was Yuan Shih-kai. This was the only time I ever saw him and his last meeting with the Dowager. If what I have been told is right, this was the occasion on which Yuan directly brought up the question of abdication. After this meeting Yuan Shih-kai used the pretext of an attempt that had been made on his life not to come to court again.

The Wuchang rising sparked off responses all over the country, and when the Manchu commander-in-chief of the imperial forces proved incapable of directing the Peiyang Army against the Republican forces the Prince Regent had no choice but to bring back Yuan Shih-kai. Yuan, who knew how to wait for his price and was kept well informed of developments in the capital, repeatedly declined the offers of reinstatement until he was offered the premiership and supreme military command. Only then did he accept the imperial edict and order the Peiyang Army to advance on the Republicans. After recapturing Hanyang he halted his troops and

---

[1] A *kang* is a low brick platform on which people sit or sleep; it can be heated in winter, and is very common in north China.

returned to Peking for audiences with the Prince Regent and the empress dowager Lung Yu.

Yuan Shih-kai was no longer the Yuan Shih-kai of before. In addition to his political and military power he had obtained some things even more valuable: some foreigners, including the British minister at Peking, were interested in him and he also had friends on the Republican side, including Wang Ching-wei[1] who had been captured after his unsuccessful attempt to assassinate the Prince Regent but whose life had been spared through the intercession of some Japanese who made it clear that Japan would be displeased to see him executed. Wang was released from jail after the Wuchang rising and served as a link between Yuan Shih-kai and some of the Republican leaders; he also kept him well-informed on developments in the revolutionary camp, and some of the constitutional monarchists were beginning to feel well disposed towards Yuan.

With all his new and old friends and his clear intelligence picture Yuan's position was stronger than ever. Within a month of his return to Peking he used Prince Ching to get the regent dismissed. Then he took over the palace treasury of the empress dowager Lung Yu on the pretext that it was needed to meet military expenses, and at the same time made the members of the royal family and the nobility hand over funds for the army. With political, military and financial power in his hands he went on to arrange for the Chinese diplomatic envoys in Russia and other countries to telegraph the Ching court requesting the emperor's abdication, while at the same time he presented the Empress Dowager with a secret memorial in the name of the whole cabinet saying that a republic was the only solution. He must have presented the memorial on the occasion when I saw him, and this would explain why Lung Yu was weeping so copiously as the memorial said that there was no hope for the

---

[1] Wang Ching-wei later became a notorious Kuomintang leader and pro-Japanese traitor. He openly surrendered to the Japanese invaders in December 1938 when he was vice-chairman of the Kuomintang and chairman of its People's Political Council. In March 1940 he became president of the puppet central government then formed in Nanking. He died in Japan in November 1944.

dynasty even in flight and that delay in abdicating might lead to a fate similar to that suffered by Louis XVI and his family in the French revolution.

The terror-struck Dowager called an emergency meeting of the imperial council to hear the opinions of the members of the royal family. When they were told of the secret memorial and of what Yuan Shih-kai had said they were very alarmed, not by the reference to Louis XVI but by the sudden change in Yuan's loyalties.

At first Yuan Shih-kai had opposed the setting up of a republic and had advocated a constitutional monarchy in the negotiations with the Republican side. Later the Ching and Republican sides had agreed in principle that the question of the state structure should be decided by a provisional national assembly; but obstruction from the Ching side had prevented agreement on its composition, time and place. With these questions still unresolved the Republicans set up a Provisional Government at Nanking and elected Sun Yat-sen as Provisional President. This prompted Yuan Shih-kai to withdraw the credentials of his delegate in the negotiations and to deal directly with the Republican representatives by cable. The suggestion of Yuan's cabinet that the dynasty should abdicate at a time when the structure of the state was still undecided naturally came as a severe shock to the royal house.

Yuan Shih-kai already had foreign support and he now had enough friends on the Republican side to be able to influence its actions. Those among the revolutionaries who had originally been constitutional monarchists had for some time been aware that Yuan was their hope, and their attitude had infected some of the more naive of the Republicans. Thus it was that the Republican side decided that if Yuan consented to it a republic could be rapidly achieved and that Yuan should be invited to be the first president. This was just what Yuan wanted; he knew, moreover, that the former Prince Regent was surrounded by a group implacably hostile to himself who intended to eliminate him whether he succeeded in defeating the revolutionaries or not. He had decided to accept the Republican offer and was considering how to deal with the Ching house when the unexpected news that Sun Yat-sen had taken office as Provisional

President in Nanking made a solution to the question much more urgent. If the Republicans went on to set up a national assembly in the south it would be impossible for him to get rid of it; he decided therefore to put pressure on the imperial house by frightening the empress dowager Lung Yu while at the same time offering her the bait of the Articles of Favourable Treatment. In this way he hoped that she would announce the abdication voluntarily and give him full powers to organize a provisional government. This, then, was the explanation for Yuan Shih-kai's sudden volte-face.

Although Yuan had betrayed the Ching house one would never have guessed it from his tearful countenance at his private audience with the empress dowager Lung Yu. But even the members of the royal house who had trusted Yuan Shih-kai before knew that they had been betrayed.

Some of the princes and nobles who had always been anti-Yuan were in favour of putting up a desperate last-ditch fight and of avenging the slaughter of Manchu bannermen that had taken place in some parts of the country, and when the empress dowager Lung Yu called the first meeting of the imperial council the atmosphere was charged with anger. A proposal by Yuan Shih-kai's old ally Prince Ching and others that the court should agree to abdicate was fiercely attacked. Prince Ching did not come to court the next day and his chief supporter in the council changed his tune.

This situation did not last long. From various accounts one can tell that one of the long series of imperial council meetings went approximately as follows. Having established that all present were in favour of the monarchy and opposed to a republic the Dowager went on to say that she had been told by Prince Ching that the imperial forces were incapable of defeating the Republicans and that the foreigners would come to the help of the Ching government after the Prince Regent resigned.

Pu Wei, a leader of the anti-Yuan group among the nobility, protested that this was obviously a lie as the regent had already resigned and the foreigners had done nothing to help them. He and others then said that the rebels were nothing to be afraid of and reported that Feng Kuo-chang, a Peiyang general, maintained that three months' military funds would be enough to defeat them. But, as the Dowager pointed out, Yuan Shih-kai had taken over the funds of the Palace Treasury so that she had no money. "Besides," she went on, "what if we lose? Surely we won't be able to fall back on the Articles of Favourable Treatment then?"

Pu Wei objected that the Articles were a trick, but when the Dowager asked about the state of the army she only got a non-committal reply.

As one inconclusive meeting of the imperial council followed another the advocates of fighting it out became fewer and fewer. Tuan Chi-jui, another Peiyang general, sent a telegram requesting the abdication of the Ching emperor. Two leaders of the war party in the royal family left Peking. One hastened to German-occupied Tsingtao and the other to Japanese-held Lushun, but they were prevented from going on to plead the imperial case in Germany and Japan by the local officials of the two countries.

On February 12, 1912 the empress dowager Lung Yu proclaimed my abdication. Some of the royal family and the nobility fled to the Legation Quarter while Prince Ching took his family and his valuables to the foreign concessions in Tientsin. My father, who had said not a word throughout the imperial council meetings, returned home to "hug his children". Yuan Shih-kai meanwhile was organizing a provisional Republican government as he had been ordered to by the Empress Dowager while at the same time he acted on an agreement with the revolutionaries and changed from premier of the cabinet of the Great Ching Empire to Provisional President of the Republic of China. And I became the President's neighbour as I started my life in the "Little Court" according to the articles providing for the favourable treatment of the Ching house.

These articles, the "Articles providing for the Favourable Treatment of the Great Ching Emperor after his Abdication", were as follows:

1. After the abdication of the Great Ching Emperor, his title of dignity is to be retained and not abolished. The Republic of China will treat him with the courtesy due to a foreign sovereign.

2. After the abdication of the Great Ching Emperor he shall receive an annual allowance of four million taels, or four million dollars after the minting of the new currency. This allowance shall be paid by the Republic of China.

3. After the abdication of the Great Ching Emperor he may live temporarily in the Imperial Palace; later he shall move to the Summer Palace. He may retain his usual bodyguard.

4. After the abdication of the Great Ching Emperor the sacrifices at his ancestral temples and the imperial tombs shall be maintained for ever. The Republic of China shall provide guards to ensure their protection.

5. The uncompleted tomb of Te Tsung (Emperor Kuang Hsu) shall be finished according to the original plan. The funeral ceremonies shall be observed in accordance with the ancient rites. The actual expenses shall be borne by the Republic of China.

6. All the persons of various grades working in the palace may continue to be employed as before; with the provision that no further eunuchs be engaged.

7. After the abdication of the Great Ching Emperor his existing private property shall receive the special protection of the Republic of China.

8. The existing Palace Guard shall be incorporated into the Army of the Republic of China; its numbers and salary shall be continued as before.

Living as an Emperor

The "Articles for Favourable Treatment" stipulated that I could live temporarily in the Imperial Palace without fixing any definite time limit. Apart from three large halls that were handed over to the Republic, the rest of the Forbidden City continued to belong to the Imperial Palace. It was in this tiny world that I was to spend the most absurd childhood possible until I was driven out by the soldiers of the National Army in 1924. I call it absurd because at a time when China was called a republic and mankind had advanced into the twentieth century I was still living the life of an emperor, breathing the dust of the nineteenth century.

Whenever I think of my childhood my head fills with a yellow mist. The glazed tiles were yellow, my sedan-chair was yellow, my chair cushions were yellow, the linings of my hats and clothes were yellow, the girdle round my waist was yellow, the dishes and bowls from which I ate and drank, the padded cover of the rice-gruel saucepan, the material in which my books were wrapped, the window curtains, the bridle of my horse . . . everything was yellow. This colour, the so-called "brilliant yellow", was used exclusively by the imperial household and made me feel from my earliest years that I was unique and had a "heavenly" nature different from that of everybody else.

When I was ten my grandmother and mother started to come and visit me on the orders of the High Consorts[1] and they brought my brother Pu Chieh and my first sister to play with me for a few days. Their first visit started off very drearily: I and my grandmother sat on the *kang* and she watched me playing dominoes while my brother and sister stood below us very properly, gazing at me with a fixed stare like attendants on duty in a yamen. Later it occurred to me to take them along to the part of the palace in which I lived, where I asked Pu Chieh, "What games do you play at home?"

"Pu Chieh can play hide-and-seek," said my brother, who was a year younger than me, in a very respectful way.

"So you play hide-and-seek too? It's a jolly good game." I was very excited. I had played it with the eunuchs but never with children younger than myself. So we started to play hide-and-seek and in the excitement of the game my brother and sister forgot their inhibitions. We deliberately let down the blinds to make the room very dark. My sister, who was two years younger than me, was at the same time enraptured and terrified, and as my brother and I kept giving her frights we got so carried away that we were laughing and shouting. When we were exhausted we climbed up on to the *kang* to get our breath back and I told them to think of some new game. Pu Chieh was thoughtful for a while, then started to gaze at me wordlessly, a silly smile on his face.

[1] Dowager Consorts of the first degree, widows of the emperors Tung Chih and Kuang Hsu.

"What are you grinning at?"

He went on grinning.

"Tell me! Tell me!" I urged him impatiently, thinking that he must certainly have thought out some new game. To my surprise he came out with, "I thought, oh, Pu Chieh thought that Your Majesty would be different from ordinary people. The emperors on the stage have long beards. . . ." As he spoke he pretended to be stroking his beard.

This gesture was his undoing. As he raised his hand I noticed that the lining of his sleeve was a very familiar colour. My face blackened.

"Pu Chieh, are you allowed to wear that colour?"

"But . . . bu . . . but isn't it apricot?"

"Nonsense! It's imperial brilliant yellow."

"Yes, sire, yes, sire. . . ." Pu Chieh stood away from me, his arms hanging respectfully by his sides. My sister slipped over to stand with him, frightened to the point of tears.

"It's brilliant yellow. You have no business to be wearing it."

"Yes, sire."

With his "yes, sire" my brother reverted to being my subject. The sound "yes, sire" died out long ago and it seems very funny when one thinks of it today. But I got used to it from early childhood, and if people did not use the words when replying to me I would not stand for it. It was the same with kneeling and kotowing. From my infancy I was accustomed to having people kotow to me, particularly people over ten times my own age. They included old officials of the Ching Dynasty and the elders of my own clan, men in the court robes of the Ching Dynasty and officials of the Republic in Western dress.

Another strange thing which seemed quite normal at the time was the daily pomp.

Every time I went to my schoolroom to study, or visited the High Consorts to pay my respects, or went for a stroll in the garden I was always followed by a large retinue. Every trip I made to the Summer Palace must have cost thousands of Mexican dollars: the

40

Republic's police had to be asked to line the roads to protect me and I was accompanied by a motorcade consisting of dozens of vehicles.

Whenever I went for a stroll in the garden a procession had to be organized. In front went a eunuch from the Administrative Bureau whose function was roughly that of a motor horn: he walked twenty or thirty yards ahead of the rest of the party intoning the sound "chir . . . chir . . ." as a warning to anyone who might be in the vicinity to go away at once. Next came two chief eunuchs advancing crabwise on either side of the path; ten paces behind them came the centre of the procession — the Empress Dowager or myself. If I was being carried in a chair there would be two junior eunuchs walking beside me to attend to my wants at any moment; if I was walking they would be supporting me. Next came a eunuch with a large silk canopy followed by a large group of eunuchs of whom some were empty-handed and others were holding all sorts of things: a seat in case I wanted to rest, changes of clothing, umbrellas and parasols. After these eunuchs of the imperial presence came eunuchs of the imperial tea bureau with boxes of various kinds of cakes and delicacies, and, of course, jugs of hot water and a tea service; they were followed by eunuchs of the imperial dispensary bearing cases of medicine and first-aid equipment suspended from carrying poles. The medicines carried always included potions prepared from lampwick sedge, chrysanthemums, the roots of reeds, bamboo leaves, and bamboo skins; in summer there were always Essence of Betony Pills for Rectifying the Vapour, Six Harmony Pills for Stabilizing the Centre, Gold Coated Heat-Dispersing Cinnabar, Fragrant Herb Pills, Omnipurpose Bars, colic medicine and anti-plague powder; and throughout all four seasons there would be the Three Immortals Beverage to aid the digestion, as well as many other medicaments. At the end of the procession came the eunuchs who carried commodes and chamber-pots. If I was walking a sedan-chair, open or covered according to the season, would bring up the rear. This motley procession of several dozen people would proceed in perfect silence and order.

But I would often throw it into confusion. When I was young I liked to run around when I was in high spirits just any child does. At first they would all scuttle along after me puffing and panting with their procession reduced to chaos. When I grew a little older and knew how to give orders I would tell them to stand and wait for me; then apart from the junior eunuchs of the imperial presence who came with me they would all stand there waiting in silence with their loads. After I had finished running around they would form up again behind me. When I learnt to ride a bicycle and ordered the removal of all the upright wooden thresholds in the palace so that I could ride around without obstruction the procession was no longer able to follow me and so it had to be temporarily abolished. But when I went to pay my respects to the High Consorts or to my schoolroom I still had to have something of a retinue, and without it I would have felt rather odd. When I heard people telling the story of the last emperor of the Ming Dynasty who had only one eunuch left with him at the end I felt very uncomfortable.

The type of extravagant display that wasted the most effort, money and material was meals. There were special terms to refer to the emperor's eating and it was absolutely forbidden to fail to use them correctly. Food was called not "food" but "viands"; eating was called "consuming viands"; serving the meal was "transmitting the viands"; and the kitchen was the "imperial viands room". When it was time to eat (and the times of the meals were not set but were whenever the emperor felt like eating), I would give the command "Transmit the viands!" The junior eunuchs of the presence would then repeat "Transmit the viands" to the eunuchs standing in the main hall of the palace in which I lived and they would pass it on to the eunuchs standing on duty outside the hall; these would in turn call it out to the eunuchs of the "imperial viands room" waiting in the Western Avenue of the Forbidden City. Thus my order went straight to the kitchens, and before its echoes had died away a procession rather of the sort that used to take a bride's trousseau to her groom's house had already issued from the "viands room". It was made up of an imposing column of several dozen neatly dressed eunuchs hurrying to the Mind Nurture Palace with seven tables of various sizes and scores of red-lacquered boxes painted with golden dragons. When they reached the main hall they handed their burdens over to young eunuchs wearing white sleeves who laid out the meal in an eastern room of the palace.

Usually there were two tables of main dishes with another one of chafing-dishes added in winter; there were three tables with cakes, rice and porridge respectively; and there was another small table of salted vegetables. All the crockery was imperial yellow porcelain with dragon designs and the words "Ten thousand long lives without limit" painted on it. In winter I ate from silver dishes placed on top of porcelain bowls of hot water. Every dish or bowl had a strip of silver on it as a precaution against poison, and for the same reason all the food was tasted by a eunuch before it was brought in. This was called "appraising the viands". When everything had been tasted and laid out and before I took my place a young eunuch would call out "Remove the covers". This was the signal for four or five other junior eunuchs to take the silver lids off all the food dishes, put them in a large box and carry them out. I then began to "use the viands".

And what was the food laid out "ten cubits square"? The empress dowager Lung Yu would have about a hundred main dishes on six tables, an extravagance inherited from the empress dowager Tzu Hsi. I had about thirty. But these dishes which were brought in with such ceremonial were only for show. The reason why the food could be served almost as soon as I gave the word was that it had been prepared several hours or even a whole day in advance and was being kept warm over the kitchen stoves. The cooks knew that at least since the time of Kuang Hsu the emperor had not eaten this food. The food I ate was sent over by the Empress Dowager, and after her death by the High Consorts. She and each of the High Consorts had kitchens of their own staffed by highly skilled chefs who produced twenty or more really delicious dishes for every meal. This was the food that was put in front of me, while that prepared by the imperial kitchens was set some distance away as it was only there for the sake of appearances.

To show how they loved and cared for me the High Consorts also sent a responsible eunuch to report on how I had "consumed viands". This too was a pure formality. No matter what I had really eaten, the eunuch would go to the quarters of the High Consorts, kneel before them and say:

"Your slave reports to his masters: the Lord of Ten Thousand Years consumed one bowl of old rice viands (or white rice viands), one steamed breadroll (or a griddle cake) and a bowl of congee. He consumed it with relish."

At Chinese New Year and other festivals and on the birthdays of the High Consorts my kitchen sent a spread of food to the Consorts as a mark of my filial piety. This food could be described as expensive and showy without being good, and was neither nutritious nor tasty.

According to the record of one month of the second year of my reign, the empress dowager Lung Yu, the four High Consorts and myself used up 3,960 catties of meat (over two tons) and 388 chickens and ducks every month, of which 810 catties of meat and 240 chickens and ducks were for me, a four-year-old child. In addition there was a monthly allocation for the numerous people in the palace who served us: members of the Grand Council, imperial bodyguards, tutors, Hanlin academicians, painters, men who drew the outlines of characters for others to fill in, important eunuchs, *shaman* magicians who came every day to sacrifice to the spirits, and many others. Including the Dowager, the Consorts and myself, the monthly consumption of pork was 14,642 catties at a cost of 2,342.72 taels of silver. On top of this there were the extra dishes we had every day which often cost several times as much again. In the month in question there were 31,844 catties of extra meat, 814 catties of extra pork fat and 4,786 extra chickens and ducks, to say nothing of the fish, shrimps and eggs. All these extras cost 11,641.07 taels, and with miscellaneous items added the total expenditure came to 14,794.19 taels. It is obvious that all this money (except what was embezzled) was wasted in order to display the grandeur of the emperor. This figure, moreover, does not include the cost of the cakes, fruit, sweets and drinks that were constantly being devoured.

Just as food was cooked in huge quantities but not eaten, so was a vast amount of clothing made which was never worn. I cannot now remember much about this, but I do know that while the Dowager and the High Consorts had fixed yearly allocations there were no limits for the emperor, for whom clothes were constantly made throughout the year. I do not know what exactly was made, but everything I wore was always new. I have before me an account from an unspecified year headed "List of materials actually used in making clothes for His Majesty's use from the sixth day of the tenth month to the fifth day of the eleventh month". According to this list the following garments were made for me that month: eleven fur jackets, six fur inner and outer gowns, two fur waistcoats, and thirty padded waistcoats and pairs of trousers. Leaving aside the cost of the main materials and of the labour, the bill for such minor items as the edgings, pockets, buttons and thread came to 2,137.6335 silver dollars.

My changes of clothing were all laid down in regulations and were the responsibility of the eunuchs of the clothing storerooms. Even my everyday gowns came in twenty-eight different styles, from the one in black and white inlaid fur that I started wearing on the nineteenth of the first lunar month to the sable one I changed into on the first day of the eleventh month. Needless to say, my clothes were far more complicated on festivals and ceremonial occasions.

To manage all this extravagant pomp there was, of course, a suitable proliferation of offices and personnel. The Household Department, which administered the domestic affairs of the emperor, had under its control seven bureaus and 48 offices. The seven bureaus — the storage bureau, the guard bureau, the protocol, the counting house, the stock-raising bureau, the disciplinary bureau and the construction bureau — all had storerooms, workshops and so on under them. The storage bureau, for example, had stores for silver, fur, porcelain, satin, clothes and tea. According to a list of officials dating from 1909, the personnel of the Household Department numbered 1,023 (excluding the Palace Guard, the eunuchs and the servants known as "sulas"); in the early years of the Republic this number was reduced to something over 600, and at the time I left the Imperial Palace there were still more than 300. It is not hard to imagine an organization as large as this with so many people in it, but the triviality of some of its functions was almost unthinkable.

One of the forty-eight offices, for example, was the As You Wish Lodge (Ju Yi Kuan). Its only purpose was to paint pictures and do calligraphy for the Empress Dowager and the High Consorts; if the Dowager wanted to paint something the As You Wish Lodge would outline a design for her so that all she had to do was to fill in the colours and write a title on it. The calligraphy for large tablets was sketched out by the experts of the Great Diligence Hall or else done by the Hanlin academicians. Nearly all late Ching inscriptions that purport to be the brushwork of a dowager or an emperor were produced in this way.

The buildings all around me and the furniture of the palace were all a part of my indoctrination. Apart from the golden-glazed tiles that were exclusively for the use of the emperor, the very height of the buildings was an imperial prerogative that served to teach me from an early age that not only was everything under heaven the emperor's land, but that even the sky above my head belonged to nobody else. Every piece of furniture was "direct method" teaching material for me. It was said that the emperor Chien Lung once laid it down that nothing in the palace, not even a blade of grass, must be lost. To put this principle into practice he put some blades of grass on a table in the palace and gave orders that they were to be counted every day to see that not a single one of them was missing. This was called "taking the grass as a standard". Even in my time these thirty-six withered blades of grass were still preserved in a cloisonné canister in the Mind Nurture Palace. This grass filled me with unbounded admiration for my ancestor and unbridled hatred for the Revolution of 1911.

There is no longer any way of calculating exactly the enormous cost of the daily life of an emperor, but a record called "A comparison between the expenditure of the seventh year of Hsuan Tung (1915) and the past three years" compiled by the Household Department shows that expenditure in 1915 topped 2,790,000 taels, and that while it dropped in each of the following three years it was always over 1,890,000 taels. Thus it was that with the connivance of the Republican authorities we continued our prodigious waste of the sweat and blood of the people in order to maintain our former pomp and continue our parasitic way of life.

Some of the rules in the palace were originally not simply for the sake of show. The system by which all the food-dishes had strips of silver on them and the food was tasted before the emperor ate it, and the large-scale security precautions whenever he went out were basically to protect him against any attempt on his life. It was said that the reason why emperors had no outside privies was that one emperor had been set upon by an assassin when going out to relieve himself. These stories and all the display had the same effect on me: they made me believe that I was a very important and august person, a man apart who ruled and owned the universe.

Mothers and Son

When I entered the palace as the adopted son of the emperors Tung Chih and Kuang Hsu all their wives became my mothers. Strictly speaking, I became the adopted son of Tung Chih while only "continuing the sacrifices" to Kuang Hsu. This meant that I was now primarily the son of Tung Chih and only secondarily the son of Kuang Hsu. But Kuang Hsu's empress, the empress dowager Lung Yu, ignored this and used her authority as dowager to push the three high consorts of Tung Chih into the background for daring to argue this point with her. For the rest of her life they were not really numbered among my mothers, and Kuang Hsu's Chin Consort did not get the treatment of a secondary mother as she should have done either: when we ate together she had to stand while Lung Yu and I sat. After the death of Lung Yu the three consorts of Tung Chih combined with Kuang Hsu's consort to put their case to the princes and members of the nobility and succeeded in getting the titles of High Consorts. From then on I addressed all of them as "August Mother".

Although I had so many mothers I never knew any motherly love. As far as I can remember today the greatest concern they ever showed for me was to send me food at every meal and hear the report of the eunuch that I had "consumed it with relish".

In fact I was unable to "consume it with relish" when I was small as I had a stomach ailment, a condition that was probably caused by their "motherly love". Once when I was five I stuffed myself with chestnuts and for a month or more afterwards the empress dowager Lung Yu only allowed me to eat browned rice porridge; and although I was crying with hunger nobody paid any attention. I remember that one day when I was going for a walk by the side of one of the lakes in the palace the Dowager told them to take some stale steamed breadrolls for me to feed to the fish. I could not restrain myself from cramming one of them into my mouth. So far from feeling any regret at my display of hunger, Lung Yu actually tightened up her restrictions; but the tighter they got the stronger grew my desire to steal food. One day I noticed that the tribute food sent by the princes to the Dowager had been put down in the Western Avenue of the palace, so I made straight for one of the food containers, opened it, and saw that it was full of cold pork. I grabbed a piece and sank my teeth into it. The eunuchs with me turned pale with horror and rushed up to snatch it from me. I put up a desperate resistance, but as I was small and weak the delicious morsel was snatched away almost as soon as I had put it into my mouth.

Even after I was allowed to eat normally again I still got into trouble. Once a senior eunuch observed that I had downed six pancakes and, afraid that I had overeaten, thought up a way of helping me digest them. He had two other eunuchs pick me up by the arms and bring me hard down on to the floor as if they were ramming earth with me. Later they were very pleased with themselves and said that it was thanks to their cure that I had suffered no ill effects from the pancakes.

This may seem rather unreasonable, but there were other things more unreasonable still. Whenever I got impatient or lost my temper before I was seven or eight the chief eunuch would make the following diagnosis and prescription: "The Lord of Ten Thousand Years has fire in his heart. Let him sing for a while to disperse it." I would then be shut into some small room, usually the room in the schoolroom palace where my commode was kept. Once I was in there by myself it made no difference how much I cursed, kicked the door, implored or wailed: nobody would pay any attention. Only when I had finished howling, or, as they put it, finished "singing" and "dispersed the fire" would they let me out.

This strange cure was not an invention of the eunuchs nor, for that matter, of the dowager Lung Yu: it was a family tradition from which my brothers and sisters also suffered in my father's house.

When I was seven the empress dowager Lung Yu died. All I can remember about her "motherly love" is what I have related above.

I lived rather longer with the four High Consorts. Normally I saw very little of them and I never sat and talked with them in an ordinary, friendly way. Every morning I would go to pay them my respects. A eunuch would put down a hassock covered with yellow silk for me to kneel on, and after kneeling to them for a moment I would get up and stand to one side waiting for them to make their usual remarks. At this time of day they were having their hair combed by eunuchs and they would ask me, "Did the emperor sleep well?" or advise me to dress warmly as the weather was cold, or inquire how far I had got in the book I was studying. It was always the same — a few dry and stereotyped remarks; sometimes they would give me a few clay toys or something of the kind and then they would say, "Go away and play now, Emperor." This would be the end of our meeting and I would not see them again for the rest of the day.

The Dowager and the four High Consorts addressed me as "Emperor", as did my real parents and grandmother. Everyone else called me "Your Majesty". Although I had an ordinary name as well as a "milk name"[1] none of my mothers ever used them. I have heard others saying that when they think of their "milk names"

---

[1] "Milk name" is a name used in childhood.

49

they are reminded of their childhood and their mother's love. Mine has no such associations. I have also been told by some people that whenever they fell ill when studying away from home they would think of their mothers and of how their mothers comforted them when they were ill as children. I have often been ill in my adult life, but the thought of the visits I had from the High Consorts when I was sick as a child has never made me feel at all nostalgic.

I always caught colds or flu when the weather turned chilly. Whenever this happened the High Consorts would come to see me one after another. Each of them would ask the same question: "Is the emperor at all better? Have you had a good sweat?" and before two or three minutes were up she would be off again. I have a rather stronger memory of the swarms of eunuchs who accompanied them and crowded into my little bedroom. They would come and go again all within the space of a few minutes, thus disturbing the atmosphere in my room. As soon as one High Consort had gone another one would arrive and the room would be packed again. With four visits in a single day the atmosphere would be disturbed four times. Fortunately I always got better on the following day, and my bedroom would be quiet again.

When I was ill my medicines were made up by the dispensary in the palace of the high consort Tuan Kang, who after the death of the dowager Lung Yu managed, with the help of Yuan Shih-kai, to be made the senior of the four High Consorts and thus my chief mother.

Thus I grew to the age of twelve or thirteen under the "care" of my four mothers. Like any other child I was very fond of new toys, and some of the eunuchs tried to please me by buying me amusing things from outside. Once a eunuch had a replica of the ceremonial uniform of a general of the Republic made for me with a plume in its cap like a feather duster and a military sword and belt. When I put it on I felt very pleased with myself, but when the senior high consort Tuan Kang heard of this she was furious. She ordered an investigation, which also revealed that I had been wearing foreign stockings bought outside the palace by one of the eunuchs. She regarded all this as intolerable and summoned the two eunuchs responsible to her quarters, had each of them given two hundred strokes of the heavy rod and demoted them, sending them to the cleaning office to work as menials. Having dealt with them she sent for me and lectured me on the disgracefulness of the Great Ching Emperor wearing the clothes of the Republic and foreign stockings. I had no choice but to put away my beloved uniform and sword, take off my foreign stockings and change back into court clothes and cloth socks embroidered with dragon designs.

If the high consort Tuan Kang had limited her control over me to uniforms and foreign stockings, I would not have rebelled against her later. After all, such control as this only made me even more aware of my uniqueness and reinforced the lessons I was learning in my schoolroom. I think that it was for the sake of my education that she had the eunuchs beaten and gave me that scolding.

Tuan Kang took the empress dowager Tzu Hsi as her model and strove to emulate her, although Tzu Hsi had been responsible for the death of her own sister. The lessons she learnt from Tzu Hsi did not end with the savage flogging of eunuchs: she also sent eunuchs to spy on the emperor. After dealing with some eunuchs of mine she sent over a eunuch of her own to wait on me. He would go to her daily and report on my every action. This was just how Tzu Hsi had treated Kuang Hsu. Whatever her motive was, it hurt my pride, and my tutor Chen Pao-shen, who was very indignant about it, explained to me the theory about the difference between first wives and secondary wives, the category into which Tuan Kang fell. I seethed with repressed anger.

The explosion came not long later when one of the Imperial Physicians was dismissed by Tuan Kang. The affair really had nothing to do with me as the doctor in question was one of those attending to Tuan Kang, but I had heard some inflammatory suggestions such as the remark of my tutor, "Although she is only a consort, her high-handed behaviour is going too far." And one of the eunuchs had said to me, "Is not the Lord of Ten Thousand Years becoming another Kuang Hsu? The affairs of the College of Physicians should only be settled by the Lord of Ten Thousand Years. Even your slave cannot bear to see such things happen." Raging with fury I stormed over to the palace of Tuan Kang. As soon as I saw her I shouted, "Why did you dismiss that doctor? You're too highhanded. Aren't I the emperor? Who gives the orders? You've gone too far."

I did not wait for Tuan Kang, whose face had gone white from anger, to reply and went straight out again with a flick of my sleeve. When I returned to my schoolroom my tutors covered me with praises.

The furious Tuan Kang sent for my father and several other princes and with tears and sobs asked for advice, which none of them ventured to give her. When I was told that they had come I called them to my study and said to them with great spirit:

"Who is she? She's only a consort. Never in the history of our house has an emperor had to call a consort 'mother'. Are we to maintain no distinction between principal and secondary wives? If not, why doesn't my brother call the prince's secondary wives 'mother'? Why must I call her 'mother'? Why should I obey her?"

The princes received my tirade in silence.

Another of the High Consorts, who was on bad terms with Tuan Kang, came over specially to tell me that Tuan Kang was inviting my real mother and grandmother to come and see her, and so I had better be careful. They did in fact come, and where Tuan Kang had got nowhere with the princes her rantings had some effect on them: my grandmother in particular was terrified and ended up kneeling on the ground with my mother imploring Tuan Kang to desist from her wrath and promising to persuade me to apologize. I saw my mother and grandmother in a wing of the Lasting Peace Palace (Yung Ho Kung) in which Tuan Kang lived and heard that the High Consort was still raging in the main hall. I had orginally wanted to go and have it out with her, but unable to hold out against the tears and desperate entreaties of my mother and grandmother I relented and promised that I would apologize to Tuan Kang.

I resented making that apology. I went and greeted Tuan Kang without even looking at her, mumbled, "August Mother, I was wrong", and went away again. Her face restored, Tuan Kang stopped weeping.   Two days later I heard that my mother had killed herself.

My mother had never before been scolded in her life.   She had a headstrong personality and this shock was too much for her. When she returned from the palace she swallowed a fatal dose of opium. For fear that I might go too thoroughly into the circumstances of my mother's death Tuan Kang changed her treatment of me completely: she no longer restricted my activities in the least and became very accommodating.   With this my family life in the Forbidden City was peaceful again and the High Consorts and myself were once more mothers and son.   But for this my mother's life had to be sacrificed.

Studying in the Yu Ching Palace

When I was five the empress dowager Lung Yu chose a tutor for me and ordered an astrologer to select an auspicious day for me to begin my studies.   This day was September 10, 1911.

My first schoolroom was on an island in one of the palace lakes but later I changed to the Yu Ching Palace (Palace of the Cultivation of Happiness), a rather small building inside the Forbidden City. It contained two studies which were furnished more simply than most other rooms in the palace.   Under the southern window was a long table on which stood hat-stands and vases of flowers.   By the west wall was a *kang* on which I studied at first with the low *kang* table for a desk.   Later I sat at a table.   There were two more tables by the north wall with books and stationery on them.   On the walls hung scrolls that my grandfather, the first Prince Chun, had written out for his son the emperor Kuang Hsu.   The most eye-catching thing in the room was a huge clock about two metres in diameter whose hands were longer than my arms.   Its mechanism was on the other side of the wall, and to wind it up you had to go into the next room and use a thing like the starting handle of a car.

Where this strange and enormous object came from or why it was there I cannot remember, nor can I recall what sort of sound it made or how loud were the chimes at the hour.

But despite the colossal size of the clock in the Yu Ching Palace the boy who studied there had no idea of time, as could be guessed from the books I read. My principal texts were the Thirteen Classics, and I also read such books as the maxims and exploits of my ancestors and histories of the foundation of the Ching Dynasty. When I started English at thirteen the only two texts I used apart from an English reader were *Alice in Wonderland* and an English translation of the Chinese classical *Four Books*. I had some basic lessons in Manchu, but before I was even able to use the alphabet my teacher Yi Ko Tan died and my lessons stopped. So from 1911 to 1922 I learnt nothing of mathematics, let alone of science. As for my own country, I read only about such events as the "Tung Chih and Kuang Hsu Restoration"; my knowledge of foreign countries was limited to my trip with Alice to Wonderland. I was totally ignorant of George Washington, Napoleon, Watt's invention of the steam engine, and Newton and his apple. All I knew about the universe was that "the great Pole produced the two Forms, the two Forms produced the four Symbols, and the four Symbols produced the eight Trigrams."[1] If my tutors had not been prepared to chat with me about things that were not in the texts and had I not read more widely myself I would not even have known where Peking was in relation to the rest of China or that rice grew in the ground. In history no one dared to explode the myths about the origins of the ancestors of the Ching house, and as for economics, I had no idea of the price of a catty of rice. So for a long time I believed that my earliest ancestor was born after the goddess Fokulun swallowed a red fruit, and that the common people always had a table covered with dishes at every meal.

As I read a considerable number of ancient books over quite a long period of time I should have known classical Chinese very well. In fact I did not as I was not in the least conscientious. Apart from

---

[1] A quotation from the ancient classic, *Book of Changes.*

using minor illnesses as pretexts, I would sometimes tell a eunuch to inform my tutors that they were to take a day's holiday if I was not feeling like studying and had no better excuse. Up to the age of ten I was far more interested in a big cypress tree that grew outside the Yu Ching Palace than in my books. In summer there were always ants crawling up and down this tree. I got very interested in them and would often squat by their tree so absorbed in watching them or feeding them crumbs of cake and helping them to move their food that I would forget my own meals. Later I developed an interest in crickets and earthworms, so I had many an ancient porcelain bowl and urn brought over for me to keep them in. I was never very keen on my schoolbooks, and when reading them became intolerably tiresome my only thought was of going out to see those friends of mine.

In my early teens I began to understand that my textbooks had something to do with me and grew interested in how to be a "good emperor", in why an emperor was an emperor, and in what heavenly significance there was in this. It was the content rather than the language of the books that held my attention, and the content was far more concerned with the emperor's rights than with his duties. One of the sages did, it is true, say, "The people are important, the spirits of the land and grain come next and the sovereign is unimportant", "If the sovereign regards his subjects as so much grass the subjects will regard the monarch as their enemy", and other things of the kind. Far more of their admonitions, however, were directed at the ministers and common people. An example of this is the saying, "The ruler should be a ruler, the subjects should be subjects, the fathers should be fathers and the sons should be sons." The very first textbook, the *Classic of Filial Piety,* laid down the moral principle that one should "start by serving one's parents and end by serving one's sovereign". Before I started to read about this morality which seemed so delightful to me I had heard about it from the conversation of my tutors and later on they had even more to say about it than the texts. Ancient literature did not make nearly so deep an impression on me as their ancient talk.

Many of the people who studied in old-fashioned schools had to learn books by heart, and the great efforts involved are said to have had some good results. I never enjoyed any of these benefits as my tutors did not make me memorize my texts, being content with making me read them through a few times.

Perhaps it was to help me remember what I had read that they decided that I should read my text aloud to the dowager Lung Yu when I went to pay my respects to her and that the chief eunuch should stand outside my bedroom when I got up in the morning and read out the previous day's lessons several times. Nobody was interested in how much I remembered or in whether I wanted to remember it or not.

My teachers never examined me on my work and set me no compositions to write. I remember that I wrote some couplets and verses but the tutors would never comment on them, let alone correct them. Yet I was very keen on writing things when I was a child. As the tutors did not think much of such trifles I wrote them secretly for my own amusement. From the age of twelve or thirteen I read a lot for pleasure. I read most of the books of essays and the unofficial histories of the Ming and Ching Dynasties, the historical romances, tales of knights and fighters with magic powers and detective stories of the late Ching and early Republican period and the series of novels published by the Commercial Press. When I was a little older I read some English stories. Imitating all these works, Chinese and Western, ancient and modern, I concocted and illustrated many romances out of my daydreams just for my own enjoyment. I even submitted them for publication under assumed names, but I was nearly always disappointed. I remember that I once copied out a poem by a Ming writer and sent it to a small newspaper under the pseudonym of "Teng Chiung-lin". The editor was taken in and printed it. He was not the only person to be deceived: my English tutor Reginald Johnston translated it into English and put it into his book *Twilight in the Forbidden City* as evidence of his pupil's "poetic gifts".

The subject at which I was worst was Manchu: I only learnt one word in all the years I studied it. This was *yili* (arise), the reply

I had to make when my Manchu ministers knelt before me and said a set phrase of greeting in the language.

When I was eight they thought of another way of making me study better: I was provided with some fellow-students. Each of them received a stipend of the equivalent of eighty taels of silver a month and was granted the coveted privilege of being allowed to ride a horse in the Forbidden City. Although it was the time of the Republic this was still regarded as a great honour by the young men of the imperial clan. The three recipients of these favours were my brother Pu Chieh, Yu Chung (a son of my cousin Pu Lun), and Pu Chia, the son of my uncle Tsai Tao. Yet another honour conferred on these three was that of being scolded on behalf of their emperor in the schoolroom: when I made a mistake in reading out my lessons the teacher would tell one of my fellow-students off. As Pu Chieh was my brother the victim was nearly always Yu Chung, whose studies naturally suffered when he found himself being scolded whether he read well or badly.

When I had no fellow-students I was very naughty. If I felt like it I would take my shoes and socks off while I was reading and put the socks on the table. The tutor had to put them back on for me. Once I took a fancy to the long eyebrows of my tutor Hsu Fang and told him to come over so that I could stroke them. When he came obediently with his head bowed I suddenly plucked a hair from them. When he died later the eunuchs all said that this was because the "Lord of Ten Thousand Years" had pulled out his eyebrow of longevity. Another time I made my tutor Lu Jun-hsiang so angry with me that he forgot the distinction between ruler and subject. I was refusing to read my text as I wanted to go out into the garden and watch my ants. At first Lu tried to persuade me to pay attention by quoting such classical tags as "One can only be a true gentleman when one has both polish and substance", but I could not understand what he was talking about and went on fidgeting and looking around the room. Seeing that I was still unsettled my tutor went on to cite another classical saying: "If the gentleman is not serious he carries no authority; his learning will not be solid", but I naughtily got up and was about to go away from the table when

57

suddenly he lost his temper and roared at me, "Don't move!" I started with fright and did in fact behave a little better, though it was not long before I was thinking of my ants and fidgeting again.

When I had some fellow-students, things were rather better and I was able to bear sitting in the schoolroom. My teachers had ways of reproving me when I misbehaved: I remember one occasion when I came scampering into the classroom and the teacher said to Yu Chung, who was sitting there like a good boy, "Look how frivolous you are."

I studied Chinese every day from eight to eleven in the morning and English in the afternoon from one to three. At eight o'clock every morning I would be carried in a yellow-canopied sedan-chair to the Yu Ching Palace. At my command of "Call them" a eunuch would go and call out the tutor and the fellow-students from a waiting room. They always went into the schoolroom in a set order: first a eunuch carrying books, then the tutor for the first lesson, and finally my fellow-students. Once through the door the tutor would stand and gaze at me as a form of greeting. By the rules of protocol I was not obliged to return his salutation as although he was my teacher he was still my subject, and although I was his pupil I was still his sovereign. Then Pu Chieh and Yu Chung would kneel and pay their respects to me. These formalities over, we would all sit down. I sat by myself at the north side of the table, facing south, the teacher faced west and my fellow-students sat beside him. The eunuchs arranged the others' hats on the hat-stands and filed out. With that the lesson began.

I came across some pages of my diary dating from 1920, when I was fourteen. An excerpt may serve to give an idea of the life I led while I was studying.

27th. Fine. Rose at four, wrote out eighteen sheets of the character Prosperity in a large hand. Classes at eight. Read *Analects, Chou Ritual, Record of Ritual,* and Tang poetry with Pu Chieh and Yu Chung: listened to Tutor Chen lecturing on the *General Chronological History with Comments by Emperor Chien Lung.* Finished eating at 9:30, read *Tso Commentary, Ku Liang Commentary,* heard Tutor Chu on the *Explanation of the Great Learning,* wrote couplets.

Lessons finished at 11, went to pay respects to four High Consorts. Johnston did not come today as he had mild flu, so returned to Mind Nurture Palace and wrote out thirty more sheets of characters Prosperity and Longevity. Read papers, ate at four, bed at six. Read *Anthology of Ancient Literature* in bed: very interesting.

My tutor Lu Jun-hsiang, a Kiangsu man, was a former Grand Secretary who died before he had been teaching me for a year. Yi Ko Tan, who taught me Manchu for over nine years, was a Manchu of the Main White Banner who had qualified in the palace examination as a translator of Manchu. Chen Pao-shen, a Fukienese who came at the same time as Lu Jun-hsiang and Yi Ko Tan, had been a sub-chancellor of the Grand Secretariat and Vice-President of the Board of Rites; of all my tutors he was the one who was with me longest. After the death of Lu Jun-hsiang I had three more teachers of Chinese: the deputy head of the imperial academy Hsu Fang, Hanlin academician Chu Yi-fan, and Liang Ting-fen who became famous for planting trees at the tomb of Kuang Hsu.

The tutor who had the deepest influence on me was Chen Pao-shen; the next most influential was my English tutor Reginald Johnston. Chen had a considerable reputation as a scholar in his native Fukien. On passing the palace examination during the Tung Chih period he had been appointed a Hanlin academician at the age of nineteen, and after entering the Grand Secretariat he made a name for himself with his remonstrances to the empress dowager Tzu Hsi. As he did not show Chang Chih-tung's willingness to trim his sails to the political winds he was demoted five grades in 1891 and on a pretext of incompetence returned home to live in retirement for twenty years. On the eve of the 1911 Revolution he was reinstated and was appointed governor of Shansi, but before he left to take up his post he was kept at Peking as my tutor. From then until I went to the Northeast he never left me. He was regarded as the most stable and careful of the Ching veterans in my entourage, and at the time I thought him the most loyal to myself and the "Great Ching". Before I regarded his caution as too much of an encumbrance to me he was the one and only authority to whom I referred all matters whether great or trivial for decision.

"Although the king is small he is a worthy Son of Heaven," was a phrase that Chen Pao-shen often quoted in approval of me, smiling till his eyes became slits behind his spectacles and stroking his thin, white beard.

I always found his conversation interesting. As I began to grow up I asked him almost every day to tell me the latest news about the Republic. When he had finished discussing this he would nearly always go on to talk about "the Tung Chih and Kuang Hsu restoration" and "the Golden Age of Kang Hsi and Chien Lung". He was, naturally enough, particularly fond of telling stories about how he had remonstrated with the empress dowager Tzu Hsi. Whenever he referred to former Ching officials who were now serving the Republic it was always with indignation as he regarded them as turncoats. He spoke as if the Revolution and the Republic were the roots of all evil, and the people associated with them were no better than brigands. "Those who defy the sages have no law; those who defy filial piety have no parents: this is the source of great disorder" was his general conclusion about everything that displeased him. He told me the story of the king of the defeated state of Yueh who slept on firewood and frequently tasted gall to remind himself of his humiliation, and explained the principle of retiring from public affairs and waiting for one's opportunity. After explaining the current situation he would almost invariably come up with this opinion: "The Republic has only been in existence for a few years, but both heaven and the people have from the beginning been angry and dissatisfied with it. Because of the great goodness and bounty of the dynasty over more than two hundred years the people think of the Ching in their hearts: heaven and the people will inevitably end by returning it to power."

Of my other tutors Chu Yi-fan liked to play mahjong all night with the result that he tended to lethargy during the day, and Liang Ting-fen was fond of telling stories about himself. I used to find the bookish air of my tutors intolerable at times; they showed nothing of the scholar's ignorance of profit, however, when I invited them to choose themselves presents from the palace's collections of antiques and art treasures. They were also expert at fishing for honours, and knew how to wheedle congratulatory scrolls out of me.

All these tutors received posthumous titles after their deaths that were the envy of the other Ching survivals. One might almost say that they got whatever they wanted out of me and that they gave me whatever they wanted to in return. My achievements under their coaching were never tested in any examination, but there was one matter — a judgement on "loyalty" — in which I gave them great satisfaction when I was eleven.

The year Prince Ching died his family submitted a request that he be granted a posthumous title, and the Household Department sent me a list of suggestions. Normally such a matter should have been discussed with the tutors, but as I was ill with flu at the time I had not gone to class, so I had to make a decision by myself. As I found the Household Department's list completely unsatisfactory I tossed it aside and wrote out a list of very offensive titles which I sent back. This brought my father over to see me, and in his stammering voice he begged me to remember that the prince belonged to the imperial family. I adamantly refused on the grounds that Prince Ching had been a traitor to the dynasty.

When I went to the schoolroom the next day and told Chen Pao-shen about the affair he was so delighted that he smiled until his eyes were mere slits, and expressed his whole-hearted approval of the way I had stood up to my father. The title finally chosen for Prince Ching was one which I originally thought insulting but which, as I found out too late, implied that I had pardoned him.

Eunuchs

No account of my childhood would be complete without mentioning the eunuchs. They waited on me when I ate, dressed and slept; they accompanied me on my walks and to my lessons; they told me stories; and had rewards and beatings from me. There were times when other people did not have to be with me, but they never left my presence. They were the main companions of my childhood; they were my slaves; and they were my earliest teachers.

While I am not sure when the employment of court eunuchs began, I do know exactly when it ended: the day on which I was dethroned for the third time at the victorious conclusion of the Second World War. This was perhaps the time when the eunuchs were fewest as there were only about ten of them left. It is said that they were most numerous during the Ming Dynasty (1368-1644), when they reached a strength of 100,000. Although there were limits set to their numbers and functions during the Ching Dynasty, there were still over three thousand at the time of the empress dowager Tzu Hsi. Most of the eunuchs fled after the 1911 Revolution, and although the Articles of Favourable Treatment specified that no more eunuchs were to be engaged the Household Department continued to take them on secretly. According to a list dating from 1922 there were still 1,137 then. Two years later, after I had ordered a mass expulsion of the eunuchs, there were about 200 left, of whom the great majority were in the service of the High Consorts and my wives (who also had nearly a hundred maids). From that time on the palace staff was made up of members of the greatly depleted palace guard or else genuinely male servants known as "attendants".

In the past there was a time of day after which there were no true males apart from the guards on duty and the men of the emperor's own family left in the Forbidden City. The duties of the eunuchs were very extensive. In addition to being in attendance at all hours, carrying umbrellas and stoves, and other such jobs their tasks, according to the *Palace Regulations,* included the following: transmitting imperial edicts, leading officials to audiences, and receiving memorials; handling official documents of the various offices of the Household Department, receiving money and grain sent by treasuries outside the palace, and keeping a fire watch; looking after the books of the library, the antiques, calligraphy, paintings, clothing, fowling-pieces, bows and arrows; keeping the ancient bronzes, the *objets de vertu,* the yellow girdles granted to meritorious officials, and fresh and dried fruit; fetching the Imperial

Physicians to attend in the various palaces, and obtaining the materials used in the palace by outside builders; burning incense before the records and precepts of the emperor's ancestors, their portraits, and the gods; checking the comings and goings of the officials of various departments; keeping the registers of the attendance of the Hanlin academicians and of the watches of the officers of the guard; storing the imperial seals; recording the actions of the sovereign; flogging offending eunuchs and serving women; feeding the various living creatures in the palace; sweeping the palace buildings and keeping the gardens tidy; checking the accuracy of the chiming clocks; cutting the emperor's hair; preparing medicine; singing opera; reciting classics and burning incense as Taoist monks in the City Temple; becoming lamas in the Yung Ho Kung as substitutes for the emperor; and many other duties.

The eunuchs in the palace fell into two main categories: Those in attendance on the empress dowager, the emperor, the empress and the imperial consorts on the one hand, and all the rest of the eunuchs on the other. They were very strictly graded and could be divided roughly into chief eunuchs, head eunuchs and ordinary eunuchs. There were chief and head eunuchs in the service of the empress dowager and the empress: the consorts only had head eunuchs. The highest rank normally ever reached by a eunuch was the third grade, but Li Lien-ying, the favourite of the empress dowager Tzu Hsi, had created a precedent for a eunuch being accorded the even higher second grade, so that Chang Chien-ho, the chief eunuch in my service, was given this honour. Other eunuchs were placed in the third to the ninth grade, and below them came the ordinary, ungraded eunuchs, of whom the very lowest in rank were those who had been sent as a punishment to work as menials in the cleaning office. The official salaries of the eunuchs were rather low, with the very highest being eight taels of silver, eight catties of rice and one string plus three hundred copper cash a month; with various legal and illegal "extras", however, their actual incomes were much higher, particularly those of the senior ones. Juan Chin-shou, for example, the deputy chief of my entourage, was so rich that he could wear a different fur gown every day in the winter, and although these gowns included a number of different sables he never wore the same one twice. The sea otter cloak that he wore on New Year's Day alone would have represented a lifetime's expenditure for a petty official. Nearly all the other chief eunuchs and many of the head eunuchs had their own private kitchens, and some even had their own "families" complete with serving women and maid-servants.

The life of the humbler eunuchs on the other hand was extremely hard; they ate poorly, had to endure beatings and other punishments and were left with nobody and nothing to support their old age. They had to live on a very meagre imperial "bounty", and if they were driven out for making some mistake they could only expect a future of begging and starvation.

The eunuchs with whom I was in the closest contact were those of the Mind Nurture Palace, particularly the junior eunuchs of the presence who dressed me and waited on me at mealtimes. They lived in two alleyways behind the Mind Nurture Palace, each of which was under a head eunuch. The eunuchs responsible for cleaning this palace were under another head. All of these eunuchs came under the control of the chief eunuch Chang Chien-ho and the deputy chief eunuch Juan Chin-shou.

When the empress dowager Lung Yu was alive she sent one of her chief eunuchs to be my *anda*, a post in which his duties included looking after me and instructing me in the palace etiquette. But I felt for him nothing of the trust and warmth that I did for Chang Chien-ho, my first teacher in fact if not in name, who was at the time an older man of about fifty with a slight hunchback. On the orders of Lung Yu he taught me to recognize characters printed large on cards and then read through elementary texts with me: the *Three Character Classic* and the *Hundred Surnames*. After I started my formal schooling he used to stand outside my bedroom and read aloud the previous day's lessons to help me to remember them. Like the chief eunuch of any emperor, he would take every opportunity to show his loyalty to me. I could often tell about the developments in the external situation from the changes of his mood,

64

and could even judge from the tone of his voice as he read my lessons to me in the morning whether he was anxious or happy about my prospects.

Chang Chien-ho was my first travelling companion. He used to play at racing me, though of course I always won easily. I also remember that one New Year when the high consort Ching Yi invited me to go over and play dice he was banker; the number I staked my money on always won until I cleaned out the bank. He did not mind — the money was all the High Consort's.

Just like any other child I was fond of being told stories. The stories that Chang Chien-ho and many other eunuchs told me could be divided into two sorts: ghost stories about the palace and myths about "all the spirits helping the sacred Son of Heaven". According to them everything in the palace — bronze cranes, golden jars, trees, wells, stones and so on — had at some time turned into a spirit and shown its magic powers, not to mention the clay images of Kuan Yu, the god of war, and of the Taoist gods. Through these stories, which I never tired of hearing, I believed that all the ghosts and spirits tried to win the emperor's favour and that there were even some that did not succeed, which all went to show that the emperor was the most exalted creature in existence.

The eunuchs said that a bronze crane in one of the halls of the palace had a dent in its left leg because when it had turned itself into a spirit to protect the emperor Chien Lung during a trip to the south of China it had been hit by an arrow from the emperor's bow. It had been so disappointed that it had slipped back to stand in its original position in the palace. The rusty dent on its left leg was supposed to be the arrow wound. They also said that an ancient pine that grew by the Western Fish Pond in the Imperial Garden had shaded Chien Lung throughout one of these southern tours; after his return he had written a poem to it to be inscribed on a nearby wall. What this poem said was something about which the illiterate eunuch did not concern himself.

There was even a myth about the big pearl in the imperial hat. It was said that one day when Chien Lung was strolling beside a stream in the Yuan Ming Yuan Palace he noticed something gleaming in the water which disappeared when he shot at it with a fowling-piece. He had the stream dragged, and a large clam was found with this huge pearl inside. After it became a hat pearl it would often fly away by itself until a hole was bored through it on imperial orders and it was given a golden mount; then it stayed put.

When I was a child I believed all these stories implicitly, as can be seen from the following incident. Once when I was ill at the age of about seven or eight Chang Chien-ho brought me a purple pill to take. When I asked him what sort of medicine it was he said, "Your slave has just had a dream. An old man with a white beard held a pill in his hand and told me that it was a pill of immortality that he had especially brought as a humble present to the Lord of Ten Thousand Years." I was so pleased to hear this that I forgot about my own illness and, remembering the stories of the twenty-four filial sons, I took the pill to the quarters of the four High Consorts to share it with them. Chang Chien-ho must have made some sign to my four mothers as they all looked overjoyed and praised my filial piety. When I happened to go to the Imperial Dispensary to get some medicine some time later I noticed some ordinary pills which looked just like the "pill of immortality". Believe it or not, although I was a little disappointed I still believed the story about the old man with the white beard.

While making me inordinately proud of myself these stories also made me afraid of ghosts from an early age. According to the eunuchs there were ghosts and spirits in every corner of the palace. The lane behind the Lasting Peace Palace was where ghosts grabbed people by the neck; the well outside the Ching Ho Gate was the home of a swarm of she-devils, and had not a piece of iron over the gate kept them in they would have come out every day; every three years a ghost would come and drag a passer-by off one of the bridges in the lakes in the palace grounds. The more I heard such stories the more frightened I got, and the greater my fear the keener my appetite for them. From the age of about eleven I became an addict of books of stories of the supernatural (which the eunuchs bought for me) and these, combined with the incessant sacrifices to gods and Buddhist worship, the spirit dances of the *shaman* wizards and so on, made me even more afraid of ghosts and spirits, of the dark, of thunder and lightning, and of being alone in a room.

Every evening at dusk when all the people who came to the palace on business had gone away a spine-chilling call came from the Chien Ching Palace (Palace of Cloudless Heaven), the still centre of the Forbidden City: "Draw the bolts, lock up, careful with the lanterns." As the last drawn-out sounds of this died away there arose waves of ghostly responses from the eunuchs on duty in all the corners of the palace. This practice, which had been instituted by the emperor Kang Hsi to keep the eunuchs alert, filled the palace with an eerie atmosphere. I did not dare to go out of doors for the rest of the evening and felt as if all the ghosts and demons in the stories were gathered around the windows and doors.

It was not just with the intention of frightening me and pandering to me that the eunuchs used to feed me with such stories, they were extremely superstitious themselves. Chang Chien-ho was no exception, whenever he was faced with some problem he would always consult the *Record of the Jade Box* before making a decision. The ordinary eunuchs were very devout in their offerings to the "palace gods": snakes, foxes, weasels and hedgehogs. There was a great variety of other forms of worship in the palace that were carried out by the imperial house; the palace gods, however, were the protectors of the eunuchs and were not included in the offerings made by the royal family. According to the eunuchs the palace gods had been made immortals of the second grade by some emperor. A eunuch once told me that one evening when he was standing on the steps outside the Palace of Cloudless Heaven a man wearing a hat button of the Second Grade and official robes and insignia had grabbed him and thrown him down the steps: this had been one of the palace gods. The eunuchs would not eat beef, and one of them told me that if they offended this taboo the palace gods would punish them by making them rub their lips against the bark of a tree until they bled. Whenever a eunuch went into an empty hall they would shout in a loud voice "Opening the palace" before they opened the door: thus they avoided being punished for accidentally meeting a palace god. On the first and fifteenth of every month, at New Year and at other festivals they would make offerings to them, usually of eggs, dried bean curd, spirits, and cake; at the New Year and other festivals, they would also offer whole pigs and sheep as well as large quantities of fruit. For the poorly paid eunuchs of the lowest ranks their share in all this was a burden, but it was one which they gladly undertook as they hoped that the palace gods would protect them from the beating and other forms of ill-treatment from which they often suffered.

The eunuchs had many ways of augmenting their incomes. There are descriptions in plays and novels of how the emperor Kuang Hsu had to give money to Li Lien-ying, the chief eunuch of the palace of the empress dowager Tzu Hsi, as otherwise he would make things difficult for him and refuse to announce him when he went to pay his respects to Tzu Hsi. While such things as this could not have happened I did hear a great deal about how the eunuchs used to extort money from high officials. At the time of Emperor Tung Chih's marriage the Household Department missed out one part of the palace in a distribution of bribes. On the wedding day the eunuchs of the section that had been overlooked sent for an official of the Household Department saying that a pane of glass in one of the windows of the palace in question was cracked. As a Household Department official he was not allowed to mount the terrace of the palace unless he had been specially summoned, so he could only see the crack from a distance. He was terrified, as he would be in very deep water if Tzu Hsi heard that there was something as ill-omened as a broken window on the wedding day. The eunuchs then said that there was no need to go and look for a workman as they could discreetly change the pane themselves. Although he realized that this was a racket the Household Department man had no option but to send over a sum of money; and as soon as this was done the window was repaired. This was not very difficult as the "crack" in the glass was only a strand of hair stuck on to it.

When Chung Lun, the father of Shih Hsu, was comptroller of the Household Department he once failed to distribute enough bribes. One of the eunuchs who was dissatisfied with his portion lay in wait for him one day when he was going to an audience with the Empress Dowager and deliberately threw a basinful of water out of a room and drenched his sable jacket. The eunuch pretended to be distraught and begged to be punished. Chung Lun, knowing that he was in no position to make a scene as the Dowager was waiting to see him, desperately begged the eunuch to think of some way out. The eunuch produced another sable jacket, saying, "This humble place of ours would be very grateful to be able to share in your good fortune; we know you will be very bountiful." The eunuchs always kept a complete range of court clothing to be hired out at short notice to officials. Chung Lun had no choice but to submit to this extortion and pay a very considerable "rental".

A former official of the Household Department told me that when I got married my chief eunuch Juan Chin-shou (who had replaced Chang Chien-ho) extorted a sizable sum of money from them. As the Department had been ordered by me to keep the expenses of the wedding within a limit of 360,000 taels there had been little left over above the actual costs for the eunuchs, so that the chief eunuch blocked the whole plan. One of the officials of the Household Department had to go to Juan Chin-shou's quarters to intercede with him, but his pleas and flattery were of no effect until he accepted Juan's way of doing things.

But I believe that Chang Chien-ho and Juan Chin-shou were no comparison with Chang Yuan-fu, the chief eunuch of the empress dowager Lung Yu. When I was in Tientsin he was living there too in a magnificent mansion in the British concession in the style of a warlord with several concubines and a host of servants. One of his concubines fled to the police station of the British concession to escape his cruelty; but such was the miraculous power of his wealth that so far from protecting her the police station sent her back to that hellish household. He had her beaten to death, but nobody dared touch him.

My Nurse

In the journal of my actions and utterances kept by my tutor Liang Ting-fen there is an entry for February 21, 1913:

> His Majesty frequently beats the eunuchs; he has had seventeen flogged recently for minor offences. His subject Chen Pao-shen and others remonstrated but His Majesty did not accept their advice.

That goes to show how by the age of eleven flogging a eunuch was a part of my daily routine. My cruelty and love of wielding my power were already too firmly set for persuasion to have any effect on me.

Whenever I was in a bad temper or feeling depressed the eunuchs would be in for trouble; and their luck was also out if I was in high spirits and wanted some sort of amusement. In my childhood I had many strange tastes, and apart from playing with camels, keeping ants, rearing worms, and watching fights between dogs and bulls I took the greatest delight in playing unkind tricks on people. Long before I learnt how to make the Administrative Bureau beat people many a eunuch came to grief through my practical jokes. Once when I was about seven or eight I had a brainwave: I wanted to see whether those servile eunuchs were really obedient to the "divine Son of Heaven". I picked on one of them and pointed at a piece of dirt on the floor. "Eat that for me," I ordered, and he really knelt down and ate it. Another time an aged eunuch almost died as a result of my soaking him with a fire pump.

Growing up as I did, with people pandering to my every whim and being completely obedient to me, I developed this taste for cruelty. Although my tutors tried to dissuade me from it with their talk about the "way of compassion and benevolence", at the same time they acknowledged my authority and taught me about that authority. No matter how many stories they told me about illustrious sovereigns and sage rulers of history I still remained the emperor and "different from ordinary people", so that their advice had little effect.

70

The only person in the palace who could control my cruelty was my nurse Mrs. Wang. Although she was completely illiterate and incapable of talking about the "way of compassion and benevolence" or illustrious sovereigns and sage rulers of history, I could not disregard the advice she gave me.

Once I was so pleased with a puppet show given by one of the eunuchs that I decided to reward him with a cake; then an evil inspiration came to me. I opened up a bag filled with iron filings that I used for doing exercises and put some of them into the cake. When my nurse saw what I was doing she said to me, "Master, who will be able to eat those filings?"

"I want to see what he looks like when he eats the cake."

"But he'll break his teeth. If he breaks his teeth he won't be able to eat anything, and if he can't eat anything then where will he be?"

I could see that she was right, but I did not want to miss my fun, so I said, "I just want to see him breaking his teeth this once." Nurse then suggested that I put dried lentils in instead as it would be great fun when he bit them. Thus she saved that eunuch from disaster.

One time when I was playing with an air-gun, shooting lead pellets at the eunuchs' quarters and making little holes in the paper of their windows, I was really enjoying myself. Then somebody sent for my nurse to come to the eunuchs' rescue.

"Master, there are people in there. You'll hurt someone, if you shoot into the house!"

Only then did it occur to me that there might be people in the room and that they might get injured. My nurse was the only person who ever told me that other people were just as human as myself. I was not the only person to have teeth: other people had them too. Mine were not the only teeth not made for biting iron filings. Just as I had to eat so did others get hungry when they did not eat. Other people had feelings; other people would feel the same pain as I would if they were hit by air-gun pellets. This was all common knowledge which I knew as well as anybody; but in that environment I found it rather hard to remember it as I never would consider others, let alone think of them in the same terms as myself. In my mind others were only my slaves or subjects. In all my years in the palace I was only reminded by my nurse's homely words that other men were the same as myself.

I grew up in my nurse's bosom, being suckled by her until I was eight, and until then I was as inseparable from her as a baby from its mother. When I was eight the High Consorts had her sent away without my knowledge. I would gladly have kept her in exchange for all four of my mothers in the palace, but no matter how I howled they would not bring her back. I see now that I had nobody who really understood humanity around me once my nurse had gone. But what little humanity I learnt from her before the age of eight I gradually lost afterwards.

After my wedding I sent people to find her and sometimes had her to stay with me for a few days. Towards the end of the "Manchukuo" period I brought her to Changchun and supported her there until I left the Northeast. She never once took advantage of her special position to beg any favours. She had a mild nature and never quarrelled with anybody; on her comely face there was always a slight smile. She did not talk much and was often silent. If someone else did not take the initiative in talking with her she would just smile without saying a word. When I was young I used to find these smiles of hers rather strange. Her eyes seemed to be fixed on something far, far in the distance, and I often wondered if she had seen something interesting in the sky outside of the window or in a picture hanging on the wall. She never spoke about her own life and experiences. After my special pardon I visited her adopted son and found out what suffering and humiliation the "Great Ching Dynasty" had inflicted on this woman who suckled a "Great Ching Emperor" with her own milk.

She was born in 1887 to a poor peasant family named Chiao in a village of Jenchiu County in Chihli (now Hopei Province). There were three other people in her family: her parents and a brother six years older than herself. The fifty-year-old father rented a few *mou* of low-lying land which was parched when it did not rain and flooded when it did. What with rents and taxes they did not get enough to eat even in good years. In 1890 there were disastrous floods in northern Chihli and her family had to leave their village as refugees. Her father thought of abandoning her several times during their wanderings, but he always put her back into one of the baskets slung from his carrying pole. The other basket contained the tattered clothes and bedding that was all the property they had in the world. They did not have a single grain of food. When she later told her adopted son about how she had been in such danger of being abandoned she had not a word of complaint against her father; she only repeated that he had been hungry for so long that he could no longer carry her. He had not been able to beg a scrap of food on their journey as everyone they met had been reduced to more or less the same state.

Finally the two parents with their son of nine and daughter of three managed to drag themselves to Peking. They had originally planned to take refuge in the house of a eunuch who was a relative of theirs, but when he refused to see them, they had to drift round the streets as beggars. Peking was full of tens of thousands of refugees who slept in the streets moaning with hunger and cold. At this very time the court was carrying out large-scale building at the Summer Palace and my family was spending money like dirt on my grandfather Prince Chun's funeral. Meanwhile the victims of the floods, whose sweat and blood had provided that money, were on the brink of death and selling their own children. The Chiao family wanted to sell their daughter but could find no buyer. The prefect of Shuntienfu opened a congee kitchen as a measure to prevent disturbances and so they were able to stay for a while. A barber took on the nine-year-old boy as an apprentice, and this enabled them to last out the winter, albeit with difficulty.

With the coming of spring the refugees thought of their land and faced the prospect that the congee kitchen would soon close, so they drifted off home again. Back in the village the Chiaos spent several more cold and hungry years, and in 1900 the allied armies of the foreign powers devastated the district. The daughter of the family was now a girl of thirteen, and she fled again to Peking where she stayed with her brother the barber. But he was unable to support her, so when she was sixteen she was half sold and half married to a yamen runner named Wang. Her husband developed tuberculosis, but lived a rather loose life. After three years as a downtrodden slave she gave birth to a daughter, shortly after which her husband died, leaving his wife, daughter and parents destitute.

This was just about the time that I was born, and the household of Prince Chun was looking for a wet-nurse for me. She was chosen from among twenty applicants for her healthy and pleasant appearance and the richness of her milk. For the sake of the wages with which she could support her parents-in-law and her daughter she accepted the most degrading conditions: she was not allowed to return home or to see her own child, she had to eat a bowl of unsalted fat meat every day, and so on. For two ounces of silver a month a human being was turned into a dairy cow.

In the third year in which she was my nurse her own daughter died of malnutrition, but my family kept this news from her lest it should affect the quality of her milk.

In the ninth year a woman servant quarrelled with a eunuch and the High Consorts decided to expel them and my nurse as well. This docile and long-suffering woman, who had borne everything in those nine years with a slight smile and a set stare, only then discovered that her own child had long been dead.

CHAPTER THREE

FROM THE FORBIDDEN CITY TO THE JAPANESE LEGATION

The Yuan Shih-kai Period

It was a peculiarity of morning in the Forbidden City that deep in the palace one could sometimes hear the sounds of the outside world. You could make out the cries of pedlars quite distinctly, as well as the rumbling of the wooden wheels of heavy carts and, at times, sounds of soldiers singing. The eunuchs used to call this phenomenon the "city of sounds". After I left the Forbidden City I often used to recall the "city of sounds" and the strange images it conjured up for me. What made the deepest impressions were the military bands that sometimes could be heard playing in the neighbouring palace of the President of the Republic. "Yuan Shih-kai has been eating," the chief eunuch Chang Chien-ho said to me once. "He has music at mealtimes, which is even grander than Your Majesty."

From the way he screwed his face up it was clear that he felt very indignant. Even though I was only about eight at the time I could detect the touch of sadness in his voice. The sound of the bands brought the most humiliating picture to my mind: Yuan Shih-kai sitting there with even more dishes spread in front of him than the Empress Dowager, and an army of servants waiting on him, making music for him and fanning him.

There was another "city of sounds" in which I became more and more interested as I grew older, and which I heard about from my tutors: the rumours about my restoration.

Restoration, in the language of the Forbidden City, was "recovery of the ancestral heritage"; in the language of the former officials of the Ching it was "the glorious return of the old order" or "returning government to the Ching". Activities with this aim in view did not begin with my brief restoration in 1917, nor did they end with my flight to the Japanese Legation in 1924. One would be safe

77

in saying that they did not cease for a day from the abdication proclamation in 1912 to the establishment of the "Empire of Manchukuo" in 1934.[1]   At first I played my role under the direction of adults, but later I was able to act on my own initiative, guided by my class instincts.   In my childhood my tutors were my directors, and behind them there were of course the senior officials of the Household Department and my father, who supervised the affairs of the imperial house with the consent of the President of the Republic. Although their fervour was not a whit less than that of anyone outside the palace, I gradually came to understand that they had not got the real power to bring about a restoration; they even realized this themselves.   Comical though it may seem, the Forbidden City pinned its hopes on the very men who ruled the country in place of the Ching.   The first object of these illusions was President Yuan Shih-kai, for all that he did to arouse the palace's resentment.

On December 31, 1912 my tutor Chen Pao-shen came into the schoolroom, sat down, and, instead of taking up his red brush to punctuate our text, looked at me for a moment with a quizzical smile before saying:

"Tomorrow is New Year's Day by the Western calendar, and the Republic is going to send someone over to convey greetings to Your Majesty.   He will be the representative of their president."

I cannot remember whether this was the first time that he acted as my political director, but it was the first time I had seen him in one of the rare moments when he looked pleased with himself. He told me that when I received this formal visitor from the Republic I should treat him as I would the minister of a foreign country.   I would not have to say anything and Shao Ying, the Comptroller of the Household Department, would be there to look after everything; all I would have to do would be to sit behind the dragon table and observe the proceedings.

----

[1] Strictly speaking, the restoration movement did not come to an end then as some people worked for the establishment of a "Later Ching" after the Japanese invasion of north China.   As their Japanese masters did not approve, their efforts came to nothing.

The next day I was dressed in the full imperial regalia of golden dragon coat and gown, hat with a pearl button, pearl necklace, and I sat solemnly on the throne in the Cloudless Heaven Palace. A Minister of the Presence stood on either side of me, and beside them were Companions of the Presence and sword-bearing imperial bodyguards. Chu Chi-chien, the envoy of President Yuan, entered the hall and bowed to me from a distance, advanced a few more steps, bowed again, came up to my throne dais, made a third and very low bow; then he delivered his congratulatory address. When he had finished Shao Ying ascended the throne dais and knelt before me. I took the reply that had been written out beforehand from a wooden box covered with yellow silk and handed it to Shao Ying, who stood up to read it to the envoy. Then he gave it to Chu Chi-chien, who bowed once again and withdrew. The ceremony was over.

The change in the atmosphere was even more marked the next morning. Chang Chien-ho's voice rang clear as he read the previous day's lessons to me, and in the schoolroom my tutor Chen Pao-shen twirled his white beard into a ball and wagged his head as he said, "The Articles of Favourable Treatment are stored in the national archives and recognized by all the powers. Even that president of theirs can't flout them."

Not long after this the President sent envoys to convey his congratulations on my birthday, which falls on the 13th of the first month in the Chinese calendar. These attentions from Yuan Shih-kai encouraged those princes and former Ching officials who had been lying low throughout the first year of the Republic to put on their robes with official insignia and to wear their red hat buttons and peacock feathers; some of them even went so far as to revive the practice of having outriders to clear the way and a retinue crowding around them when they went through the streets. The northern gate of the palace and the Forbidden City were bustling with activity for a while. In the first year of the Republic these people had nearly all come to the palace in ordinary clothes and only changed into court dress after their arrival, but from the beginning of the second year they dared to go along the street in full imperial costume.

The birthday and then the death of the empress dowager Lung Yu in 1913 were the occasions when the splendour of the old days was fully restored. Lung Yu's birthday was on March 15 and she died seven days later. Yuan Shih-kai sent Liang Shih-yi, the head of his secretariat, to congratulate her on her birthday; in his official letter he wrote solemnly, "The President of the Great Republic of China writes to Her Majesty the Great Ching Empress Dowager Lung Yu." After this envoy had gone Chao Ping-chun, the prime minister, arrived with the whole of the cabinet to pay his respects.

Yuan Shih-kai's reaction to the death of Lung Yu was even more impressive: he himself wore a black armband; he ordered that flags were to be flown at half-mast throughout the country and that civil and military officials were to wear mourning for 27 days; and he sent the whole cabinet to pay their last respects to her. A so-called National Memorial Assembly was held in the Palace of Supreme Harmony with the Head of the Senate as master of ceremonies, and a similar meeting conducted by the army at which another of Yuan's trusted henchmen, General Tuan Chi-jui, presided. In the Forbidden City men in black court robes and Western dress came and went side by side to the sound of the wails of the eunuchs. The members of the royal family and the nobility, who had been ordered to wear mourning for 100 days, were beaming with delight. What gave them most pleasure was the presence of Hsu Shih-chang from Tsingtao and his acceptance of the honour conferred on him by the Ching house of wearing a peacock feather. After the Ching abdication this Grand Tutor of the Ching house had fled to the German-occupied Tsingtao as a refugee. I shall have something to say later about the significance of his arrival in Peking.

Before the obsequies for Lung Yu were over the expedition against Yuan Shih-kai that was known as the "second revolution" started in the south of China and ended not many days later in Yuan's victory. After this Yuan surrounded the National Assembly with his military police and forced it to elect him as full president (instead of acting president as he had been before). He sent a report to me saying that he had previously organized a provisional Republican government in obedience to the edict of the empress dowager Lung Yu and that he had now been elected full president, thanks to the regard for the common good of the "Great Ching Empress Dowager Lung Yu" and the "Great Ching Emperor". He was going to lead the people to good government and order, and strictly observe the Articles of Favourable Treatment to console Lung Yu's spirit in heaven.

Many of the veteran officials changed their views on Yuan Shih-kai. They said that Yuan had only agreed to a republic as a trick to defeat the South, that the term used for my abdication might really only mean a temporary retirement, and that when he referred to "running" a republic it meant that it was only an experiment. Indeed, such was the mood of the time that when the cabinet came to the funerals of the emperor Kuang Hsu and the empress dowager Lung Yu the Republican premier changed into court mourning robes and performed the ninefold kotow before the coffins. When my tutor Liang Ting-fen saw that the Republic's foreign minister, who had been a Ching official, was still in Western dress he upbraided him to his face and made him admit that he was less than nothing.

When 1914, the third year of the Republic, began there was a feeling that this was to be the year of restoration. One thing after another made the Ching loyalists more and more excited: Yuan Shih-kai sacrificed to Confucius, reverted to using feudal administrative titles, established an institute to write an official history of Ching, and promoted former officials of the Ching. What most dazzled them was the appointment of Chao Erh-sun, a former Ching Viceroy of the Northeastern Provinces, as head of the Institute for Ching History. My tutor Chen and others regarded him as a turncoat, but he said of himself, "I am a Ching official, I edit the Ching history, I eat the Ching's rice, and I do the Ching's business." Lao Nai-hsuan, a former vice-minister of education and chancellor of the Metropolitan College under the Ching who had taken refuge in Tsingtao, openly advocated in an article that government should be handed back to the Ching and urged Hsu Shih-chang in a letter to persuade Yuan Shih-kai to do this. Hsu Shih-chang, then both a

Grand Tutor of the Ching house and Secretary of State of the Republic, showed Lao Nai-hsuan's article to Yuan Shih-kai, and Yuan invited Lao to come to Peking as an adviser. Other writers too were advocating a Ching restoration, and there was even said to be a bandit in Szechuan known as Thirteenth Brother who wore Ching court dress and rode in a green wool-covered litter with all the airs of an elder statesman of the late dynasty, waiting to enjoy his share of the fruits of restoration.

In the Forbidden City there was no more talk of moving out to the Summer Palace as there had been shortly after the abdication. To be on the safe side, Shih Hsu, the cautious head of the Household Department, went to see Yuan Shih-kai, who was his sworn brother, and brought back some even more exciting news. Yuan had said to him, "Don't you see, brother, that these articles were just made to cope with the southerners? The imperial ancestral temple is in the Forbidden City, so how could it do for His Majesty to move? Besides, who could live in the palace if His Majesty didn't?" I was told about this a long time later by a man who had worked in the Household Department; in those days Shih Hsu and my father never discussed such matters with me directly, and would only do so through my tutor Chen Pao-shen when it was necessary. My tutor's line at the time was, "By the look of things that president of theirs still gives special treatment to the Great Ching. The Articles of Favourable Treatment are stored in the national archives. . . ."

Chen Pao-shen always seemed to leave something unsaid. Looking back on it now, it would seem to be an indication of his "cautious" attitude. The optimism in the Forbidden City in those days was undoubtedly cautious and reserved compared with that of some of the veterans of the Ching outside the palace. Of course, many of Yuan Shih-kai's actions — from his open references to not forgetting Lung Yu's "spirit in heaven" to his secret assurance that "His Majesty" would not have to leave the imperial palace and ancestral temple — gave rise to a number of illusions inside the Forbidden City; but this was as far as they expected him to go, so that the excitement of the palace had to be partly concealed.

The change in the political climate in Peking at the end of what had at first been called the "year of restoration" showed that this reserve had been justified.

The change in the political climate started when an official of the Republic's Inspectorate proposed that the rumours about a restoration should be investigated. Yuan Shih-kai instructed the Home Ministry to "examine and deal with" the case, and as a result Sung Yu-jen, one of the advocates of the Ching restoration, was sent back to his hometown under an escort provided by the army command. This news caused a panic in some circles: no more was heard about returning the Ching to power, and Lao Nai-hsuan decided not to leave his refuge in Tsingtao and come to Peking to take the post as adviser that Yuan had offered him. But there was still considerable confusion: on the document about the investigation of restoration activities Yuan had written the enigmatic words "Rumours about a restoration are severely prohibited, but do not go into them too thoroughly", and when Sung Yu-jen was sent back to his hometown Yuan sent him 3,000 Mexican dollars and arranged that all the government yamens on his route should feast him; thus it was not clear whether Sung was being punished or rewarded. In 1915, the fourth year of the Republic Frank J. Goodnow,[1] an American adviser in the office of President Yuan, published an article in which he maintained that a Republican system was not suited to Chinese conditions. After this came the appearance of the Chou An Hui (Society for the Preservation of Peace), an organization entirely under the control of Yuan Shih-kai which recommended that Yuan should become the emperor of China. The type of restoration that Yuan had in mind was now clear for everyone to see, and now that this was so obvious the atmosphere in the Forbidden City changed markedly.

It was at this time that I heard military bands playing in the presidential palace. The three great halls in the southern part of

---

[1] Goodnow had been a professor of Columbia University in America. This article of his, entitled "On Republic and Monarchy", laid the theoretical foundation for Yuan Shih-kai's monarchy by asserting such nonsense as "a monarchy is better suited than a republic to China".

the imperial palace were then being renovated and one could get a clear view of the painters at work on their scaffolding from the top of the steps of the Mind Nurture Palace in which I lived. The eunuch Chang Chien-ho told me that these were preparations for Yuan Shih-kai's accession to the throne. Later Pu Lun, a member of the royal clan, submitted a petition to Yuan in the name of the imperial house and the eight banners requesting him to take the throne. Pu Lun was rewarded with the title of prince of the first rank and sent to the palace to demand the weapons carried in imperial processions and the imperial seals from the High Consorts. This news was both mortifying and frightening to me as although my tutor Chen Pao-shen would not say so in as many words I knew the old saying that "there are neither two suns in the sky nor two rulers in the country". When Yuan made himself emperor he was not likely to tolerate my continued existence as a superfluous sovereign. There were too many historical examples pointing the other way: had not the Grand Historian of antiquity counted that "in the Spring and Autumn Period (770 to 475 B.C.) there were thirty-six cases of monarchs being killed."

Everyone in the palace was passionately concerned about the activities in the three great halls. Whenever people walked across the courtyard they would take an anxious look in that direction to see whether the work of painting and renovation with which their fate was so closely bound was finished yet. The High Consorts would burn incense and pray every day to the tutelary god of the Ching Dynasty to lend them aid. The processional weapons were hastily handed over but the imperial seals were not taken away as they were inscribed in both the Han and the Manchu languages and thus unsuitable for Yuan's purposes.

The big change in the schoolroom was that the tutors became very polite to my fellow-student Yu Chung as he was the son of Yuan Shih-kai's protégé Pu Lun. One day when Yu Chung was out of the schoolroom on a visit to the High Consorts' quarters, Chen Pao-shen looked out of the windows to make sure that there was not anybody outside, produced a piece of paper, and said to me furtively:

"Your subject made a divination last night. Please look at what it omened, Your Majesty."

I took the paper, which read "My enemy has a sickness; he is not able to approach me. Auspicious." Chen explained that it meant that my enemy Yuan Shih-kai faced a bleak future and would be unable to endanger me. This was a good omen. In addition to making this divination by the trigrams of the *Book of Changes* he had scorched the tortoise shell and consulted the milfoil and they had given favourable omens too. He told me this so that I could stop worrying. The old fellow had used all the methods of divination of the primitive society of antiquity to ascertain my fate. He announced his happy conclusion that the nefarious Yuan could not come to a good end and that the Articles of Favourable Treatment were inviolable.

Activity by my tutors, my father and the Household Department to protect my position and the Articles of Favourable Treatment was not confined to consulting the oracles, and though I was told nothing about it officially I was not completely in the dark. They made a deal with Yuan Shih-kai by which the Ching house would support Yuan as emperor and he would observe the Articles. Documents to this effect were exchanged, including an assurance in Yuan's own handwriting that he would observe the Articles and incorporate them into his constitution. It was even arranged that I would take one of his daughters as my empress, but before any of these agreements could be put into effect Yuan died in June 1916, after only 83 days as emperor, with a storm of opposition ringing in his ears.

The Restoration of 1917

The news of Yuan Shih-kai's death was received with great rejoicing in the Forbidden City. The eunuchs rushed hither and thither spreading the news, the High Consorts went to burn incense to the tutelary god, and there were no lessons that day in the Yu Ching Palace.

New opinions were expressed in the palace.

"Yuan died because he wanted to usurp the throne."

"It's not that a monarchy is impracticable, it's just that the people want their old sovereign."

"Yuan Shih-kai was different from Napoleon III: he had no such ancestry on which to rely for support."

"It would be much better to return things to the old sovereign than to have a Mr. Yuan as emperor."

All these voices were in tune with the saying of my tutor that "because of the great goodness and rich benefit conferred by our dynasty the people of the whole country are thinking of the old order."

I was now old enough to be interested in the papers, and it was not many days after Yuan's death before they were full of reports of "Failure of Rising by Imperial Clan Party" and "Mongol and Manchu Bandit Threat". From these news items I learnt that four Manchu noblemen who had been open opponents of the Republic from the beginning still were acting on my behalf. Of these four one had taken refuge in a foreign concession in Tientsin and the others were staying in the Japanese-leased Lushun and Talien and, acting through Japanese *ronin*, were co-operating with Japanese militarists and financiers in armed activities for a restoration. The most important of these was Shan Chi, Prince Su, who had got a million yen from the financier Ohira Kihachiro and had Japanese officers training an army of several thousand Manchu and Mongol bandits. They started making trouble after the death of Yuan Shih-kai. One group of them under the Mongol noble Babojab came close to Changchiakou (Kalgan) and was quite dangerous until Babojab was killed by one of his subordinates. Even at the height of the crisis, while "loyalist" and Republican troops were fighting in various places in the Northeast, the Republic and the "little court" continued their exchanges of courtesy visits. The rising excitement in the Forbidden City after the death of Yuan Shih-kai was not influenced by Babojab and Shan Chi's armed rising, and neither was it affected by their defeat.

After Yuan's death, Li Yuan-hung succeeded him as president with Tuan Chi-jui as premier. The palace sent a representative to congratulate President Li and Li Yuan-hung returned to the palace the imperial processional weapons that Yuan had taken. Some of the Ching princes, nobles and senior officials were even given Republican decorations, including a few who had been in hiding during Yuan Shih-kai's time. The Household Department was busier than ever conferring such honours as posthumous titles, the permission to ride a horse in the Forbidden City or wear a peacock's feather; bringing girls for the High Consorts to select ladies-in-waiting from; and secretly recruiting more eunuchs despite the prohibition in the Articles of Favourable Treatment. And of course there were all sorts of contacts being made that I did not know about, from private dinners to public banquets for the members of the Republic's parliament.

In short, the Forbidden City was as active as it had been in the old days; and with Chang Hsun's audience with me in 1917 the restoration movement reached a climax.

I had not received many people in audience before then and they had all been Manchus. Those parts of my day that were not devoted to studying in the Yu Ching Palace or reading newspapers in the Mind Nurture Palace I mostly spent playing. I was very excited to see how many people wearing court clothes were always coming and going in the palace; the news of the rising of the "loyalist" troops of Prince Su and Babojab thrilled me even more, and their defeat naturally depressed me. But generally speaking I soon forgot about such matters; and while I could not help worrying about the flight of Prince Su to Lushun and his uncertain fate, the highly amusing sight of a camel sneezing was enough to make me forget all about his predicament. With my father, my tutors and my ministers to look after things what need was there for me to concern myself? When my tutors told me about any matter it meant that everything had already been discussed and agreed. So it was on June 16, 1917.

Chen Pao-shen, who had recently been granted the title of "Grand Guardian", and Liang Ting-fen, a newly appointed tutor, came into the schoolroom together that day; and before they had sat down Chen Pao-shen said, "Your Majesty will have no lessons today. A high official is coming for an audience with Your Majesty, and a eunuch will be here to announce him very shortly."

"Who is he?"

"Chang Hsun, the Viceroy of Kiangsi, Kiangsu and Anhwei and Governor of Kiangsu."

"Chang Hsun? The Chang Hsun who won't cut his queue off?"

"Yes, that's the man," said Liang Ting-fen, nodding in approval. "Your Majesty's memory is very good." Liang missed no opportunity to flatter me.

This had in fact been no feat of memory as Chen Pao-shen had told me the story of Chang Hsun not long before. From the beginning of the Republic he and his troops had kept their queues. Yuan Shih-kai owed his successful crushing of the "second revolution" in 1913 to the capture of Nanking by his pigtailed soldiers. When in the sack of the city Chang Hsun's men had mistakenly injured some of the personnel of the Japanese consulate he went and apologized to the Japanese consul in person and promised to pay full damages. He announced national mourning for the death of the empress dowager Lung Yu in a telegram of condolences and went on to say that "all we Republican officials are the subjects of the Great Ching". After the death of Yuan Shih-kai another telegram of Chang's was published in the press in which he made known his political position. Its first item was "I attach the greatest importance to all of the Articles of Favourable Treatment of the Ching house". I believed that he was a loyal subject and was interested to see what he looked like.

According to the practice of the Ching house nobody else could be present when a high official was received in audience by the emperor. For this reason my tutor would have to give me some coaching and tell me what to say before I received anyone who did not come regularly. This time Chen Pao-shen told me very seriously that I must praise Chang Hsun's loyalty, that I should remember that he was the High Inspecting Commissioner for the Yangtse River and had sixty battalions of troops in the region of Hsuchow and Yenchow; I could ask him about the military situation in Hsuchow and Yenchow and was to make it very clear that I was interested in him. Finally Chen repeated two or three times, "Chang Hsun is bound to praise Your Majesty. You must remember to reply modestly so as to display Your Majesty's divine virtue."

I had tried to form a picture of what Chang Hsun looked like from the picture magazines that the eunuchs bought for me, but I had not yet succeeded when I got down from my carrying chair. Soon after I reached the Mind Nurture Palace he arrived. As I sat on the throne he knelt before me and kotowed.

"Your subject Chang Hsun kneels and pays his respects. . . ."

I waved to him to sit on a chair as the court had ended the practice of having officials report in a kneeling position. He kotowed again to thank me and then sat down. I dutifully asked him about the military situation in the Hsuchow and Yenchow area, but I did not pay any attention to his reply. I was somewhat disappointed at the appearance of this "loyal subject" of mine. He was dressed in a thin silk jacket and gown, his face was ruddy and set with very bushy eyebrows, and he was fat. The sight of his short neck made me think that but for his whiskers he would have looked like one of the eunuch cooks: he was far from perfect. I looked carefully to see if he had a queue and indeed he did: a mottled grey one.

Then he started to talk about me and, as Chen Pao-shen had expected, spoke in very respectful terms.

"Your Majesty is truly brilliant," he said.

"I am not up to much," I replied. "I am young and I know very little."

"Emperor Sheng Tsu of this dynasty (Kang Hsi) acceded to the throne when of tender years. He was only five."

"How can I be compared with my august ancestor? He was my ancestor, after all. . . ."

This audience was not much longer than an ordinary one, and he went after five or six minutes. I found his speech rather coarse and reckoned that he was probably not a second Tseng Kuo-fan:[1] I was not very excited by him. But when Chen Pao-shen and Liang Ting-fen came to me the next day beaming with smiles to tell me that Chang Hsun had praised my modesty and intelligence I was very pleased with myself. I did not ask myself why Chang had come for an audience, or why my tutors were so visibly excited, or why the Household Department had given him such lavish presents, or why the High Consorts had held a banquet for him.

About a fortnight later, on July 1, my tutors Chen Pao-shen, Liang Ting-fen and the newly arrived Chu Yu-fan came to the schoolroom together with very grave faces. Chen Pao-shen spoke first.

"Chang Hsun is here. . . ."

"Has he come to pay his respects?"

"No, he has not just come for that. All preparations have been made and everything has been settled. He has come to bring Your Majesty back to power and restore the Great Ching."

Seeing that I was startled he went on to say, "Your Majesty must allow Chang Hsun to do this. He is asking for a mandate on behalf of the people; heaven has complied with the wishes of the people."

I was stunned by this completely unexpected good news. I stared at Chen Pao-shen in a daze, hoping that he would go on to tell me a little about how to be a "true emperor".

"There is no need to say much to Chang Hsun. All you have to do is to accept." Chen Pao-shen spoke with great confidence. "But it wouldn't do to accept at once; you must refuse at first and only finally say, 'If things are so then I must force myself to do it.' "

I returned to the Mind Nurture Palace and received Chang Hsun in audience again. What Chang Hsun said was much the same as had been written in his memorial requesting a restoration, except that it was less elegantly expressed.

---

[1] Tseng Kuo-fan (1811-72), a Han landowner and bureaucrat from Hunan, played a major role in suppressing the revolutionary Taiping Heavenly Kingdom, thus helping to save the Ching Dynasty from well-deserved destruction.

"The empress dowager Lung Yu was not prepared to inflict a disaster on the people for the sake of one family's illustrious position, so she issued a decree ordering that a republic be organized. But who would have thought it, it was run so badly that the people have no way to make a living. . . . A republic does not suit our country. . . . Only Your Majesty's restoration will save the people."

When he had finished gabbling I said, "I am too young; I have neither talent nor virtue. I could not undertake so great an office." He lavished praises on me and droned on about how Emperor Kang Hsi had come to the throne at the age of five. While he talked I thought of a question: "What about their President? Will we give him favourable treatment?"

"Li Yuan-hung has already memorialized asking that he be allowed to resign. All that is necessary is for Your Majesty to grant his request."

"Ah. . . ." Although I did not understand what was going on I thought that my tutors must have settled everything and that I had better end this audience quickly. "If things are so I must force myself to do as you say." With this I regarded myself as the emperor of the "Great Ching Empire" again.

After Chang Hsun's departure hosts of people came to kotow to me, some to pay their respects, some to thank me, and some both to thank me and pay their respects. After this a eunuch brought in a pile of nine "imperial edicts" that had already been written out. The first of these proclaimed my return to the throne, and another created a board of seven regents, including Chang Hsun and Chen Pao-shen.

Old Pekinese remember how on that morning the police suddenly told all the households in the city to hang out imperial dragon flags; the people had to improvise them with paper and paste. Then Ching clothes that had not been seen for years reappeared on the streets worn by people who looked as if they had just stepped out of their coffins. The papers brought out special issues for the restoration at a higher price than usual, so that amid the strange sights one could hear news-vendors shouting as they sold the "Edicts of Hsuan Tung", "Antiques, six cash only! This nonsense will be an antique in a few days — six cash for an antique — dead cheap."

Some of the shops outside the Chien Men Gate did a booming trade in those days. Tailors sold Ching dragon flags as fast as they could make them; the second-hand clothes shops found that newly appointed officials were struggling to get hold of Ching court dress; and theatrical costumiers were crowded with people begging them to make false queues out of horsehair. I still remember how the Forbidden City was crowded with men wearing court robes with mandarins' buttons and peacock feathers on their hats. From the back of everyone's head dangled a queue. When later the Army to Punish the Rebels approached Peking one could pick up real queues all over the place: these were said to have been cut off by Chang Hsun's pigtailed soldiery as they fled.

If those visitors to the Forbidden City had shared any of the foresight of the news-vendors about the fate of "imperial edicts" and queues they would not have got so excited in the first days of the restoration.

The princes and nobles of the royal clan were very disappointed in those few days as they did not see their personal ambitions realized. On the morrow of the restoration an "imperial edict" was issued banning them from interfering in state affairs. My father became the leader of a group of nobles who were opposed to this, and he wanted to argue this point with Chang Hsun and myself. When my tutor Chen heard this he hurried over to tell me to refuse them as it was their extreme incompetence that had brought about the abdication in 1912. I followed his advice, and before the princes had time to do anything about it the early collapse of the restored monarchy paradoxically saved them from being held responsible for its establishment.

Chen Pao-shen, who was normally a stable and sensible man, was quite carried away by the restoration, surprising me with his opposition to the princes and the violence of his views on how to deal with President Li Yuan-hung who had refused to resign when urged to by one of my tutors. The three tutors came into the Yu Ching

Palace and Chen, his face livid with anger, had burst out uncontrollably:

"Li Yuan-hung has actually dared to refuse to accept the order. Will Your Majesty please instruct him to commit suicide at once."

I was startled to hear so extreme a suggestion. "It wouldn't do at all for me to tell Li Yuan-hung to kill himself so soon after my return to the throne. Didn't the Republic give me favourable treatment?"

This was the first time that Chen Pao-shen had been openly rebuffed by me, but he was so carried away by his hatred for the President that, oblivious to everything else, he went on, "Li Yuanhung is not only refusing to resign, he is even hanging on to the Presidential Palace, the rebellious brigand and traitor. How could you mention him in the same breath as yourself, Your Majesty?"

Seeing how determinedly I refused to follow his advice he had to drop his proposal. When an emissary went to make another attempt at persuading Li Yuan-hung he found that Li had already fled with his seals of office to the Japanese Legation.

In the first few days of the restoration I spent half of my time in the Yu Ching Palace. Although my lessons were suspended I was obliged to see my tutors as I had to follow their directions in whatever I did. For the rest of my time I looked over the "imperial edicts" that were to be issued, read the official papers of the cabinet, and received homage and salutations; apart from this I would watch ants crawling from one hole to another or tell the eunuchs of the Imperial Stables to bring out some camels for my entertainment. But before five days of this kind of life were up the bombs dropped by the aircraft of the Army to Punish the Rebels changed things completely. Nobody came to kotow to me any longer, there were no more "imperial edicts", and all my regents had disappeared except for Chen Pao-shen and one other, Wang Shih-chen.

On the day of the air-raid I was sitting in the schoolroom talking to my tutors when I heard an aeroplane and the unfamiliar sound of an explosion. I was so terrified that I shook all over, and the colour drained from my tutors' faces. With everything in chaos eunuchs hustled me over to the Mind Nurture Palace as if my bedroom were the only safe place. The High Consorts were in an even worse state, some of them lying in the corners of their bedrooms, and some of them hiding under tables. The air was filled with shouts and the whole palace was in confusion. This was the first air-raid in Chinese history and the first time a Chinese air force was used in civil war. Here are the first air-raid precautions, for what they may be worth: everyone lay down in their bedrooms and the bamboo blinds in the corridors were let down. As far as the knowledge of the eunuchs and the palace guard went, these were the wisest measures they could take. Fortunately the pilot did not mean business and gave us nothing worse than a fright, dropping only three tiny bombs about a foot long. One of them fell outside the Gate of Honouring the Ancestors (Lung Tsung Men) wounding one of the carriers of sedan-chairs; one fell into a pond in the Imperial Garden, damaging a corner of the pond; and the third fell on the roof of one of the gateways in the Western Avenue of the palace striking dread into the hearts of a crowd of eunuchs who were gambling there although it failed to explode.

Soon after this the sound of approaching gunfire was heard in the Forbidden City. Wang Shih-chen and Chen Pao-shen did not come to court and the palace had no more contact with the outside world. A little later a false report was brought from the commander of the palace guard that Tuan Chi-jui's Republican army had been defeated by Chang Hsun's men, but the next morning the news of Chang Hsun's flight to the Dutch embassy swept away the smiles of the day before.

My father and Chen Pao-shen now appeared, dejection written all over their drooping faces. Reading the abdication edict that they had drafted both frightened and saddened me, and I wept out loud. The decree ran like this:

On the twentieth day of the fifth month of the ninth year of Hsuan Tung the Cabinet receives this Imperial Edict: Formerly we followed the memorials of Chang Hsun and others who, saying that the nation was in a state of fundamental disorder and that the people longed for the old way, advised us to resume the government. As our years are tender and we live deep in the Forbidden City we have heard nothing about the people's livelihood and the affairs of the nation. Remembering with reverence the great benevolence and the instructions of the late August Empress Hsiao Ting Ching (Lung Yu) who yielded the government out of pity for the people, we had not the least intention of treating the world as our private property; it was only because we were asked to save the nation and the people that we forced ourselves to accede to the requests made of us and assume power.

Now yesterday Chang Hsun reported armed risings in every province, which may lead to military insurgencies in a struggle for power. Our people have been suffering hardships for years, and their state is as desperate as if they were being burned or drowned. How could we then compound their miseries with war? Thinking upon this we were disturbed and unable to rest. We therefore resolved that we would not keep this political power for ourselves and thus besmirch the living soul of the August Empress Hsiao Ting Ching by turning our back on her abundant virtue.

Let Wang Shih-chen and Hsu Shih-chang inform Tuan Chi-jui at once, that the transfer of power may be arranged and the present troubles brought to an end, so calming the people's hearts and avoiding the calamity of war.

By the command of the Emperor.

The Chieftains of the Peiyang Clique

This abdication edict was never issued. All that was published at the time was a statement of the Household Department that was quoted in an order of the President of the Republic.

By order of the President:

The Home Ministry reports that it has received the following communication from the Household Department of the Ching house:

"This day the Household Department received an Edict:

" 'Formerly on the twenty-fifth day of the twelfth month of the third year of Hsuan Tung a Decree was issued by the August Empress Dowager Lung Yu in which, recognizing that the whole people were inclined towards a republic, she and the Emperor returned sovereign power to the whole country. She ordained that there should be a republic and settled that the Articles of Favourable Treatment for the Ching house should be adhered to for ever; for the past six years the Ching house has been very well treated and has never had any intention of using the political power for its own ends; what cause could it have had for going back on its word?

" 'But contrary to expectation Chang Hsun led his soldiery to occupy the palace on July 1. He fraudulently issued edicts and decrees and altered the state structure, thus disobeying the instructions of the Empress Dowager of the former dynasty. I, a child living deep in the Forbidden City, had no choice in the matter; in these circumstances I should have allowances made for me by the whole world. The Household Department has been instructed to request the Government of the Republic to make this generally known both within the country and abroad.' "

When the Ministry received this letter they thought it right to report this matter.

As it is common knowledge that Chang Hsun the traitor and usurper was the originator of the disturbances, let the details of this document be speedily proclaimed.

For general information,

Issued by the Prime Minister Tuan Chi-jui

July 17, sixth year of the Republic of China

It was through the collaboration of the three bosses of the Peiyang clique and the Forbidden City that the admission in the abdication edict that I had decided to "assume power" was changed in the Household Department's statement into Chang Hsun occupying the palace and the "child" having no choice in the matter. The man who thought out this clever formulation was the Grand Tutor Hsu Shih-chang, and it was carried out by President Feng Kuo-chang and Premier Tuan Chi-jui. The role of the Forbidden City in the restoration was glossed over, and its new activities after the failure of this attempted restoration received little attention.

As the palace was able to draw a veil over its role in the restoration public attention was focused on its unsuccessful supporters outside the Forbidden City. I was able to get a picture of what had really happened from articles I read in the press and what I was told by my tutors.

After the failure of Yuan Shih-kai's usurpation in 1916 Hsu Shih-chang and Chang Hsun had agreed that a restoration of the Ching monarchy was their only chance of resisting the southern Republicans. After Yuan's death Chang Hsun called a conference of warlords at his headquarters in Hsuchow (the "Second Hsuchow Conference") at which it was decided that the first thing was to get foreign support, particularly from Japan. When their plan met with the approval of the commander of the Japanese garrison in Tientsin, Chang Hsun established contact with the "loyalist" troops led by Babojab and Prince Su in Inner Mongolia and the Northeast. He arranged with some other warlords that they would march on Peking on the pretext of defending the capital against the "loyalist" army, but this scheme fell through when Babojab was killed by one of his subordinates.

The other leader of the restoration conspiracy, Hsu Shih-chang, tried to win the support of the Japanese cabinet for his plans, but when Chang Hsun realized that Hsu was trying to make himself regent he was furious, and the monarchist movement was split.

Meanwhile a power struggle was going on in Peking between Peiyang warlord Tuan Chi-jui, who was prime minister at the time, and President Li Yuan-hung. When Tuan was dismissed from his premiership and went to Tientsin, Chang Hsun, who had been promised the support of various other warlords and the Peiyang leaders Tuan Chi-jui and Feng Kuo-chang at his fourth Hsuchow Conference, saw this as his opportunity to lead his troops north. He tricked Li Yuan-hung into inviting him to come and mediate between him and Tuan Chi-jui. Having contacted the Peiyang chiefs in Tientsin he entered Peking and enacted his restoration on July 1.

Most of the press attributed Chang Hsun's failure to the way he monopolized power and to two other major blunders: giving only an empty title to Hsu Shih-chang and underestimating Tuan Chi-jui. Thinking that he had the Peiyang leaders in his pocket, he was astounded to hear that Tuan Chi-jui had administered an oath to his troops in Tientsin that they would "punish the rebels" and that the other local warlords had all changed sides and become "supporters of the Republic". This volte-face paid Tuan Chi-jui and

97

Feng Kuo-chang handsomely as the former became premier once more and the latter won the presidency.

But although the blame for the restoration was put on Chang Hsun, he was treated very leniently by the new Republican authorities as he told them that he possessed a case of incriminating documents that proved that they had originally supported his monarchist schemes. When Hsu Shih-chang became president the following year the warrant for his arrest was withdrawn.

What interested me about all these revelations was that all the chiefs of the Peiyang clique and some other leading figures in the Republic had been enthusiastic monarchists, and that they were now making Chang Hsun the scapegoat so as to protect me. They explicitly stated that the palace had been blameless. Feng Kuo-chang in his telegram announcing his support for the Army to Punish the Rebels even went so far as to say, "I was not a supporter of Republicanism in the former Ching Dynasty but the pressure of events created a republic at the time of the Revolution of 1911." Why were they covering up for the Forbidden City and announcing their own monarchist sympathies so frankly? The only conclusion I could draw was that these men were not really opposed to a restoration and that the only problem at issue was the question of who was to lead it.

From the point of view of the Forbidden City all cats whether tabby or white were good cats provided they caught mice. It made no difference to us whether a Mr. Chang or a Mr. Tuan restored the monarchy. Thus it was that when Feng Kuo-chang and Tuan Chi-jui came to power the hopes of the monarchists were focussed on these two new strong men. But the palace's schemes came to nothing when the Peiyang group split into a Chihli clique led by Feng Kuo-chang and an Anhwei one with Tuan Chi-jui at its head. In the friction between the two factions Feng lost his presidency. Although Tuan hinted to the palace through Shih Hsu, the head of the Household Department, that a restoration was still perfectly possible, Shih Hsu was now too cautious to attach much importance to the word of a man who had come to power by leading an expedition against a restoration.

Feng Kuo-chang was succeeded as president by Hsu Shih-chang. A commentary in the Shanghai *Hsin Wen Pao* shortly after the collapse of the 1917 restoration had contained a passage that made a big impact in the Forbidden City:

> Had the restoration been managed by Hsu Shih-chang it would certainly not have been so clumsily handled; had it not been the work of Chang Hsun the commanders of the Peiyang clique would have soon acknowledged themselves the emperor's subjects. . . .

Thus it was that not only I, who had satisfied my craving to be emperor for only a few brief days, but other monarchists as well were very excited at the beginning of Hsu Shih-chang's presidency.

A sixty-year-old Manchu resident of Peking has told me: "When Hsu Shih-chang became president in 1918 many Manchu carriages and women's hairstyles appeared in the streets of Peking, and the houses of the nobility became very lively with noisy birthday parties, theatrical performances, and feasts. There were even amateur nobles' drama groups and clubs. . . ."

Another old gentleman of Han race explained to me, "There were three occasions after the founding of the Republic when we had 'walking ancestors'[1] in the streets of Peking. The first time was the days after the death of the empress dowager Lung Yu, the next was the period of Chang Hsun's restoration, and the last was from when Hsu Shih-chang became president to the 'Great Nuptials'.[2] This last time was when things really bustled. . . ."

Hsu Shih-chang had been a friend of Yuan Shih-kai's in the days before Yuan made his name and later became the adviser Yuan consulted before making almost any important move. It was said that Yuan and Hsu Shih-chang had held a discussion with Feng Kuo-chang, Tuan Chi-jui and others before they made the empress dowager Lung Yu give up state power in 1912. At this meeting they had agreed that as the Republican Army would have to be dealt with by cunning rather than by force they should first accept

---

[1] So called because they wore Ching court dress which made them look like the figures in ancestral portraits.

[2] My wedding.

the terms of the revolutionaries and found a republic, then wait for the revolutionary army to disintegrate and bring the emperor back to power. Hsu Shih-chang was none too pleased when Yuan Shih-kai proclaimed himself emperor in 1916. A relation of mine was once told by a nephew of Hsu Shih-chang's that Yuan came to see Hsu the very day his monarchy was abolished. When Yuan entered the reception room this nephew was in the smoking room next door and did not dare come out. From what he could catch of the conversation Hsu Shih-chang was advising Yuan to "keep to the original agreement", but he could not make out Yuan's reply. As later developments showed, Yuan either did not follow this suggestion or else died before he could put it into effect. It was, however, virtually an open secret that Hsu Shih-chang never abandoned his idea of a Ching restoration.

When Hsu became president in September 1918 he announced that he could not live in the presidential palace of his predecessors (which had originally been a part of the imperial palace) and would therefore live in his own home until a new presidential palace was built. He pardoned Chang Hsun, advocated the study of the Confucian classics, honoured Confucius, sacrificed to heaven, and gave civil and military office to members of the royal family. He referred to the Ching as the "present dynasty" in public as well as in private and spoke of me as if I were the reigning emperor.

The Household Department had helped to provide Hsu with discreet financial backing in his bid for the presidency, and after it was clear that he would get it he announced at a private dinner given for him by the senior officials of the Department that his only purpose in taking office was to "act as regent on behalf of the young monarch". He also presented Shih Hsu with a pair of scrolls inscribed with a couplet in his own handwriting which implied loyalty to me.

The people around me told me nothing at the time of these events. All I knew was that Hsu's name was always mentioned in a very hopeful way. From Hsu's coming to power onwards the Forbidden City was alive with activity: posthumous titles and permission to ride a horse in the palace seemed to have become far more desirable, and officials of the previous dynasty both true and false flocked to the palace. Although my tutors never said much about the negotiations that were going on between the palace and the president, Chen Pao-shen once remarked contemptuously in the course of a conversation, "Hsu Shih-chang still wants to be Prince Regent: it's asking a bit much. A dukedom would be enough for him." On another occasion he commented, "He originally proposed that the daughter of a senior Han official should be made empress: what was the motive behind that? You can see what sort of person he really is from the fact that he has taken office under the Republic although he is a Grand Tutor of the Ching."

From this time onwards the Forbidden City never spoke about Hsu Shih-chang again with the old enthusiasm. He was not in fact in a very strong position a year after coming to power. With the Peiyang group split into two factions he could no longer achieve much in his capacity as a chief of the Peiyang clique; he was on increasingly bad terms with Tuan Chi-jui; and in 1919 the May 4th Student Movement that shook the whole of China made them devote all their energies to trying to maintain themselves in power. No matter how loyal a monarchist he had been, there was nothing Hsu could have done to bring about a restoration. But although the palace heard less and less from Hsu it never despaired of its future completely.

Undying Hope

One day as I was riding my bicycle in the Palace Garden I nearly ran into somebody as I turned a corner. For such a thing to happen in the palace was a gross solecism, but I did not care. I turned round and was about to ride off when I saw that the man was kneeling on the ground and saying, "Your humble servant pays his respects to the Lord of Ten Thousand Years."

He was wearing a dark-coloured waistcoat of the sort the eunuchs wore, but when I looked at him more closely I noticed stubble on his chin and knew he could not be a eunuch. Riding round in circles I asked him what he was doing.

"Your servant is seeing to the electric light."

"Hm, so that's your job. You were lucky not to be knocked over just now."

"Your servant's luck is very good; today I have been able to see the true dragon, the Son of Heaven. I beg the Lord of Ten Thousand Years in his celestial bounty to grant his humble servant a title."

I was amused by his absurd request and thought of the nickname that the eunuchs had told me was given in Peking to the beggars who squatted at the ends of bridges.

"Very well, I enfeoff you as the Marquis Guarding the Bridge,"[1] I said, roaring with laughter. Little did I imagine that this title-crazy fellow would take my joke seriously and go along to the Household Department to ask for a "patent of nobility". Unfortunately I never heard what the outcome of this was.

I was often told by my tutors and the eunuchs in those days that people in the countryside used to ask "How is the Hsuan Tung Emperor?" or "Who is on the throne nowadays?" or "Would the world be at peace if the true dragon, the Son of Heaven, were sitting on the throne?" My English tutor Reginald Johnston told me that according to an article in some journal even the most deeply anti-monarchical people were disappointed in the Republic, so that it was clear that even they were changing their minds. The real reason why some people were talking about the "former Ching" was, of course, that they were sick of the disasters inflicted by warlordism. My tutors, however, used all this to prove to me that people were longing for the old order.

At the end of the era of Hsu Shih-chang one often met monarchy-struck people. There was a merchant named Wang Chiu-cheng who had made a fortune out of supplying uniforms for the armies of the Chihli clique. His ambition was to be granted the old imperial honour of being allowed to wear a yellow riding-jacket and had

---

1 "Marquis" in Chinese is pronounced the same as the word for "monkey".

spent a considerable amount of time and money to this end. The eunuchs gave him the nickname of "the spendthrift". I do not know how he fixed it, but every New Year he would come along with the old-timers to kotow and offer tribute to me, and when he did this he always brought thick wads of banknotes which he scattered liberally wherever he went. The eunuchs were always very pleased to see him come as anyone who showed him the way, announced him, pulled aside the door-curtains, poured his tea or even spoke a few words to him would be sure to be the richer by a roll of bank-notes. And this is not even to mention the money he spent in more formal ways. In the end he achieved his ambition and was granted the "honour" of being allowed to wear a yellow jacket.

Men came to the Forbidden City every day or submitted memorials from distant places for the sake of a yellow riding-jacket, the right to say in their family registers that they held a Ching office, or a posthumous title for somebody. There was even one Liang Chu-chuan, known as Lunatic Liang, who threw himself into a pond to win with his dead body and a sodden "posthumous memorial" the title of "True and Upright". Later there were so many requests for posthumous titles that it was decided that they would only be given to people above a certain rank: otherwise the little court would have made itself look cheap. Even tighter restrictions were put on the granting of the privileges of riding a horse or being car-ried in a chair in the palace and on the distribution of scrolls in my writing. The result was that not only the Manchu nobility but even military commanders of the Republic regarded obtaining one of these as a "signal honour".

Some of the so-called new writers of the time, such as Hu Shih, had the same ideas. I had been told about this Doctor Hu Shih, the champion of writing in the vernacular language, by my tutor Johnston when I was fifteen. Johnston jeered at his line "Picnic by the river", written half in English and half in Chinese, but also said that there would be no harm in my looking at some of his writings as a part of my education. Having done so I got the idea that I would like to have a look at this modern personality. One day my curiosity prompted me to telephone him, and to my surprise he came to the palace when I invited him. I shall have more to say about this meeting later; meanwhile I would like to quote a letter that this foreignized doctor wrote to Johnston afterwards in which he revealed that his feelings were not unlike those of an old official of the Ching. One part of it read:

I must confess that I was deeply touched by this little event. Here I was, standing and sitting in front of the last of the emperors of my country, the last representative of a long line of great monarchs.

What was rather more important was the encouragement the palace received from foreigners' opinions. Johnston used to give me quite a lot of information on this subject: according to him many foreigners thought that a restoration was the wish of the ordinary Chinese. He would read me passages from foreign newspapers, including the following one that he later quoted in his book *Twilight in the Forbidden City*. It was a part of an article from an English paper, the Tientsin *North China Daily Mail*, of September 9, 1919 entitled "Is Another Restoration Near at Hand?":

The record of the republic has been anything but a happy one, and to-day we find North and South at daggers drawn. The only conclusion to be drawn from this is that republicanism in China has been tried and found wanting. The mercantile classes and the gentry, the back-bone of the land, are weary of all this internecine strife and we firmly believe that they would give their whole-hearted support to any form of government which would ensure peace to the eighteen provinces.

It must not be forgotten that there exists a very strong phalanx of pro-monarchical people who have never become reconciled to the republican form of government, but they have kept quiet for the last few years for obvious reasons. That they are in sympathy with the present militaristic movement goes without saying and the comings and goings of some of the better known of them to various places where officials are known to congregate are not devoid of significance.

The contention of those who secretly favour and hope for a successful restoration of the ex-emperor is that the republicans are destroying the country, and that means, however drastic, must be taken to bring it back to its former prosperous and peaceful condition.

A reversion to a monarchy is not by any means likely to be well received in all quarters. On the contrary, it will probably meet with considerable diplomatic opposition in more than one Legation, but even opposition of that kind is bound to evaporate if a successful *coup d'état* is brought off, as we all know that nothing succeeds like success.

Despite all the encouraging things that the foreign papers were saying, it was of course the men with guns in their hands who directly controlled the fate of the little court. As the *North China Daily Mail* pointed out, "the comings and goings . . . to places where [military] officials are known to congregate are not devoid of significance." I remember how in the second half of 1919 the little court had close relations with warlords other than those of the old Peiyang group. The first of these was High Inspecting Commissioner Chang Tso-lin, the head of the Fengtien clique.

The palace's dealings with Chang Tso-lin had started when my father received a sum of money sent from Fengtien (modern Liaoning in northeast China where Chang Tso-lin's power was centred) as payment for some estates there that had been the property of the emperor. My father wrote a letter of thanks and the Household Department despatched a high-ranking official with some antiques from the palace collection — a picture by Tung Yuan of the Southern Tang Dynasty (937-975) and a pair of porcelain vases with an inscription by the emperor Chien Lung — as a present to Chang Tso-lin from my father. Chang sent his sworn brother Chang Ching-hui, then the second in command of the Fengtien army and later the premier of "Manchukuo", to accompany our envoy back to Peking and convey his gratitude to my father. This marked a strengthening of the relationship between the Mansion of Prince Chun acting on behalf of the court and the Fengtien army.

Three senior officers of the Fengtien army had come to Peking in 1917 to participate in Chang Hsun's restoration and two others were now given the right to ride a horse in the Forbidden City. When the father of divisional commander Chang Tsung-chang, one of the two, celebrated his eightieth birthday in Peking my father went along to congratulate him. In 1920 the Fengtien clique aligned itself with the Chihli clique to defeat the Anhwei clique and when the Chihli chief Tsao Kun (the successor to the dead Feng Kuo-chang) and

Chang Tso-lin entered Peking the little court sent Shao Ying, an official of the Household Department, to welcome them. The Mansion of Prince Chun became more active than ever. A rumour that Chang Tso-lin was going to come to the palace for an audience caused a special meeting of the senior officials of the Household Department in my father's house to discuss what presents he should be given; it was decided that he should receive an ancient sword in addition to everything else that had been prepared. Chang Tso-lin, however, went back to Fengtien without visiting the palace. Two months later a young Manchu noble, a relation of my father, was appointed as an adviser to Chang and he went to Fengtien for a while. During the period of Fengtien-Chihli co-operation following the defeat of the Anhwei clique the Fengtien Club in Peking became the meeting-place for Fengtien commanders and was frequently visited by a number of princes and nobles. Even the chief steward of the Mansion of Prince Chun was a frequent visitor and became the sworn brother of the leading Fengtien figure Chang Ching-hui there.

These two years were much like the time leading up to Chang Hsun's restoration: the air was full of rumours of a new attempt to put me back on the throne. Two months after my father had sent the presents to Fengtien and Chang Ching-hui had come to the capital, the English-language newspaper *Peking Leader* of December 27, 1919 carried the following item from Fengtien:

> During the course of the last few days, the rumour of the coming resuscitation of the Manchu monarchy in Peking in place of the existing so-called republican government of China has been in circulation among all classes of the natives especially among the militarists under general Chang Tso-lin. According to current allegations, the monarchy will this time be started by general Chang Tso-lin with the co-operation of certain monarchical and military leaders of northwest China, and ex-general Chang Tsun . . . will play a very important part in it . . . even president Hsu and ex-president Feng, in view of the existing unsettled political situation of the country and external dangers, are inclined to accept the resuscitation of monarchy without strong opposition or dissatisfaction. With regard to Tsao Kun, Li Shun and other lesser military leaders, it is said that these men can be satisfied by

making them princes, dukes or marquises in addition to permitting them to hold their present posts in the various provinces. . . .

When Johnston told me of this some time later I remember that he also told me some other rumours about Chang Tso-lin's restoration activities. News of this sort circulated until Chang returned to the Northeast a defeated man in 1922. Such news made a deep impression on me and made me feel very happy. It also enabled me to understand why the commanders of the Fengtien army were so enthusiastic about the Forbidden City, why Chang Ching-hui went with the princes and Ching officials to kotow to the high consort Tuan Kang on her birthday, why the Fengtien Club was said to be so busy, and why some of the princes were in such a state of excitement. But before my joy had lasted very long it was swept away by the open split between the Chihli and Fengtien cliques and the consequent defeat of the Fengtien army which withdrew to the Northeast.

Disturbing reports arrived in quick succession. Hsu Shih-chang had suddenly resigned. The Chihli army controlled Peking. Li Yuan-hung, who had been forced out of office during Chang Hsun's restoration, had become president again. A new panic swept the Forbidden City; the princes and officials begged Johnston to take me to the British Legation for safety. Johnston arranged with the British Minister Sir Beilby Alston that the British Legation would let him have some rooms in which he could keep me as his private guest if necessary. He also arranged with the Portuguese and Netherlands Legations that other members of the royal family would be allowed to take refuge in the Legation Quarter. I did not agree with this idea: I thought it would be better to go abroad straight away. I proposed to Johnston that he should take me abroad at once. The suddenness with which I sent for him and asked this stunned him. He had no time to think out his answer: "That would be very awkward. Your Majesty should think it over calmly: President Hsu has only just left Peking and if Your Majesty were to disappear from the Forbidden City immediately afterwards it would lead to suggestions that there had been some kind of conspiracy between the palace and Hsu Shih-chang. Moreover Britain would not be able to receive Your Majesty in the present circumstances."

In those days I neither had the sense to work out for myself nor did anyone else tell me that there had been some kind of secret links between Chang Tso-lin and Hsu Shih-chang or between Chang, Hsu and the little court; I was even less aware of any connection between the Legation Quarter and the outbreak of war between the Chihli and Fengtien factions. So when I heard that my request was impossible I let it go at that. When the situation became more stable the matter of taking refuge in the legations was no longer raised, let alone that of going abroad.

A year later, in 1923, the head of the Chihli clique, Tsao Kun, bought the votes of the members of parliament at 5,000 dollars apiece and had himself elected president. The little court had only just stopped being frightened of him when another rising Chihli commander, Wu Pei-fu, attracted their attention. Cheng Hsiao-hsu, later a close adviser of mine, told me that Wu was a soldier with a very bright future who wished to preserve the Great Ching and who could very probably be persuaded to support us. That same year I sent Cheng Hsiao-hsu to Wu Pei-fu's headquarters at Lo-yang with lavish presents to congratulate him on his fiftieth birthday. Kang Yu-wei, the reformer of 1898 who was now a monarchist, also went to try and win him over but did not get any definite reply. As it turned out, Wu Pei-fu's success was short-lived as the year after this birthday celebration his subordinate Feng Yu-hsiang changed sides in the fighting between the Chihli and Fengtien cliques. This led to Wu's total defeat and I was driven out of the Forbidden City by the National Army of Feng Yu-hsiang.

Reginald Johnston

The first time I saw foreigners was at the last reception that the empress dowager Lung Yu held for the wives of the foreign ambassadors. I thought that their strange clothes and their hair and eyes of so many colours were both ugly and frightening. At that time I had never seen foreign men, but I had got a rough idea of what they looked like from illustrated magazines: they wore moustaches on their upper lips; there was always a straight line down the legs of their trousers; and they invariably carried sticks. The eunuchs said that foreigners' moustaches were so stiff that one could hang lanterns from the ends of them and that their legs were rigid. Believing this one senior official had suggested to the empress dowager Tzu Hsi in 1900 that when fighting foreigners it was only necessary to knock them over with bamboo poles for them to be incapable of getting up again. The eunuchs said that the sticks in their hands were "civilization sticks" for hitting people with. My tutor Chen Pao-shen had been in Southeast Asia where he had seen foreigners, and what he told me about the outside world gradually replaced the impressions of my childhood and the stories of the eunuchs. All the same, I was very surprised and disconcerted when I was told that I was to have a foreigner as a tutor.

It was on March 4, 1919 that my father and my Chinese tutors introduced me to Mr. Reginald Fleming Johnston in the Yu Ching Palace. First of all he bowed to me as I sat on a throne according to the protocol for receiving foreign officials and then I got up and shook hands with him. He bowed once more and withdrew. Then he came in again and I bowed to him: this was the way in which I acknowledged him as my teacher. Once these ceremonies were over he started to teach me in the company of my tutor Chu Yi-fan.

I found that Johnston was not so frightening after all. His Chinese was very fluent and much easier to understand than Chen Pao-shen's Fukienese or Chu Yi-fan's Kiangsi dialect. He must have been at least forty at the time and was clearly older than my father, but his movements were still deft and skilful. His back was so straight that I wondered whether he wore an iron frame under his clothes. Although he had no handlebar moustache or "civilization stick" and his legs did bend, he always gave me an impression of stiffness. It was his blue eyes and greying fair hair in particular that made me feel uneasy.

During one lesson about a month after he first came he suddenly turned round and glared furiously at the eunuch who was standing by the wall. His face red with anger, he protested to me in Chinese spoken with an English accent:

"The Household Department is treating me very discourteously. Why do I alone have to have a eunuch standing here when the other tutors don't? I don't like it. I don't like it and I'm going to bring the matter up with President Hsu as it was he who invited me to take this post."

He did not have to go and see President Hsu. At least half of the reason why the Ching house had invited him was to get his protection, and so they did not dare offend him. He only had to go red in the face for my father and the high officials to give way and withdraw the eunuch. I found him very intimidating and studied English with him like a good boy, not daring to talk about other things when I got bored or ordering a holiday as I did with my Chinese tutors.

After two or three months I realized that he was getting more and more like my Chinese tutors. He used the same reverential form of address to me as they did and would push the textbook aside and chat with me when I got tired of reading, telling me stories about things old and new and places near and far. On his suggestion a fellow-student was provided for my English lessons. His way of doing things was the same as that of my Chinese tutors.

This old Englishman was an M.A. of Oxford University who had been formally invited by the Ching house after discussions between the British Legation and President Hsu Shih-chang. He had been a colonial official in Hongkong and was Commissioner of the British-leased territory of Weihaiwei before coming to the palace. As he said himself, he had already been in Asia for over twenty years, had visited every province of China, had seen her famous mountains, rivers and antiquities. He was well versed in Chinese history, familiar with all parts of the country, expert in Confucianism, Mohism, Buddhism and Taoism, and a connoisseur of ancient Chinese poetry. I do not know how many classical Chinese books he had read and

I used to see him wagging his head as he chanted Tang poems just like a Chinese teacher, his voice rising, falling and pausing.

He was as honoured to receive presents from me as the other tutors. After I had awarded him the mandarin hat button of the highest grade he had a full set of Ching court clothes specially made. He posed for a photograph in these clothes standing under a tablet in my handwriting in front of his country house in Cherry Valley in the Western Hills, and distributed prints of it to his family and friends. The Household Department rented an old-style Peking house for him and he furnished it just as a veteran of the Ching would have done: as soon as one entered the front gate one could see red tablets on which were written in black letters "Companion of the Yu Ching Palace", "Entitled to Be Carried in a Chair with Two Porters in the Palace", "Awarded the First Grade Hat Button", and "Entitled to Wear a Sable Jacket". Every time he received a major award he would write a memorial thanking me for my benevolence.

He coined himself a literary name from the saying in the *Analects* of Confucius that "a scholar sets his mind on truth". He was a lover of Chinese tea and peonies and was fond of talking with the Ching veterans. When he retired and went back to England he set aside a room in his house in which to display the things I had given him and his Ching court robes and hat button. He even flew the flag of "Manchukuo" from an island he had bought to show his loyalty to the emperor. But what brought about the closeness between teacher and pupil was his patience. Looking back on it now, I realize that it can have been no easy matter for that testy Scot to adopt the attitude he did to a pupil like myself. One day he brought me some foreign magazines full of pictures of the First World War, mostly showing the aircraft, tanks and artillery of the allied armies. I was intrigued by these funny things. Seeing that I was interested he explained the things in the pictures to me and told me what tanks were for, which country's aircraft were best, and how brave the soldiers of the allies were. I was fascinated at first but as usual I got bored after a while, emptied the contents of a snuff-bottle on the table and started to doodle in it. Without a word Johnston tidied up the magazines and waited there till the end of the lesson while I played.

Another time he brought me some foreign sweets and I was delighted by the tin box, the silver wrapping-paper and their different fruit flavours. He started to tell me how the fruity tastes were produced by chemical techniques and how the neat shape of the sweets was made by machines. I could not understand any of this and did not even want to, and when I had eaten two of the sweets I thought of my ants on their cypress tree and wanted to let them try the flavour of chemistry and machinery. I rushed into the courtyard and old Johnston waited with the sweet tin until the lesson was over.

As I gradually realized how diligently Johnston was teaching me I was very pleased and willing to be more obedient. He did not only teach me English; or rather teaching me the English language was not so important in his eyes as training me to be like the English gentlemen he talked about. When I was fourteen I decided to dress like he did and sent some eunuchs out to buy me a large amount of Western clothing. I put on an outfit that did not fit me at all, and I must have looked a strange sight with my tie hanging outside my collar like a length of rope. When I went to the schoolroom Johnston quivered with anger at the sight of me and told me to go back and take those clothes off at once. The next day he brought a tailor along to measure me and make me clothes that would have done for an English gentleman. Later he explained to me, "It is better to wear your Manchu robes than ill-fitting Western dress. If you wear clothes from a second-hand shop you won't be a gentleman, you'll be. . . ." But what I would be he did not go on to say.

"If Your Majesty ever appears in London you are bound to be invited to tea very often. Tea parties are informal but important occasions that usually take place on Wednesdays. At them one can meet peers, scholars, celebrities and all sorts of people Your Majesty will need to meet. There is no need to be too dressed up but manners are most important. It is very bad to drink tea as if it were water, to eat cakes as if they were a real meal, or make too much noise with your fork or teaspoon. In England tea and cakes are *refreshment* (he used the English word) and not a meal. . . ."

I forgot much of Johnston's careful instruction and threw the caution with which I ate the first cake to the winds by the time I came to the second, but all the same the Western civilization represented by guns and aircraft in the magazines, the sweets made by chemistry and the etiquette of tea parties made a deep impression on my mind. The magazines about the First World War gave me a taste for foreign publications. First of all I was struck by the advertisements and I immediately told the eunuchs to buy dogs and diamonds for me from abroad like the ones shown in them. I made the Household Department buy me foreign furniture and had the red sandalwood table with brass fittings on the *kang* changed for one painted with foreign paint and fitted with white porcelain handles. I also had a wooden floor laid down so that the room was a complete hotch-potch, being neither properly Chinese nor completely Western. Imitating Johnston I bought all sorts of trinkets to hang about myself: Watches and chains, rings, tiepins, cuff-links, neckties and so on. I asked him to give foreign names to myself, my brothers and sisters, my "empress" and my "consort": I was called Henry and my empress Elizabeth. I even imitated his way of talking in a mixture of Chinese and English when I was with my fellow-students:

"*William* (Pu Chieh), sharpen this *pencil* (I used the English word) for me . . . good, put it on the *desk*."

"*Arthur* (Pu Chia), tell *Lily* (my third sister) and the others to come round this *afternoon* to *hear* some foreign military music."

I felt very pleased when talking like this, but when Chen Pao-shen heard me he screwed his face up as if he were suffering from toothache.

I thought that everything about Johnston was first-rate and even went so far as to regard the smell of mothballs about his clothes as fragrant. He made me feel that Westerners were the most intelligent and civilized people and that he was the most learned of Westerners. I do not think that even he realized how deep an influence he was exercising on me: the woollen cloth that he wore made me doubt the value of all the silks and satins of China and the fountain pen in his pocket actually made me ashamed of the writing brushes and hand-made paper that Chinese used to write with. After he had brought a military band from the British barracks to play in the palace I felt that Chinese music was not worth listening to and even found the ancient ceremonial music far less majestic.

A mere remark by Johnston that Chinese queues were pigtails was enough for me to cut mine off. Ever since 1913 the Home Ministry of the Republic had been writing to the Household Department asking that the Forbidden City should co-operate with them in persuading the Manchu bannermen to cut off their queues; they also hoped that the queues in the palace would go. The tone of these letters was very polite and they did not refer to the queues hanging from my head and the heads of the senior officials. The Household Department used all kinds of excuses to put off the Home Ministry, even going so far as to say that queues were a useful way of distinguishing who should be allowed in and out of the palace. Several years after the matter was first brought up the Forbidden City was still a world of queues. But now Johnston's one piece of propaganda was enough to make me have mine off. Within a few days at least a thousand disappeared and only my three Chinese tutors and a few of the senior officials of the Household Department kept theirs.

The High Consorts wept several times at the loss of my plait and my tutors went round with long faces for days. Later Pu Chieh and Yu Chung used the pretext of "obeying an imperial decree" to cut off theirs at home. That day Chen Pao-shen shook with fury at his bald-headed students and finally remarked to Yu Chung with a bitter smile, "If you sold your queue to a foreign woman you could get a good price for it."

The people who most hated Johnston were the staff of the Household Department. In those days expenditure in the palace was still enormous although the payments under the Articles of Favourable Treatment were in arrears every year. In order to meet running expenses the Household Department had to sell or pawn antiques, pictures, calligraphy, gold, silver and porcelain every year.

I gradually learnt from what Johnston said that there was something fishy about this. Once when the Household Department wanted to sell a golden pagoda as tall as a man I thought of Johnston's remarks that by selling gold and silver objects for the value of the metal in them instead of as works of art the Household Department was losing a lot of money. According to Johnston only a fool would act like this. I therefore sent for the officials of the Department and asked them how they intended selling it. When they said they would sell it according to its weight I burst into a fury:

"Only fools would do that. Haven't you got an ounce of sense between you?"

The Household Department reckoned that Johnston was ruining their racket and so they thought out a way of dealing with him: they sent the pagoda to Johnston's house and claimed that the emperor had asked him to sell it for him. Johnston saw through their trick at once, exploded with anger and said, "If you don't take it away I shall report this to His Majesty immediately." The result was that the Household Department officials carried the pagoda away again without making any more trouble.

By my last year of studying in the Yu Ching Palace Johnston had become the major part of my soul. Our discussions of extracurricular topics occupied more and more of our lesson-time and ever widened in scope. He told me about the life of the English royal family, the politics of different countries, the strength of the powers after the Great War, places and customs all over the world, the "great British Empire on which the sun never sets", China's civil wars and her "vernacular writing movement" (as he called the May 4th Movement of 1919) and its links with Western culture. He also talked about the possibility of a restoration and the unreliable attitude of the warlords.

"One can see clearly from all the papers," he said once, "that the Chinese people are thinking of the Great Ching and that everybody is tired of the Republic. I do not think that there is any need for Your Majesty to worry about those military men; nor need Your Imperial Majesty waste so much time trying to find out their attitudes from the papers; nor is there anything to be gained from discussing what difference of ultimate motives they have in supporting a restoration or defending the Republic. Tutor Chen is quite right in saying that the most important thing is for Your Majesty daily to renew your sage virtue. But this must not only be done in the Forbidden City. Your Majesty can acquire much essential knowledge and widen your horizons in Europe, particularly at Oxford University in the land of His Majesty the King of England where the Prince of Wales studied. . . ."

Before I got the idea of studying in England he had already done quite a lot to widen my "vision". He introduced English admirals and the British governor of Hongkong who were all polite and respectful, addressing me as "Your Imperial Majesty".

My intoxication with a European way of life and the way I tended more and more to ape him was not too pleasing to Johnston. On the subject of clothes, for example, our opinions differed as he had a special interest in me. On my wedding day I appeared at the reception given for foreign guests and drank a toast with them; but when I got back to the Mind Nurture Palace I changed my dragon robes for an ordinary gown worn over Western trousers and a peaked cap. Just then Johnston came along with some friends of his. A sharp-sighted old foreign lady saw me standing by the verandah and asked him, "Who is that young man?"

When Johnston spotted me and saw the clothes I was wearing his face went quite red. This gave me a fright, and the disappointed expressions of the foreigners mystified me. Johnston was still in a temper after they had gone and he said to me furiously:

"What do you mean by it, Your Majesty? For the Emperor of China to wear a hunting-cap! Good lord!"

My Wedding

If I was at all interested when the princes told me on the orders of the High Consorts that I was old enough for my "Grand Nuptials" it was because marriage would mark my coming of age and would mean that others could no longer control me as if I were still a child.

The people who felt most concern over the matter were the old ladies. Early in 1921, when I was just fifteen, the High Consorts summoned my father for a number of consultations on the subject and then called a meeting of about ten of the princes to discuss it. Almost two years later the wedding took place. There were a number of reasons why the delay was so long. One was that it would have been wrong for me to marry too soon after the deaths first of the high consort Chuang Ho and then of my own mother. The more important reason was that the political situation was unsettled and there were complicated quarrels over the choice of my bride. This was why my tutors counselled postponing it.

The quarrels occurred because the high consorts Tuan Kang and Ching Yi each wanted to choose a future "empress" who would be friendly to herself. Each put forward her own candidate and would not give way, and each was supported by one of my uncles. The situation was deadlocked.

In the last resort the choice had to be made by the "emperor". The way that this had been done in the time of Tung Chih and Kuang Hsu was for the girls who were candidates to stand in a line and the future bridegroom to select one of them. I have heard two versions of how he indicated his choice. One was that he handed a jade symbol to the girl who took his fancy; the other was that he hung a pouch on the girl's buckle. When it came to my time the princes felt that lining up a row of maidens would no longer be suitable and decided that I should choose from photographs instead. I was to pencil a mark on the picture of the one I liked best.

Four photos were sent to the Mind Nurture Palace. To me the girls seemed much the same and their bodies looked as shapeless as tubes in their dresses. Their faces were very small in the pictures so that I could not see whether they were beauties or not. The only comparison I could make was between the styles of their clothes. It did not occur to me at the time that this was one of the great events of my life, and I had no standards to guide me. I casually drew a circle on a pretty picture.

She was the daughter of Tuan Kung of the Manchu Ordet clan. She was called Wen Hsiu (her other name was Hui Hsin) and she was three years younger than me, so that she would have been twelve when I saw her picture. As she was the girl favoured by the high consort Ching Yi her rival Tuan Kang was most displeased and, overruling Ching Yi's protests, she insisted on summoning the princes to persuade me to choose her candidate. She said that Wen Hsiu came of an impoverished family and was ugly, whereas the girl she supported, Wan Jung (also called Mu Hung), was of a rich family, beautiful and the same age as me. I followed the advice of the princes, wondering why they had not explained things at the beginning, instead of letting me think that there was nothing to this business of making a pencil mark and drew a circle on the photo of Wan Jung.

This met with the disapproval of the high consorts Ching Yi and Jung Hui. After a series of arguments among the High Consorts and princes the high consort Jung Hui came out with this suggestion: "As His Majesty has marked Wen Hsiu's picture it wouldn't do for her to be married to one of his subjects, so he had better take her as a consort." I did not feel that I had much need for one wife, let alone two, and was not at all keen on this proposal; but when the princes and high officials pointed out to me that according to the customs of my ancestors "the emperor has to have an empress and a consort" this was an argument I could not resist. As I had to have all the prerogatives of an emperor I agreed to their suggestion.

I have rather simplified the process of choosing the empress and consort, which in fact took a whole year. After the selection had been made the Chihli-Fengtien war meant that the wedding had to be put off until the winter of 1922. Although this was after the fall of Hsu Shih-chang the large-scale preparations for the ceremony were too far under way to be stopped, so the wedding had to go ahead. The princes did not feel as much confidence in Li

Yuan-hung (now president for the second time) as they had felt for Hsu Shih-chang and were afraid that he might interfere with the pomp of the occasion. As it turned out, however, the help that Li gave far exceeded their expectations and was no less than they would have hoped for from Hsu Shih-chang. The Republic's Ministry of Finance wrote a letter in somewhat humble terms to the Household Department which said that as they were having difficulties at the moment in meeting their expenditure they were unable to pay in full the annual subsidies stipulated in the Articles of Favourable Treatment; they would, however, make a special payment from tax revenue of 100,000 dollars to help with the Grand Nuptials, of which 20,000 dollars was to be regarded as a present from the Republic. At the same time the military, gendarme and police authorities of the Republic presented plans for their men to provide protection for the double wedding, plans involving the participation of many hundreds of men.

From the entry into the palace of the trousseau of the consort to the ceremony at which I received congratulations in the Cloudless Heaven Palace the wedding lasted five days. The celebrations included three days of theatricals and the granting of new titles.

What caused the most public indignation was that after the attempted restoration in 1917 the little court was flaunting its pomp outside the Forbidden City. The ceremonial emblems of the Ching court were paraded with great majesty round the streets of Peking under the respectful protection of large numbers of Republican soldiers and police. On the day of the wedding ceremony proper two princes dressed in Ching court robes with staffs of office in their hands rode on horseback behind two Republican military bands. They were followed by more army bands and cavalry, mounted police, and mounted security police. After them came seventy-two dragon-and-phoenix parasols and flags, four "yellow pavilions" (containing the imperial patent for the new empress and her clothing), and thirty pairs of palace lanterns. This imposing procession set out for the "Residence of the Empress". At the brightly illuminated gate of the "residence" another host of police and soldiers were guarding Wan Jung's father and brothers as they knelt there to greet the "imperial decree" brought by the two envoys.

The rich presents given by leading figures of the Republic also attracted considerable attention. President Li Yuan-hung wrote "Offering of President Li Yuan-hung of the Republic of China to the Hsuan Tung Emperor" on a red card and gave the following presents: four vessels in cloisonné, two kinds of silk and satin, one curtain and a pair of scrolls wishing me longevity, prosperity and good fortune. Ex-President Hsu Shih-chang sent 20,000 dollars and many other valuable presents including twenty-eight pieces of porcelain and a sumptuous Chinese carpet with a dragon and phoenix design. Chang Tso-lin, Wu Pei-fu, Chang Hsun, Tsao Kun and other warlords and politicians also sent cash and many other kinds of presents.

The representative of the Republic at the ceremony, Yin Chang, was a chief aide-de-camp in the Office of the President, and he congratulated me formally as he would have done a foreign sovereign. When he had finished bowing to me he announced, "That was on behalf of the Republic. Your slave will now greet Your Majesty in his private capacity." With this he knelt on the floor and kotowed to me.

At the time many papers severely criticized these strange occurrences but this did nothing to dampen the enthusiasm of the princes and high officials, nor did it prevent veterans of the Ching from emerging all over the country like insects waking up after the winter and converging on Peking in swarms. They brought presents that included money and antiques from themselves and others. The valuables were not as important, however, as the power that the court now seemed to enjoy, which went beyond even their own expectations and made them feel that our prospects were very hopeful.

What caused the High Consorts, princes, high officials and veterans of the Ching the most excitement was the presence of guests from the Legation Quarter. This was the first time that foreign officials had appeared in the Forbidden City since the Revolution of 1911, and although they came in their personal capacities they were still, after all, foreign officials.

On the suggestion of Johnston a reception was given to show our gratitude to the foreigners for attending the ceremony and I read a short speech in English.

While all this hustle and bustle went on around me one question kept running through my mind: "I have an empress and a consort; I'm married. But how are things any different from before?" The answer that I gave myself was, "I've come of age. If there had not been a revolution I would start ruling without regents."

I hardly thought about marriage and my family. It was only when the empress came into my field of vision with a crimson satin cloth embroidered with a dragon and a phoenix over her head that I felt at all curious about what she looked like.

According to tradition the emperor and the empress spent their wedding night in a bridal chamber some ten metres square in the Palace of Earthly Peace (Kun Ning Kung). This was a rather peculiar room: it was unfurnished except for the bed-platform which filled a quarter of it, and everything about it except the floor was red. When we had drunk the nuptial cup and eaten sons-and-grandsons cakes and entered this dark red room I felt stifled. The bride sat on the bed, her head bent down. I looked around me and saw that everything was red: red bed-curtains, red pillows, a red dress, a red skirt, red flowers, and a red face . . . it all looked like a melted red wax candle. I did not know whether to stand or sit, decided that I preferred the Mind Nurture Palace, and went back there.

When I got back to the Mind Nurture Palace I looked at the list of the senior officials of the country during the Hsuan Tung reign that was pasted on the wall and wondered again, "I have an empress and a consort and I'm grown up, but how are things any different from before?"

How did Wan Jung feel, abandoned in the bridal chamber? What was Wen Hsiu, a girl not yet fourteen, thinking? These questions never even occurred to me as my thoughts were preoccupied. "If there had been no revolution I would now be starting to rule with full powers. I must recover my ancestral heritage."

Internal Clashes

From the time when Johnston entered the palace onwards I became a more and more difficult emperor for the princes and palace officials to deal with. About the time of my marriage my actions must have seemed stranger and stranger to them and made them more and more uneasy. One day I would order the Household Department to buy me a diamond costing 30,000 dollars and the day after I would castigate them for failing to make ends meet and accuse them of corruption and waste. In the morning I might summon the high officials and tell them to inspect the collections of antiques, calligraphy and paintings and report the same day, and in the afternoon I might want a car for a trip to Fragrance Hill outside Peking. I was bored with traditional ceremonies and did not even like to ride in the gold-canopied yellow chair. To make cycling easier I had all the thresholds in the gates of the palace, which had caused no inconvenience to my ancestors over the centuries, sawn off. I would accuse the eunuchs of disloyalty to me for trifling reasons and have them sent to the Administrative Bureau to be flogged or discharged. What made the princes and high officials most uncomfortable, however, was the way in which at one moment I would be preparing myself for a reform of the palace and a financial clean-up and the next I would be announcing that I wanted to leave the Forbidden City and go and study abroad. They were in fear and trembling all day and their queues almost went white from worry.

Some of the princes and officials had thought about my going to study abroad before it occurred to me, and this was one of the reasons why they had invited Johnston to be my tutor; and after my wedding I received a number of memorials and suggestions from Ching veterans proposing this. But when I raised the question myself almost everybody opposed it, and the most common reason given was: "If Your Majesty leaves the Forbidden City it will amount to abrogating the Articles of Favourable Treatment. Why should you want to abolish them yourself when the Republic has not done so?"

None of them, whether they sympathized with my wish to go abroad or whether they opposed it, whether they had already despaired of "restoring the ancestral heritage" or whether they still had hopes of it, none of them could do without the Articles of Favourable Treatment. Although the clause which referred to a subsidy of 4,000,000 dollars a year had been shown to be an empty promise, the clause stating that the emperor's "title of dignity is to be retained and not abolished" still held good. It was not only those who still hoped for a restoration who regarded it as important that I should stay in the Forbidden City and keep up the little court; and even those who had lost hope still saw it as the way to safeguard their ricebowls and their positions. Apart from the titles they would be given after their deaths, they could consecrate the ancestral tablets of others and write epitaphs while they were alive.

My ideas differed from theirs. In the first place I did not think that the Articles of Favourable Treatment would be observed for ever and I was more conscious than anyone else of the precariousness of my position. The new outbreak of civil war, the retreat of Chang Tso-lin to the Northeast, the fall of Hsu Shih-chang and Li Yuan-hung's return to power all made me feel that danger had suddenly become imminent. My only concern was whether or not the new authorities would kill me. There no longer seemed to be any possibility of favourable treatment. On top of all this came the report that some members of parliament were proposing the abolition of the Articles of Favourable Treatment. Even if the *status quo* could be maintained, who could tell in the political and military confusion which warlord might be in power tomorrow or which politician might be organizing a cabinet the day after. I knew from many sources, particularly Johnston, that foreign powers were behind all these changes, so would it not be better to contact the foreigners directly rather than depend upon favourable treatment from the latest Republican authorities? Might it not be too late if I waited until someone implacably hostile to me came to power before thinking of some way out? I was only too well acquainted with the way that the last emperors of dynasties had met unpleasant deaths throughout the history of China.

Of course, I did not remind the princes and high officials of these woeful tales. The argument I used with them was:

"I don't want any 'favourable treatment'. I want to let the common people and the world know that I have no hope that the Republic will treat me favourably. To do this is much better than waiting for them to abrogate the articles first."

"But the articles are stored in the state archives and internationally recognized. If the Republic were to abrogate them the foreign powers would certainly help us," was their reply.

"If the foreigners would help us then why don't you let me go abroad? Surely they would be even more helpful when they saw me in person?"

However good my reasons, they would never have agreed. All my arguments with my father, my tutors and the princes had only one result: they speeded up their preparations for my "Grand Nuptials".

There was another reason why I was so anxious to go abroad apart from those I mentioned to the princes and officials: I had been growing tired of my whole environment, themselves included, long before I got the idea of foreign travel. Since Johnston had come to the palace and filled me with knowledge about Western civilization, this and my youthful curiosity had made me dissatisfied with my surroundings and the restrictions that hemmed me in. I agreed with Johnston's diagnosis that the root of the trouble lay in the conservatism of the princes and high officials.

In their eyes everything new was terrifying. When I was fifteen Johnston noticed that I might be short-sighted and advised asking a foreign ophthalmologist to come and examine my eyes. If his guess was correct I should have spectacles. To his surprise this suggestion created as much of an uproar as if he had tipped some water into a pan of boiling oil and the Forbidden City all but exploded. What an idea! That the eyes of His Imperial Majesty should be looked at by a foreigner! His Majesty was still in the vigour of youth. How could he wear "specs" like an old man?

Nobody from the High Consorts down would consent. It was through repeated entreaties by Johnston and determination on my part that it was finally done.

I was particularly annoyed when the princes and high officials would oppose my having things that they had themselves. An example of this was a telephone.

When I was fifteen an explanation from Johnston of the uses of the telephone aroused my curiosity, and when I heard from my brother Pu Chieh that my father's house had one of these toys I told the Household Department to have one installed in the Mind Nurture Palace. On receiving this order the head of the Household Department, Shao Ying, turned pale with horror. He did not utter a word of protest, however, and withdrew with a "yes, sire". But the next day all my tutors came to offer advice.

"There is no precedent for such a thing in the ancestral code. If a telephone is installed anyone might talk to Your Majesty, a thing that never happened in the times of your ancestors. . . . The ancestors never used these foreign contraptions. . . ."

I had arguments with which to retaliate: "The chiming clocks, pianos and electric lights in the palace are all foreign things that have no place in the ancestral system, but did not my ancestors use them?"

"If outsiders can make phone calls whenever they like will they not offend the Celestial Countenance? Will this not damage the imperial dignity?"

"I have been offended by outsiders often enough in the press. What difference is there between reading insults and hearing them?"

Perhaps even my tutors did not understand at the time why the Household Department asked them to dissuade me. What really frightened the Household Department was not that the "Celestial Countenance" might be offended but that the telephone might enable me to have more contact with the outside world. It was already enough for them that I should have a talkative Johnston by my side and take over twenty different newspapers. In the Peking newspapers of the day one would find statements from the Household Department every month at least either denying that the Ching house was in contact with the authorities of this or that province or some important personality, or else refuting rumours that the palace had recently been pawning or selling some antiques. The great majority of the rumours that were denied were in fact true, and at least half of them were things that the Household Department did not want me to know about. The combination of the newspapers and Johnston kept them quite busy enough: a third link with the outside in the form of a telephone would put them in an impossible position. So naturally they did all in their power to prevent it, and when they saw that the tutors had failed to dissuade me they brought my father in.

My father had by then become a convinced believer in maintaining the existing state of affairs. Provided I made no trouble and stayed quietly in the Forbidden City, he would go on receiving his annual grant of 42,480 taels of silver and be quite contented with his lot; this made him very amenable to the direction of the Household Department. But his tongue was not as glib as the Household Department had hoped. He could produce no argument to dissuade me that my tutors had not already tried and was unable to find an answer to one question I asked him: "Hasn't there been a telephone in Your Highness's home for a long time?"

"That . . . that. . . . But it is quite different from Your Majesty having one. Let's talk the matter over again in a couple of days. . . ."

I was reminded that he had cut his queue off before me, had a telephone before me, and would not let me buy a car although he had already purchased one himself, and so I was not feeling at all pleased.

"Why should it be different for the emperor? Am I not to have even this tiny amount of freedom? No, I insist on a telephone." I turned to a eunuch. "Tell the Household Department I want a telephone installed today."

"Very well," my father nodded his head, "very well, have one then."

With the telephone installed there was more trouble.

The telephone company sent a directory along with the apparatus. In a state of high excitement I leafed through its pages thinking that

I would have some fun with the phone. I rang up a Peking opera actor and an acrobat and hung up before saying who I was, then called up a restaurant and ordered a meal to be sent round to a false address. After amusing myself like this for a while it would be fun to hear what the Dr. Hu Shih, the author of the line "Picnic by the river" whom Johnston had recently mentioned, sounded like and so I called his number. By a piece of luck he answered the phone himself.

"Is that Dr. Hu?" I asked. "Excellent, guess who I am."

"Who are you? I have no idea."

"Ha ha, no need to guess, I'll tell you. I'm Hsuan Tung."

"Hsuan Tung? Is that Your Majesty?"

"Right, I'm the emperor. I've heard your voice now, but I haven't seen you. Come round to the palace when you have time so that I can have a look at you."

This casual joke brought him along. Johnston told me that Hu Shih had come to see him especially to confirm the telephone call as he had not expected "His Majesty" to phone. He anxiously asked Johnston about palace etiquette and decided to come when he found out that he would not have to kotow to me and that I was a reasonably good-tempered emperor. I had forgotten all about our conversation and had not told the eunuchs to inform the guards, so that when Dr. Hu Shih arrived at the palace gate no amount of talking would get him in. Not knowing whether to believe him or not the guards referred the matter to me, and only let him in when I gave the word.

This meeting born of the whim of a moment lasted about twenty minutes. I asked him about the uses of vernacular writing, about his travels abroad and so on. Fishing for compliments, I ended by saying that I did not mind whether I got favourable treatment or not so long as I could study and be a "promising young man" of the sort one read about in the papers. He covered me with the expected flattery: "Your Majesty is most enlightened. If Your Majesty studies conscientiously, there is a bright future ahead of you." I did not know what he meant by this future. He went away and I thought no more of the affair, but to my surprise the princes and senior officials, particularly my tutors, were thrown into an uproar at the news that I had met this "new figure" in a private audience.

As I grew up they saw that I was becoming more and more dissatisfied; and I found them increasingly tiresome. At this time I had already made several trips outside the Forbidden City, a small freedom I had won in the face of much protest on the pretext of going to make offerings to my mother after her death. This taste of freedom had whetted my appetite and I was thoroughly sick of all these timorous and doltish officials. My accumulated impatience at all the incidents mentioned above made me more determined than ever to go abroad, and my conflict with the princes and high officials reached a climax in the summer of 1922 when I formally raised my wish to study in England.

They were not prepared to give way on this as they had done over the installation of a telephone. Even my uncle Tsai Tao, who sympathized with me most strongly, would only give permission for a house to be got ready in the English concession in Tientsin in which I could take refuge in an emergency. As it was impossible for me to leave the Forbidden City openly I asked Johnston to help me. I related in the preceding section that he thought that the time was not ripe and would not agree to my going at the moment. While I forced myself to wait for my chance I made secret preparations for an escape with the assistance of a loyal and willing helper — my brother Pu Chieh.

Pu Chieh and myself were a well-matched pair of brothers, and our feelings and ambitions were even more similar than our faces. His one thought was to escape from his cooped-up life at home, to fly high, and to find a way out; he believed that all his dreams would be realized once he went abroad. The only difference between his environment and mine was the same as that between our two bodies: his was one size smaller. Between the ages of four and seventeen he was dressed every morning by his old nurse. He could do nothing for himself, not even wash his feet or trim his nails. If he picked up a pair of scissors the nurse would shout and scream, terrified that he might cut himself. She would take him everywhere, and did not let him run, climb, or go out of the front gate. He was not allowed to eat fish for fear he might choke. He studied in a family school under a tutor who used to curse the Republic. Our mother urged Pu Chieh to help me faithfully and never to forget that he was a descendant of the Aisin-Gioro clan.

Although Pu Chieh was a year younger than me he knew more about the outside world. This was mainly because he only had to give his family the excuse of going to the palace to be able to move outside freely. The first stage of our escape plan was to provide for our expenses. The way we did this was to move the most valuable pictures, calligraphy and antiques in the imperial collections out of the palace by pretending that I was giving them to Pu Chieh and then store them in the house in Tientsin. Pu Chieh used to take a large bundle home after school every day for over six months, and the things we took were the very finest treasures in the collections. As it happened the heads of the Household Department and my tutors were checking through the pictures and calligraphy at the time, so all we had to do was to take the items they selected as being of the very highest grade. In addition to paintings and calligraphy we also took many valuable ancient editions of books. We must have removed over a thousand handscrolls, more than two hundred hanging scrolls and pages from albums, and about two hundred rare Sung Dynasty printed books. All these were taken to Tientsin and later some dozens of them were sold. The rest were taken up to the Northeast by the Kwantung Army adviser Yoshioka after the foundation of "Manchukuo" and disappeared after the Japanese surrender.

The second stage of our plan was to make a secret escape from the Forbidden City. We had learnt a most important lesson from the history of the first years of the Republic: once I was out of the palace and into the Legation Quarter the Republican authorities and the palace officials would be powerless to touch me. Johnston had thought out the details of how to do it. First I had to get in touch with the doyen of the diplomatic corps, the Dutch Minister W. J. Oudendijk, and let him make appropriate preparations. He had suggested this to me back in February 1923. Nine months previously he had opposed my going abroad on the grounds that the time was not ripe. I did not have the least idea why he thought that the time had now come, or whether he had made any further arrangements with the foreign envoys. This indication from Johnston gave me great confidence and satisfied me completely. First I asked him to go to the legations and inform them, then I spoke to Oudendijk over the phone myself. To make things even more definite I also sent Pu Chieh to visit the Dutch Legation. The results were completely satisfactory. Oudendijk agreed to my requests over the telephone, and arranged with Pu Chieh that although he could not send a car into the Forbidden City for me he would have one waiting outside the Gate of Divine Valour; once I slipped out of this gate there would be no more problems. He would take complete responsibility for everything from my first night's food and lodging right up to my entry into an English university. We fixed the day and the hour for my departure from the palace.

On February 25 the only remaining problem was how to get through the Gate of Divine Valour. I had to reckon with the eunuchs of my own entourage, the eunuchs at each of the palace gates, the sentries of the palace guard outside the palace walls and the Republican patrols outside the Gate of Divine Valour. I reckoned that once the eunuchs in my suite and at the gates were dealt with there would be no other great problem. My ideas were a little too simple, and I thought that all I had to do to win them over was to give them some money. They thanked me profusely for it and I thought that everything was now ready; but an hour before the set time one of the eunuchs who had taken my bribes informed the Household Department. Before I had even left the Mind Nurture Palace I heard that my father had given an order that nobody was to be allowed through any of the palace gates and that the whole of the Forbidden City had been put into a state of siege. Pu Chieh and I sat in the Mind Nurture Palace stupefied at the news.

Before long my father arrived in a very nervous state.

"I — I — I hear that Your — Your Majesty wa — wa — wants to go away. . . ."

He looked so ill at ease that one might have thought that he was the wrong-doer, and I could not help laughing.

"Of course I don't," I replied, suppressing my laughter.

"It's not good of you. What should we do about it?"

"But I don't want to."

My father glared suspiciously at Pu Chieh, who was frightened into bowing his head.

"I don't want to," I repeated. My father muttered a few more words before going off, taking my "accomplice" with him. When he had gone I called the eunuchs of the presence to question them about who had betrayed the plan. I intended to have the culprit flogged to within an inch of his life. I could not get the information out of them and I could not have the matter investigated by the Administrative Bureau either; I could only nurse my anger by myself.

From then onwards I hated the sight of the high palace wall.

"Prison, prison, prison," I muttered to myself as I stood on an artificial hill in the palace looking at the wall. "That the Republic should not be on good terms with me is understandable, but it is quite unreasonable for the princes and palace officials to be so hostile. It is only for the sake of my ancestral heritage of mountains and rivers that I want to go away. What are your motives in keeping me here? The worst of you are the ones in the Household Department: it must have been them who dragged my father into this."

When I saw Johnston the next day I poured my complaints out to him. After some words of consolation he advised me to put the matter out of my mind for the time being: it would be more practical to start by reorganizing the Forbidden City. He recommended me to follow the suggestions of the newly arrived Cheng Hsiao-hsu on the subject of reform.

A new hope was kindled in my mind. Even if I could not recover my ancestral heritage outside the palace walls, at least I could reform my property within the Forbidden City. I was very pleased with Johnston's suggestion. I never dreamed at the time that when he later described my attempted escape in his book he would actually claim to have had nothing to do with it and even say he had opposed it.

The Dispersal of the Eunuchs

Despite its superficial calm the Forbidden City was in complete disorder. From my earliest years I was always hearing about theft, arson and murder, to say nothing of gambling and opium smoking. At the time of my wedding robbery had got to such a state that as soon as the ceremony was over all the pearls and jade in the empress's crown were stolen and replaced by fakes.

I had been told by my tutors that the treasures of the Ching palace were world-famous and that the antiques, calligraphy and paintings alone were amazing both for their quantity and value. Apart from what had been looted by foreign troops in 1860 and 1900, nearly all of the collections that had been amassed by the Ming and Ching Dynasties were still in the palace. Most of these objects were uncatalogued and even those that were catalogued had not been checked so that nobody knew what or how much had been lost. This made things very easy for thieves.

Looking back on it today it all seems to have been an orgy of looting. The looters included everyone from the highest to the humblest; anybody who had the chance to steal did so without the least anxiety. The techniques varied: some people forced locks and stole secretly, while others used legal methods and stole in broad daylight. The former method was the one favoured by most of the eunuchs, while the officials used the latter: they mortgaged pieces, sold them openly, borrowed them "for appraisal" and asked for them as presents. The most advanced technique was the one used by Pu Chieh and myself. Of course, I did not think about it in these terms at the time, and it seemed to me then that everyone else was stealing my property.

One day when I was seventeen my curiosity prompted me to have the eunuchs open up a storeroom by the Palace of Established Happiness (Chien Fu Kung). The doors of the store were thickly plastered with strips of sealing-paper and had clearly not been opened for decades, and inside were a number of large chests. It turned out that the very valuable collection of antiques and scrolls they contained were Emperor Chien Lung's favourite pieces and that they had been put away after his death. The discovery of all this treasure made me wonder how much wealth I really had. I had taken away what I had seen, but how much more was there that I had not seen? What should I do about these enormous stores of treasure? How much of it had been stolen? How could I prevent further thefts?

Johnston told me that many new antique shops had been opened in Ti An Men Street where he lived. Some of these shops were said to be run by eunuchs and others by officials of the Household Department or relations of theirs. Later my other tutors also felt that some measures should be taken to prevent further thefts, and I agreed to a proposal of theirs that an inventory should be made. This decision, however, led to even more trouble.

First of all the number of thefts increased. The lock to the store of the Yu Ching Palace was smashed and one of the windows at the back of the Cloudless Heaven Palace forced open. The situation was getting so badly out of hand that even the big diamond I had recently bought disappeared. In an attempt to investigate the robberies the High Consorts ordered the head of the Administrative Bureau to question the eunuchs responsible for these stores, using torture if necessary; but neither torture nor the offer of rich rewards had any effect. This was not all. On the night of June 27, 1923, soon after the checking of the contents of the store of the Palace of Established Happiness had begun, a fire broke out there and everything, whether checked or not yet checked, was burnt to ashes.

The fire was apparently discovered by the fire brigade of the Italian Legation, and when their fire engine reached the palace gates the guards did not realize why they had come. The conflagration, which was fought all night by fire brigades of all sorts, reduced the whole area round the Palace of Established Happiness to ashes.

These were the places where most of the treasures of the Ching house were stored, and what was lost in the fire is still a mystery. The Household Department published a very rough account which estimated that the losses included 2,665 gold statues of the Buddha, 1,157 pieces of painting and calligraphy, 435 antiques, and tens of thousands of ancient books; but heaven only knows what they based these figures on.

When the fire was being fought the place was full of foreigners and Chinese, residents of the palace and outsiders, all coming and going hither and thither. It can be easily imagined that they were not only concerned with extinguishing the fire, but the Forbidden City expressed its gratitude to all of them. One foreign lady who came to watch the excitement started quarrelling with a Chinese fireman and actually hit her opponent on the nose with her fan. Later she showed me her bloodstained fan as evidence of her courage and I wrote a poem on it as a mark of my gratitude.

One can get an indication of the extent of the losses caused by the fire from the way the pile of cinders left over after the fire and the "salvaging" was dealt with. At the time I wanted to find a stretch of empty land for a tennis court where Johnston could teach me tennis, a game he said that all the English aristocrats played. The ruined site was just right for the purpose and so I told the Household Department to clear it up as quickly as possible. There were no traces of paintings, calligraphy or ancient porcelain in the rubble but there was a great deal of gold, silver, copper and tin. The gold merchants of Peking were invited by the Household Department to submit tenders and one of them bought the right to dispose of the ashes for 500,000 dollars; he picked out over 17,000 taels of gold from them. When he had taken what he wanted the Department packed the rest into sacks and distributed them to its personnel. One Department official later told me that four gold altars one foot in height and diameter that his uncle gave to the Yung Ho Kung Temple and the Cypress Grove Temple in Peking were all made of gold extracted from some of these sacks of ashes.

The cause of the fire is as impenetrable a mystery as the amount of damage it did. My suspicion is that it was deliberately started by thieves to cover their traces. Only a few days later another fire was started above one of the windows of the No Idleness Study in the eastern inner court of the Mind Nurture Palace. Fortunately it was detected early, and a wad of kerosene-soaked cotton wool was extinguished soon after it had been lit. My suspicions grew instantly stronger and I believed that somebody had started this fire not only to cover his traces, but also to murder me.

That there had been thefts and that the fire had been started deliberately to conceal them were facts that even my tutors did not attempt to conceal from me; but perhaps my fears of an attempt on my life were due to excessive nervousness. My suspicious nature was already quite obvious. According to the code of the Ching house the emperor had to read a page of the "instructions" of his ancestors, which were always set out for him in his bedroom, and at that time I particularly admired the "Vermilion Rescripts, Edicts and Decrees" of Emperor Yung Cheng (1723-35) for their cautious cynicism. He and Kang Hsi (1662-1722) warned against putting too much trust in anybody, particularly eunuchs. The message of these remarks was driven home by the fires.

I decided to follow the advice of Yung Cheng to "make things clear through careful investigation." I thought of two methods. One was to question the junior eunuchs of my entourage and the other was to eavesdrop on the eunuchs' conversations. I discovered at the window of one of their lodging places that they were discussing me behind my back, saying that my temper was getting worse and worse. This strengthened my suspicions. On the evening of the fire in the No Idleness Study I eavesdropped again under their windows and found that they had gone even further in their remarks about me and were saying that I had started the fire myself. I now felt that they were completely unreliable and that if I did not strike first there would be no end of trouble.

It was just then that an attempted murder was discovered. One of the eunuchs had been reported for making some mistake and had been beaten by a chief eunuch. Nursing his resentment he had gone into the room where the informer slept carrying some lime and a knife; he had thrown the lime into the man's face to blind him and then stabbed him. The attacker was still at large.

This made me think of all the eunuchs who had been beaten on my orders and I wondered whether they might not make some such attack on me. The thought was so frightening that I was too scared to sleep. There were eunuchs sleeping on mats on the floor from the room next to my bedroom all the way to the outbuildings of the Mind Nurture Palace, and if any of them was ill-disposed towards me and could stand me no longer it would be only too easy for him to finish me off. I wanted to find a reliable person to keep watch for me, and I could think of nobody but my empress. From then on I made Wan Jung sit up all night keeping watch; she was to wake me if she heard any movement, and I kept a club beside my bed ready for use. But after Wan Jung had spent several sleepless nights in a row I realized that this method was no good. Finally I decided to deal with the problem once and for all by expelling all the eunuchs from the palace.

I knew that I was bound to have some trouble doing this and that if I did not cope with my father it would be impossible. I decided to go and see him myself. Suddenly faced with this problem and having no way to discuss it with the head of the Household Department or my tutors he found it harder than ever to get his words out. With a tremendous effort he managed to produce a hotch-potch of objections: my ancestors had always had eunuchs; after all their years of service they could not plan any treachery; and so on. Finally he tried to persuade me to think it over for a few days. I replied that if he did not agree I would never return to the palace.

He was so worked up that he did not know whether to sit or to stand. Scratching his head and his cheek, and walking round in circles he knocked a bottle of lemonade to the floor with his sleeve and smashed it. I could not help giggling, and casually opened a book on the desk as if I had no intention of leaving.

Finally my father gave in and all the eunuchs, except a few from whom the High Consorts could not be parted, were driven out of the palace.

Reorganizing the Household Department

My expulsion of the eunuchs was very well received by public opinion, and under the direction of Johnston I made the Household Department the next object of my determination to govern well. The Household Department had a long tradition of corruption and graft. A friend of mine who was a former official of the Department has described how the Manchus who ran it abhorred scholarship and learning and regarded graft and corruption as practices in which they had imperial authority to indulge.

It will suffice to cite two examples of the Department's embezzlement. One is its astronomical annual expenditure, which could not have been covered by the 4,000,000 dollars annuity due under the Articles of Favourable Treatment even if it had been paid in full. It was revealed in 1924, after I left the palace, that the Department had received 5,000,000 dollars in that year from pawning gold, silver and antiques, and all of this money had been spent. Another example is the way in which the Household Department pawned a large batch of palace gold and jewellery through my father-in-law Jung Yuan at a fraction of its true value.

Although I did not have such evidence of the Department's corruption while I was still living in the palace as I did later, I knew one thing from the annual expenditure figures: they were higher than they had even been in the time of the empress dowager Tzu Hsi. In obedience to an edict of mine ordering that the finances be put in order the Household Department prepared "A Comparison Between the Expenditures of the Seventh Year of Hsuan Tung (1915) and the Past Three Years". According to their figures the Department's expenditure (excluding the set payments to the princes and high officials) was 2,640,000 taels in 1915; 2,380,000 taels in 1919; 1,890,000 taels in 1920; and 1,710,000 taels in 1921. At the beginning of the rule of Tzu Hsi annual expenditure had only been about 300,000 taels, and even in the year in which her seventieth birthday was celebrated it had only gone up to 700,000 taels. The

137

difference would have been surprising to a worse mathematician than myself. At the same time I noticed stories in the gossip columns of the press about how noble and official families had been reduced to destitution or were going steadily downhill; I read about scions of such families being found dead in the gateways of the city wall and about princesses and noble ladies becoming prostitutes. Meanwhile officials of the Household Department were opening antique shops, banks, pawnshops, building firms and so on. Although my tutors sided with the Household Department to oppose my buying a car and installing a telephone, none of them had a good word to say for such behaviour by Department officials. My Manchu tutor Yi Ko Tan said to me not long before his death in 1921 that Chen Pao-shen was guilty of "deceiving his sovereign" because he would not tell me about the corruption of the Household Department and therefore did not deserve the title of "Grand Tutor". Johnston of course regarded the Department as a bloodsucking monster, and this view of his strengthened my resolution to clean it up.

"The Household Department in the palace and the stewards of the princes are all exceedingly rich," he remarked one day. "Their masters know nothing about their own finances and are completely dependent on them: without them they cannot lay their hands on a copper cash. Never mind restoring the old order, if they don't put their stewards in their proper place they won't even keep their remaining wealth for long."

"The Household Department has a motto," he said on another occasion. "It is 'preserve the present order'. Everything from a trifling reform to a major ideal runs into this obstacle and has to stop." He emphasized the last word by putting it into English.

The first use I made of my new authority after my wedding was to choose some of those I regarded as the most loyal and capable of the Ching veterans who had come to the ceremony to be my assistants in this undertaking. They in turn recommended their friends, and in this way another twelve or thirteen pigtails came into the palace. The most important of them were Cheng Hsiao-hsu, Lo Chen-yu,

Wang Kuo-wei and Shang Yen-ying. I distributed the titles "Companion of the Southern Study" (the emperor's study) and "Companion of the Great Diligence Hall" (referring to the office that looked after the emperor's stationery). I also put two bannermen in charge of the Household Department: my father-in-law Jung Yuan and the Mongol Chin Liang, the former tutor of Chang Hsuehliang (the "Young Marshal").

They offered me very full advice on what I should do. In a document dated "First Month of the Sixteenth Year of Hsuan Tung" (1924), which would have been about two months before his appointment to the Household Department, Chin Liang wrote:

"In your subject's opinion the most important thing today is secretly to plan a restoration. To carry out this great enterprise of changing the world there are many things to do. The first priority is to consolidate the base by protecting the court; the next most important task is to put the imperial property into order so as to secure our finances. For it is necessary to have the wherewithal to support and protect ourselves; only then can we plan a restoration." He went on to suggest in more detail how these principles could be carried out, and one of his proposals with which I thoroughly agreed was that we should begin by reforming the Household Department.

Even the majority of the more apathetic Ching survivals supported the domestic reform plans. One group of them, however, led by Chen Pao-shen shook their heads at all talk of cleaning up the Household Department, reckoning that the situation had gone too far to be remedied; attempts to do so had been made in earlier reigns but without success. They thought that reorganization would only lead to trouble. But even they had not a good word to say for the Department.

At the urging of Johnston I had tried unsuccessfully to put my property in order shortly before my wedding, but I attributed the failure of this attempt to my minority and to choosing the wrong man for the job rather than to the machinations of the Department. Now that I had come of age and had all these new assistants I felt that I was in a much stronger position and entrusted Cheng Hsiao-hsu with the responsibility for the reform.

Cheng Hsiao-hsu was a fellow-provincial of Chen Pao-shen's who had served the Ching as a consul in Japan and later as a border commissioner in Kwangsi. Chen Pao-shen and Johnston both recommended him to me, particularly Johnston, who said that he was the man he had most admired in his twenty-odd years in China, and that his character, learning and ability were unmatched in the country. I also knew that he had refused to serve the Republic and had heard that he made his living from selling his calligraphy. I thought that he must be an exceptionally loyal subject.

After Cheng Hsiao-hsu became a "Companion of the Great Diligence Hall" he came to see me several times to explain to me how necessary it was to clean up the Household Department in order to "accomplish the great enterprise", and he told me about his plans for doing so. He thought that four sections would be quite enough to do the work of the Department; great numbers of its staff should be dismissed and enormous economies made. In this way the drain on resources could be stopped and the material position strengthened. If his plan were carried out the financial basis of a restoration could be assured. I was so struck by him that I broke precedent and appointed him Comptroller of the Household Department and "Keeper of the Keys and Seals" although he was a Han and not a Manchu. He thus became the leading official of the Household.

But to imagine that the vulgar and unlettered Household Department could be worsted by Cheng Hsiao-hsu was to underestimate this office which had over two hundred years of running the palace behind it. For all his eloquence and all the support and trust I gave him Cheng Hsiao-hsu only lasted three months.

I never found out who in the Department got rid of him. Did Shao Ying make trouble for him? This would seem unlikely as Shao Ying was famed for his cautious timidity. Was it Chi Ling? He was an outsider where the business of the Department was concerned and took little interest in it. As for the third of the high officials, Pao Hsi, he was a new arrival and unlikely to have been able to operate as effectively as that. Yet it was not likely that their subordinates would have dared to act against Cheng on their own initiative.

The first thing that Cheng Hsiao-hsu encountered on taking office was a backlog of files dating back to the Revolution of 1911. His response was to make a display of his authority by dismissing the holder of a key job and giving it to his friend Tung Chi-hsu. The Household's response was to behave as if it had been paralysed. If he wanted money, there was no money and accounts in black and white proved it; if he wanted some object nobody knew where it was stored, and this too was clearly stated in the records.

In order to win over his subordinates Cheng made a great show of humility and of listening to what they had to say. He held a discussion every week at which they were invited to offer suggestions for reform. One proposal made was that the expenditure on fruit and cakes used in offerings at the various shrines in the palace was too high and that as these offerings were only symbolic it would be just as dignified to use wooden or clay replicas. This suggestion met with Cheng Hsiao-hsu's strong approval and orders were given that it was to be put into effect; the proposer was promoted one grade. But the eunuchs who regarded the offerings as their legitimate income (there were about a hundred eunuchs left after the expulsion) all hated Cheng bitterly for it. Within a few days of taking office Cheng had become the most unpopular man in the Forbidden City.

When he would not abandon his position he received threatening letters saying that he was depriving people of their livelihood and that he had better be careful if he wanted to keep his head on his shoulders. Johnston received similar communications, and neither he nor Cheng paid any attention to them.

I was the person who finished off the reform episode. Soon after I had appointed Cheng Hsiao-hsu to the Household Department I heard some most unwelcome news: a group of members of the Republic's Parliament were reintroducing a bill to abolish the Articles of Favourable Treatment and make the Forbidden City over to the Republic. A bill like this had been presented two years previously on the grounds that the palace had staged a restoration in 1917 and that by granting peerages and posthumous titles to Republican officials it was putting itself above the Republic and clearly still plotting a restoration. Now that the bill was being reintroduced they were saying that I had given a posthumous title to Chang Hsun, the criminal instigator of the 1917 restoration, and had acted illegally in making a Han, Cheng Hsiao-hsu, Comptroller of the Household Department and giving him the right to ride a horse in the Forbidden City.

The appearance of this news in the papers was the signal for a series of attacks on the actions of the Household Department; various forms of corruption that had gone unremarked before now came in for public criticism. The inventory of paintings and calligraphy that was being made by Lo Chen-yu and others of my new batch of pigtailed advisers also came under fire: they were selling rubbings of bronzes and prints of pictures, and the originals themselves became fewer and fewer as the process went on. Then the Republic announced a "Bill for the Protection of Old Books, Antiques and Ancient Relics" that was clearly intended to prevent the palace from selling its art treasures.

My father came to see me and suggested in a roundabout and fawning way that I should carefully reconsider Cheng Hsiao-hsu's methods and think what trouble there might be with the Republican authorities disapproving of them.

One day Shao Ying, the former Household Comptroller, appeared before me looking very timid and said that the commander of the army of the Republic was deeply dissatisfied with Cheng Hsiao-hsu's actions; if Cheng made any more trouble and the Republic took action he would be able to do nothing to help me. I was terrified by this news, and then Cheng memorialized asking to be relieved of his duties. The result of it all was that Cheng reverted to being a "Companion of the Great Diligence Hall" and Shao Ying resumed control of the Household Department.

The Last Days in the Forbidden City

Although my attempt to reform the Household Department had ended in failure I did not abandon my efforts to improve my situation.

Apart from the men in the palace planning for my restoration there were others working for me all over the country. Kang Yu-wei, for example, was operating in China and abroad under the sign of his "Imperial Chinese Constitutional Monarchist Party". Through Johnston I received extravagant and fanciful reports of the support the party was supposed to be gaining, and although nearly all this support was imaginary I believed in it at the time.

I also gave money to charity. I can no longer remember which of my tutors suggested the idea, but the motive behind it was clear enough to me as I knew the value of public opinion. At that time the social pages of the Peking papers would carry items almost every day about gifts to the poor by the "Hsuan Tung Emperor". My "benefactions" generally fell into two types. Sometimes I would send money to a newspaper office to distribute when the paper carried some news about poor people and at other times I would send emissaries with money direct to destitute families. Whichever method I used, the newspapers would carry an item within the next day or two about it. I was able to get good publicity for the price of a few dollars and the papers were glad to help me for the publicity they could gain for themselves.

My biggest donation was made after the Japanese earthquake of 1923. Japan's losses from this disaster had shocked the world, and I thought I would take the chance to display the "benevolence" of the "Hsuan Tung Emperor". My tutor Chen Pao-shen showed more foresight than I did, and after praising "the magnificence of the imperial bounty and the humanity of the celestial mind" he told me that "this action will make its influence felt in the future". As I was short of ready cash I sent antiques, paintings and calligraphy that were valued at about US $300,000. The Japanese minister Yoshizawa came with a delegation from the Japanese Diet to thank me, and the excitement in the palace was like that created by the presence of foreign envoys at my wedding.

In these last days in the Forbidden City I became more absurd and inconsistent than ever. While I upbraided the Household Department for overspending there was no limit to my own extravagance. I told the Household Department to buy me foreign dogs like the ones I saw in Western magazines and even had their food imported from abroad. If the dogs fell ill I would spend more on getting them cured than I would for sick humans. There was a veterinary surgeon at the Peking Police School who must have understood my character and ingratiated himself with me by writing many memorials on the keeping of dogs; he received ten presents, including a green jade wristlet, a gold ring and a snuff bottle for his pains. Sometimes my interest would be drawn by an item in the papers about, say, a four-year-old who could read the ancient classic *Mencius* or somebody who had discovered a new sort of spider, and I would invite them to the palace and give them some money. At one time I had a passion for pebbles and gave huge rewards to people who bought them for me.

When I told the Household Department to reduce its staff they brought their numbers down from seven hundred to three hundred and cut the cooks from about two hundred down to thirty-seven. Yet at the same time I added a Western-style kitchen and the monthly cost of the materials used in the Western and Chinese kitchens was over 1,300 dollars.

My annual expenditure was 870,597 taels according to the reduced figures that the Household Department prepared for me in 1921, figures that did not cover my clothing, my food, or the outlay of the various bureaus and offices of the Household Department and only included my expenses and payments of "charity in obedience to the imperial edict".

This life went on until November 5, 1924, when the National Army of Feng Yu-hsiang drove me out of the Forbidden City.

The battle of Chaoyang in September of that year was the beginning of the second Chihli-Fengtien war. At first Wu Pei-fu's Chihli army was on top, but when Wu Pei-fu was attacking the forces of the Fengtien commander Chang Tso-lin at Shanhaikuan in October his subordinate Feng Yu-hsiang deserted him, marched his troops back to Peking and issued a peace telegram. Under the combined pressure of Feng Yu-hsiang and Chang Tso-lin, Wu Pei-fu's troops on the Shanhaikuan front collapsed and Wu himself fled. (Two years later he made a comeback by allying himself with Sun Chuan-fang, another warlord.) Even before the news of Wu's defeat at Shanhaikuan came through, Feng Yu-hsiang's National Army, now occupying Peking, had put Tsao Kun (the president of the Republic who had bought the votes for his election) under house arrest and dissolved the "piglet parliament". Huang Fu, a reactionary and opportunistic politician, organized a provisional cabinet with the backing of the National Army.

When the news of the *coup d'état* reached the palace I felt at once that the situation was dangerous. The palace guard was disarmed by Feng's National Army and moved out of the city. Feng's troops also took over their barracks and their posts at the Gate of Divine Valour. I looked at Coal Hill through a telescope from the Imperial Garden and saw that it was swarming with soldiers whose uniforms were different from those of the palace guard. The Household Department sent them tea and food which they accepted, and although there was nothing alarming about their behaviour everyone in the Forbidden City was worried. We all remembered that Feng Yu-hsiang had joined the "Army to Punish the Rebels" at the time of Chang Hsun's restoration and that if he had not been moved out of Peking in time he would undoubtedly have marched into the palace then. After Tuan Chi-jui had come to power Feng Yu-hsiang and some other generals had published telegrams demanding that the little court be expelled from the Forbidden City. This made us think that the *coup d'état* and the replacement of the palace guard boded ill for the future. Then we heard that all the political prisoners had been let out of jail and that "agitators" were active. The teachings of Chen Pao-shen and Johnston on the subject of "agitators" and "terrorists" had their effect on me, particularly the story that they wanted to kill every single nobleman. I sent for Johnston and asked him to go and find out the latest news from the foreign legations and arrange somewhere for me to take refuge.

All the princes were terrified. Some of them had already booked into the Wagons-Lits Hotel in the Legation Quarter, but when they heard that I wanted to leave the palace they said that it was not yet necessary: the foreign powers all recognized the Articles of Favourable Treatment and nothing serious could happen.

The inevitable at last occurred.

At about nine o'clock on the morning of November 5 I was sitting in the Palace of Accumulated Elegance (Chu Hsiu Kung) eating fruit with Wan Jung when the senior officials of the Household Department came rushing in. Shao Ying held a document in his hand and panted:

"Your Majesty, Your Majesty ... Feng Yu-hsiang has sent soldiers with an envoy saying that the Republic is going to annul the Articles of Favourable Treatment. They want your signature to this."

I jumped up, dropped my half-eaten apple to the floor, and grabbed the paper he was holding. On it was written:

> By order of the President
> Lu Chung-lin and Chang Pi have been sent to arrange with the Ching house for the revision of the Articles of Favourable Treatment.
> November 5, 13th Year of the Republic of China
> Acting Premier Huang Fu

The Revision of the Articles of Favourable Treatment

Whereas the emperor of the Great Ching Dynasty wishes to enter thoroughly into the spirit of the Republic of the Five Races and is unwilling to continue any system which is incompatible with the Republic, the Articles of Favourable Treatment of the Ching house are revised as follows:

1. The imperial title of the Hsuan Tung Emperor of the Great Ching is this day abolished in perpetuity, and he shall henceforward enjoy the same legal rights as all citizens of the Republic of China.

2. From the time of the revision of the Articles the Government of the Republic will grant the Ching house an annual subsidy of 500,000 dollars and will make a special payment of 2,000,000 dollars for the founding of a factory for the poor of Peking in which impoverished bannermen will have the first priority for admission.

3. In accordance with the third clause of the former Articles of Favourable Treatment the Ching house will leave the palace this day. They will be free to choose their own place of residence, and the Government of the Republic will continue to be responsible for their protection.

4. The sacrifices at the ancestral temples and the mausolea of the Ching house will be continued for ever, and the Republic will provide guards for their protection.

5. The Ching house will retain its private property, which will enjoy the special protection of the Government of the Republic. All public property will belong to the Republic.

> November . . . , 13th Year of
> the Republic of China

Frankly speaking, these revised articles were not nearly as bad as I had expected. What startled me was a remark of Shao Ying's: "They say that we must move out within three hours."

"But is that possible? What about all our property? What about the High Consorts?" I was pacing around in circles in my distress. "Telephone Johnston."

"The telephone has been cut," replied Jung Yuan.

"Send someone to fetch His Highness.[1] I always said there would be trouble, but you wouldn't let me go away. Get His Highness. Get His Highness."

"We can't get out," said someone else. "They've posted men outside and they won't let anyone out."

"Go and negotiate for me."

"Yes, sire."

As Tuan Kang had died a few days previously there were only two High Consorts left in the palace, and they absolutely refused to move out. Using this as an excuse Shao Ying went to negotiate with Lu Chung-lin, the Republic's envoy, and succeeded in getting an extension of the time limit until 3 p.m. After midday it was arranged that my father should be allowed into the palace and when he came my tutors Chu Yi-fan and Chen Pao-shen had also been let in, only Johnston being kept out.

---

[1] My father.

When I learnt that my father had come I went out to meet him, and as soon as I caught sight of him coming through the gate I shouted to him, "Your Highness, what are we going to do?"

At the sound of my shout he stood stock-still as if a spell had been cast on him. He neither came any closer to me nor did he answer my question; his lips quivered for a while and then he got out a completely useless sentence:

"I, I obey the edict, I obey the edict. . . ."

Now angry as well as worried I swung round and went back into my room. Later I heard from a eunuch that when my father heard that I had put my signature to the revised articles he pulled his hat with a peacock feather off and threw it on the floor, muttering, "It's all over, it's all over. I won't need this again."

Before long Shao Ying came back to my room, his face an even more dreadful sight than it had been earlier. He was shaking as he said, "Their envoy Lu Chung-lin is pushing us. He says we can only have another twenty minutes, and that if we aren't out by then . . . they'll open fire with artillery from Coal Hill."

Although the Republic's envoy had only brought twenty soldiers armed with pistols his threat was most effective. My father-in-law was so frightened that he rushed to the Imperial Garden to find somewhere to shelter from the artillery fire and refused to come out again. Seeing the terror of the princes I decided to accept Lu Chung-lin's demands at once and go to my father's house.

The National Army had laid on five cars for us. Lu Chung-lin rode in the front one, I followed in the second, and Wan Jung, Wen Hsiu, Shao Ying and others came behind.

When I got out of the car at the main gate of the Northern Mansion (my father's house), Lu Chung-lin came up and shook hands with me.

"Mr. Pu Yi, do you intend to be emperor in future, or will you be an ordinary citizen?" asked Lu.

"From today onwards I want to be an ordinary citizen."

"Good," said the envoy with a smile, "then we shall protect you." He went on to say that as China was a republic it was not right to have someone calling himself an emperor, and that I should now do my best for the country as a citizen.

"As a citizen," added another republican official, "you will have the right to vote and to stand for election. You could even be elected president one day."

The word "president" made me feel uneasy. As I understood that now I should retire from public life and wait for my opportunity I said:

"I have felt for a long time that I did not need the Articles of Favourable Treatment and I am pleased to see them annulled, so I fully agree with what you say. I had no freedom as an emperor, and now I have found my freedom."

When I finished this little oration the soldiers of the National Army who were standing nearby applauded.

My last sentence was not entirely untrue. I was sick of the restrictions with which the princes and high officials surrounded me. I wanted "freedom", freedom to realize the ambition of regaining my lost throne.

In the Northern Mansion

After speaking these fine words I hurried past the National Army guard and through the main gate of the Northern Mansion. As I sat in my father's study I thought that this was more like the tiger's mouth than a princely mansion. The first thing I had to do was to find out how dangerous my situation was. Before leaving the Forbidden City I had sent messages to my most loyal ministers outside the palace asking them to think up as quickly as possible some way of rescuing me from the clutches of the National Army. Up till now I had not heard any news of their activities nor had I received any other information about what was happening outside. I desperately wanted someone to talk things over with, even if it was only to hear a few words of consolation. In this situation my father was a big disappointment to me.

He was even more flustered than I was. From the time I entered the Northern Mansion he never stood still for a moment. When he was not walking up and down muttering to himself he was rushing in and out in a panic, making the atmosphere very tense. When I could not bear it any longer I said to him:

"Your Highness, sit down and talk it over. We must decide what to do, and before we do that we must get some news from outside."

"Decide what to do? Very well." He sat down, but before two minutes were up he leapt to his feet, exclaimed irrelevantly, "Tsai Hsun has not appeared either," and started pacing up and down again.

"We must get some news."

"Get some news? Very well." He went out and came back again a moment later. "They wo . . . won't let us out. There are soldiers at the main gate."

"Use the telephone then."

"Telephone? Yes, yes." But before he had gone many steps he came back to ask, "Who shall I telephone?"

I saw that the only thing to do was to have the eunuchs fetch the senior officials of the Household Department. But it turned out that Jung Yuan had entered the foreign hospital with nervous disorders, Chi Ling was moving out my clothing and other effects and dealing with the eunuchs and palace maids, and Pao Hsi was looking after the two High Consorts who were still in the palace; only Shao Ying was left with me, and he was in much the same state as my father and incapable of making a single phone call. Fortunately other princes and officials came later, as did my tutors; otherwise I do not know how bad the confusion in the Northern Mansion would have become. The best news was that brought by Johnston in the evening: through his speedy efforts the Dutch minister Oudendijk, the doyen of the diplomatic corps, the British minister Macleay, and the Japanese minister Yoshizawa, had already "protested" to the new foreign minister Wang Cheng-ting (Dr. C. T. Wang) and Wang had guaranteed the safety of my life and possessions to them. This news calmed everyone in the Northern Mansion except my father, for whom the dose was not strong enough.   Johnston described the scene in *Twilight in the Forbidden City*:

> He received me in a large reception room which was nearly full of Manchu notables and of officers of the imperial household. . . . My first duty was to announce the result of the visit of the three ministers to the Foreign Office.   They had already heard from Tsai Tao of the consultation in the Netherlands Legation that morning and were naturally eager to know what happened at the interview with Dr. Wang.   They listened attentively to what I had to say, all but prince Chun, who while I was speaking moved nervously round the room for no apparent purpose. Several times he suddenly quickened his pace and ran up to me uttering a few half incoherent words.   The slight impediment in his speech seemed to be more marked than when he was in a normal state.   The purport of his words was the same each time he spoke: "Ask *huang-shang* (his majesty) not to be frightened" — a totally unnecessary remark from one who was himself obviously in a state of much greater alarm than the emperor.   When he had run up to me four or five times with this inane observation I became slightly irritated and said, "His majesty is here, standing beside me. Why not address him direct?"   But he was too much upset to notice the rudeness of my remark and resumed his aimless circumambulations.

Another action of my father's that evening made me particularly cross with him.   Soon after Johnston's arrival Cheng Hsiao-hsu came with two Japanese.   (Ever since the donation for the relief of the Tokyo earthquake my ministers had been in touch with the Japanese Legation, and when Lo Chen-yu and Cheng Hsiao-hsu came to the palace they also had contacts with the Japanese barracks.)   Cheng had made a plan with Colonel Takemoto, the Japanese commander in Peking, by which a subordinate of Takemoto's would come in civilian clothes with a doctor and escort me to the Japanese barracks while pretending to take me to hospital.   When Cheng arrived with the Japanese officer and doctor and explained his scheme it met with the unanimous opposition of the princes, officials and tutors.   They thought that it would be very difficult to smuggle me past the soldiers guarding the main gate, and that even if I succeeded in evading them there were National Army patrols in the streets.   If I were discovered by one of them things would be even worse.   My father took the strongest line, and explained his reasons thus: "Even if His Majesty reaches the Legation Quarter, Feng Yu-hsiang will come and ask me about him, and then what will I do?" In the end Cheng Hsiao-hsu and his Japanese were sent away.

The restrictions at the gates of the Northern Mansion were tightened up the next day and people were allowed to enter but not to leave. Later they were relaxed a little, but still only my tutors Chen Pao-shen and Chu Yi-fan and the senior officials of the Household Department were allowed in and out; foreigners were absolutely barred. This really alarmed the Northern Mansion: if the National Army had no respect for foreigners there was no guarantee for the future at all. Later the two tutors went into this question and decided that there had never been any authorities that were not afraid of foreigners and that as the foreign minister of the provisional cabinet had given an undertaking to the three diplomats it was unlikely that he would differ from his predecessors. Although everyone else thought that their analysis was correct I was still worried: who knew how the soldiers at the gates felt? There was a saying in those days:

> Even when right a scholar never can
> Win an argument with a military man.

What difference did the word of the provisional government make to the soldiers who were only a few yards away? If they made trouble no guarantee would make the slightest difference. The more I thought about it the more frightened I got. I wished I had gone away with the Japanese that Cheng Hsiao-hsu had brought and cursed my father for only thinking of his own interests at the expense of my security.

Just then Lo Chen-yu came back from Tientsin where he had gone by the international train[1] to get help when Feng Yu-hsiang was taking over the palace guard. At the headquarters of the Jap-

---

[1] During the civil wars trains were often detained by warlords, so that the service between Peking and Tientsin was very irregular. This international train was organized at the wishes of the foreign legations, and neither side dared to interfere with it.

anese garrison in Tientsin he had been told by a staff officer about the capture of the Forbidden City and asked on behalf of the garrison commander to go and see Tuan Chi-jui. Tuan Chi-jui had also received a telegram asking for help from Cheng Hsiao-hsu that had been sent on by Colonel Takemoto in Peking. Tuan Chi-jui issued a circular telegram opposing Feng Yu-hsiang's "oppressive" measures against the palace. When he saw the draft of the telegram Lo Chen-yu realized that as Tuan Chi-jui was going to come back into public life the situation was not so serious. To be on the safe side, he asked the Japanese command in Tientsin to declare itself openly as my "protector". He was told that Colonel Takemoto in Peking would look after me. Acting on the Tientsin commander's instructions Lo Chen-yu returned to Peking and went to see Takemoto. Takemoto asked him to tell me that Japanese cavalry were patrolling near the Northern Mansion and that if the National Army were to start anything the Japanese barracks would take "decisive action". Chen Pao-shen also told me that the Japanese barracks wanted to send some military carrier pigeons to the Northern Mansion that could be used to give the alarm, and although we did not accept them for fear that the National Army might hear of it I felt more grateful than ever to the Japanese. After this Lo Chen-yu won a position in my affections equal to that of Cheng Hsiao-hsu, and I felt even more alienated from my father.

When I saw Tuan Chi-jui's telegram opposing Feng Yu-hsiang's measures against the palace and heard the news that Feng's troops were going to clash with the Fengtien army of Chang Tso-lin I gained new confidence. At the same time Chen Pao-shen brought me a secret telegram from Tuan Chi-jui, sent via the Japanese barracks in Peking, which included this sentence: "I will support the imperial house with all my strength and protect all its property." After this the control on the gates was relaxed a little more and everyone from princes to Dr. Hu Shih was allowed in, only Johnston being excluded.

Soon afterwards there was a new development in the relationship between Chang Tso-lin and Feng Yu-hsiang in which the Northern Mansion was so interested, when it was reported that Feng Yu-hsiang had been detained in Tientsin by Chang Tso-lin's Fengtien army. Although this story later proved to have been only a rumour, it was rapidly followed by some news that was even more exciting to the Northern Mansion: the provisional cabinet of Huang Fu that was supported by Feng Yu-hsiang's National Army met with refusals when it invited the foreign diplomats to a banquet. The Northern Mansion optimistically reckoned that the days of the provisional government with which I could not coexist were numbered and that it would be replaced by Tuan Chi-jui, who was far more to the liking of the Legation Quarter, particularly the Japanese Legation. The next day's news confirmed Lo Chen-yu's report: Feng Yu-hsiang had to accept Chang Tso-lin's proposal and allow Tuan Chi-jui to return to public life. Within a few days both Chang Tso-lin and Tuan Chi-jui were in Peking.

The news of the alliance between Tuan Chi-jui and Chang Tso-lin changed the atmosphere in the Northern Mansion. The first thing the princes did was to write a secret letter to Chang asking for his protection. After he and Tuan had entered the capital the princes sent their representatives along with Cheng Hsiao-hsu to welcome them, and later they divided their efforts. They sent Cheng Hsiao-hsu to see Tuan Chi-jui and the chief steward of the Northern Mansion, who was Chang Tso-lin's sworn brother, to see Chang. What most delighted the Northern Mansion was the invitation that Chang sent Johnston asking him to come and see him. Chang's aim in inviting Johnston was to sound him on the attitude of the Legation Quarter towards himself, while the Household Department hoped to find out Chang's attitude to me through Johnston. I gave Johnston a signed photograph of myself and a ring set with a large diamond to take with him. Chang Tso-lin accepted the photograph, refused the ring, and expressed his sympathy. At the same time Tuan Chi-jui indicated to Cheng Hsiao-hsu that he might consider restoring the Articles of Favourable Treatment. With the "sympathy" of the Legation Quarter and the support of these two men the Northern Mansion dared to "counter-attack" although Feng Yu-hsiang's troops were still in Peking.

On November 28, the day after the National Army soldiers were withdrawn from the front gate of the Mansion and Feng Yu-hsiang issued his telegram of resignation, the Northern Mansion sent an official communication to the Home Ministry in the name of the Household Department:

> . . . According to the provisions of the principles of jurisprudence as applied to criminal law, all those who use violence to compel others to do things may be held guilty of assault; and according to the principles of civil law anything that is extorted through violence or terror has no legal validity. We wish to make it known through this letter that the Ching house is unable to recognize the legal validity of the five revised articles imposed by the provisional cabinet. . . .

Letters appealing for the support of foreign ministers were published at the same time as this. The Northern Mansion also ceased to recognize the "Committee for the Readjustment of the Affairs of the Ching House" although the Ching house sent representatives to participate in its first few meetings.

That day I was interviewed by a reporter from the Japanese-run paper *Shuntien Times* (a paper supported by the Japanese Legation which openly backed me and printed absurd atrocity stories about the expulsion from the palace), and what I said to him was the exact opposite of what I had said on the day I had been forced to leave the palace:

"I certainly did not gladly assent when I was forcibly compelled to sign the document by the soldiers of the National Army pretending to act in the name of the people."

Decision at the Crossroads

Although the people in the Northern Mansion shared the same excitement their views on what we should do differed. One of them, Chin Liang, later wrote in his *Journal of the Coup*:

After Tuan Chi-jui and Chang Tso-lin entered the capital they appeared to be very friendly to us but their friendship extended only to words, not to deeds. Everyone was deceived into believing that a return to the palace was imminent; when it did not take place people were of various opinions. Some said that we should not allow a word of the original Articles to be altered; some that the emperor should return to the palace with his title restored; some that he should change his title to Retired Emperor; some that annual expenditure could be cut, but foreign guarantees should be obtained; some that he should move to the Summer Palace; and some that a house should be bought in the eastern part of the city. But as real power was in the hands of others all these plans were dreams: I do not know what cause they had to think as they did.

The storm of November 5, 1924 blew me out of the Forbidden City and dropped me at the crossroads. Three roads stretched out before me. One was to do what the revised Articles suggested: to abandon the imperial title and my old ambitions and become an enormously wealthy and landed "common citizen". Another was to try and get the help of my "sympathizers" to cancel the new Articles and restore the old Articles in their entirety, to regain my title and return to the palace to continue to live my old life. The third possible course was the most tortuous: first to go abroad and then to come back to the Forbidden City, the Forbidden City as it had been before 1911. In the words of the time, this course was "using foreign power to plan a restoration".

As I faced this decision I was surrounded by men who argued endlessly over the merits of the different choices. They regarded the first possibility as not worthy of serious consideration, but fought stubbornly over the other two; and even the advocates of the same course would differ in their specific proposals.

The argument centred on whether I should stay in the Northern Mansion or take refuge in the Legation Quarter, and the party led by my father which advocated my staying put was successful at first. But their victories were insecure as their attempts to keep me in the Mansion made me more and more determined to get out. Although I had no definite ideas about my future one thing was clear in my mind from the moment I entered the portals of the

Northern Mansion: come what might I was going to leave. I had not left a big Forbidden City just to stay in a miniature one, particularly when I was in such danger there.

At this stage a new advocate of my going abroad appeared: my old friend Dr. Hu Shih.

Not long before I had seen in the papers an open letter of his to the foreign minister of the provisional cabinet in which he had roundly abused the National Army and expressed his "indignation" at the revision of the Articles of Favourable Treatment through "military intimidation". Although my tutor Chen Pao-shen still regarded him as a reptile Cheng Hsiao-hsu had made friends with him, and some of the former Ching officials thought that he was better at any rate than the revolutionaries and the National Army. Nobody tried to keep him out of the Northern Mansion. I welcomed him and praised his open letter. He inveighed against the National Army once more and said, "In the eyes of Europe and America this is all oriental barbarism."

This visit of Hu Shih's was not just a courtesy call: it sprang from his "concern" for me. He asked me what plans I had for the future. I replied that the princes and high officials were working for a restoration of the old order but that I was not in the least interested as I wanted to lead an independent life and acquire some learning.

"Your Majesty has high ideals," he said with a nod of approval. "After my last visit to the palace I told my friends that Your Majesty had high ideals."

"I want to go and study abroad but there are so many difficulties."

"Of course there are difficulties, but they can't be too serious. If you go to England Mr. Johnston can look after everything, and you will have no trouble in finding people to help you if you go to America."

"The princes and high officials won't let me go, particularly His Highness."

"That was what Your Majesty said at my last audience in the palace. I think that you will have to take some decisive action."

"I am not sure whether the Republican authorities would let me go."

"That will be no problem. The important thing is for Your Majesty to make a firm decision."

Although I felt instinctive reservations about this "modern personality" his remarks encouraged me. He made me realize that my plan of going abroad would have the sympathy of quite a lot of people. He also made me feel more tired than ever of the princes and officials who were opposed to the idea.

I felt that those who wanted to go back to the old life in the palace only wanted to do so for the sake of their titles. What enabled them to feed their families was not the emperor but the Articles. Only under the old order could they continue to occupy their lucrative sinecures or draw their pensions.

Johnston came back to me after my meeting with Hu Shih and conveyed Chang Tso-lin's concern to me. I thought that Hu Shih was right in saying that the authorities would not prevent me from going abroad. While Johnston and I were discussing how to arrange this, Chang Tso-lin indicated that I would be welcome to go and stay in the Northeast. I thought that it might be a good idea to spend some time in the Northeast first as once I was there I would be able to go abroad whenever I liked, but just when I had come to this decision a new problem arose.

The atmosphere had become much more relaxed after the withdrawal of the National Army guard from the gate and I had been very bold in cursing the National Army to the journalist as I mentioned above. Then Cheng Hsiao-hsu suddenly appeared and asked me if I had seen the papers or not.

"I've seen them, but there isn't much in them."

"Your Majesty, look at the *Shuntien Times*." He showed me a headline reading "Reds Advocate People's Self-rule". This news item said that since the entry of Feng Yu-hsiang's troops into the capital "reds" had started activities; recently tens of thousands of leaflets had appeared advocating "self-rule, not government; freedom, not laws" and so on. I had often been told by Cheng Hsiao-hsu, Chen Pao-shen, Johnston and others and read in the *Shuntien Times* that Communists were reds and radicals and that communism meant "raging floods and wild beasts", common property and common wives. I had also heard that Feng Yu-hsiang's army had contacts with the "reds" and "radicals" and various other stories. Now Cheng Hsiao-hsu explained to me that the country was on the brink of violent upheavals and that there was no question but that the "reds" would murder me.

My alarm became even worse when Lo Chen-yu came in with a grim expression on his face. I had always attached great importance to the news that Lo obtained from Japanese sources, and this time he reported that the Japanese had heard from their intelligence that Feng Yu-hsiang and the "reds" were planning action against me. "Feng's troops are now occupying the Summer Palace," he said, "and something may happen in the next day or two. Your Majesty must leave here as soon as possible and take refuge in the Legation Quarter."

Johnston then turned up with the news from the foreign press that Feng Yu-hsiang was going to make a new move against Peking. I was no longer able to restrain my anxiety and even Chen Pao-shen was so alarmed that he agreed to the suggestion that I should take shelter in the Legation Quarter while Feng Yu-hsiang's troops were not at the Northern Mansion. He suggested that I first enter the German Hospital as a doctor there was an acquaintance of mine. Chen Pao-shen, Johnston and myself discussed these plans secretly as they had to be kept not only from the Republican authorities but also from my father.

We acted according to the secret plans and carried out the first stage: I went with my tutor Chen Pao-shen to visit the two High Consorts, who had moved out of the palace a few days after me and were now living in Chilinpei Lane, and then came back to the Northern Mansion. This was to make the Northern Mansion feel that I was trustworthy. We decided to carry out stage two the following day. I was to say that I was going to inspect a house that we were intending to hire in Piaopei Lane and then slip into the Legation Quarter and enter the German Hospital. The third stage would be to go to a legation. Once I was in the Legation Quarter the third stage and the fourth one of bringing Wan Jung and Wen Hsiu to rejoin me would be quite easy. But when we had got into the cars and were about to start on stage two my father sent his chief steward to come with us. I rode in the first car with Johnston and the steward sat behind Chen Pao-shen in another.

"That's a bit awkward," said Johnston in English with a frown when he had got into the car.

"Never mind him." I was furious. I told the driver to start and we drove out of the Northern Mansion. I never wanted to enter those gates again in my life.

Johnston thought that we could not ignore the steward and would have to think of some way of shaking him off. As we drove along he decided that we should stop at a shop to buy something and send him back.

There was a foreign-run shop selling watches, clocks and cameras situated at the entrance to the Legation Quarter. When we reached the shop I went in with Johnston. After looking around I chose a French pocket-watch, but although I dillied and dallied for a long time the steward waited outside and obviously had no intention of going. Johnston had to fall back on his last resort and tell the steward that I did not feel well and was going to visit the German Hospital. He was suspicious and he followed us there, but once we arrived we pushed him aside. Johnston told Dr. Dipper why I had come and showed me into an empty ward to rest. The steward, seeing that something was wrong, disappeared at once. We knew that he would be bound to go back to the Northern Mansion to report to my father, so Johnston lost no time in going to negotiate with the British Legation. As time passed and I had no news from him I became extremely anxious, fearing that the steward would fetch my father. Just then Chen Pao-shen arrived followed by Cheng Hsiao-hsu. This is how Cheng Hsiao-hsu described the events that followed in his journal:

> I recommended to His Majesty that he go to the Japanese Legation and he ordered me to go and tell the Japanese. I thereupon visited Colonel Takemoto, and told him of the emperor's arrival, and he informed Mr. Yoshizawa. Takemoto then asked me to invite the emperor to come to the legation forthwith. A strong wind was blowing at the time and the sky was filled with yellow sand so that one

could only see for a distance of a few paces. When I returned to the hospital I was worried that the chauffeur might disobey orders and so advised His Majesty to travel in my carriage. I was also concerned about the crowd of people outside the front entrance of the hospital, so I took the carriage round to the back door. A German doctor with the keys and a nurse led the way and the emperor got into the carriage with myself and a servant. The distance between the German Hospital and the Japanese Legation is about one *li* (half a kilometre), and there are two routes, one going from east to west through the Quarter and turning north, and the other along Changan Street[1] and turning south. I told the coachman to go back to the Japanese Legation. As the second route was slightly shorter he drove into Changan Street. His Majesty exclaimed in alarm, "Why did we come this way? There are Chinese policemen in the street." As the carriage was going at a good speed I said, "We will be there in a moment. Nobody could know that this carriage contains an emperor. Please do not be alarmed, Your Majesty."

When we turned south along the bank of the stream I was able to report that we were in the Legation Quarter again, and then we arrived at the Japanese Legation. Takemoto met the emperor and took him to the barracks, where Chen Pao-shen joined us.

Cheng Hsiao-hsu was very pleased with the role he had played in my flight and wrote two poems and painted a symbolic picture to commemorate the occasion. His main cause for satisfaction was that he had beaten his secret rival Lo Chen-yu in this struggle for mastery. Lo had been unable to rise to the occasion and had even allowed his valuable connections with Colonel Takemoto to be delicately filched by Cheng. The rivalry between the two men had at first been concealed behind their common struggle against the princes, but from now on the battle was on.

In *Twilight in the Forbidden City* Johnston corrected a mistake in Cheng's account of the flight to the Legation Quarter. Cheng thought that Colonel Takemoto had gained the consent of the Japanese minister before he received me in the barracks. Such was the relationship between the military and civil officials in the Japanese Legation, however, that Takemoto did not in fact report his con-

---

[1] Changan Street was outside the Legation Quarter and thus not under foreign control.

versation with Cheng to the minister as he did not want his guest
to be taken away from him.

But taken away from Takemoto I was. As soon as the minister
heard that I had arrived at the barracks he invited me to move over
to the legation proper and I accepted the invitation.

From Legation Quarter to Concession

In those days the Legation Quarter and the foreign concessions
were definitely "hospitable" places. Seven years previously President Li Yuan-hung had been driven to take shelter in a legation by
Chang Hsun when I became emperor for the second time, and Chang
Hsun himself had become a "guest" of the Dutch Legation a few
days later. Whenever a legation was going to receive such guests
the hotels and hospitals in the Legation Quarter would always be
very busy. Many nervous people whose status was too low to get
into a legation would pack these places so full that some of them
were willing to pay even for a place under the stairs.

My reception was the first and probably the last of its kind. When
I sent for my wives from the Northern Mansion the Republican
police there would not let them out, so the Japanese Legation sent
a secretary to arrange the matter. When his efforts were unavailing
the minister went to see Chief Executive Tuan Chi-jui himself, and
as a result Wan Jung and Wen Hsiu with their eunuchs and ladies-
in-waiting rejoined me.

Seeing the size of my entourage the minister realized that three
rooms were clearly inadequate to accommodate us, and he cleared a
whole building for us to live in. There was room for everyone, from
Companions of the Southern Study and senior officials of the Household Department to dozens of attendants, eunuchs, ladies-in-waiting,
maids and scullions. The essential administrative offices of the
Great Ching Emperor functioned once more in the Japanese Legation.

What was more important was that Yoshizawa persuaded the Provisional Government to take an understanding attitude to me. Apart from explaining its views to Yoshizawa the Provisional Government sent an envoy to visit Colonel Takemoto and repeat: "The Provisional Government has every intention of respecting the Retired Emperor's wish for freedom and will do all within the bounds of possibility to protect the security of his life, his property and his dependants."

A group of princes led by my father came to try and persuade me to return to the Northern Mansion. They said that it was now safe as the presence of Tuan Chi-jui and Chang Tso-lin in the capital kept the National Army under restraint; in addition, Tuan and Chang had offered guarantees of my safety. But I believed Lo Chen-yu and the others who said that these guarantees had only been offered because I had entered the legation, and that if I were to return to the Northern Mansion with the National Army still in Peking no guarantee would have any force. I refused to go back. The princes were in fact finding themselves places to stay in the Legation Quarter themselves at the time.

The enthusiasm with which the Japanese Legation looked after me stirred many Ching veterans who were previously unknown to me into action. They sent telegrams from all over the country asking Chief Executive Tuan Chi-jui to restore the original favourable treatment; they sent me money to cover my expenses; and some of them even came to Peking to pay their respects and offer me grand strategies. The Mongol princes acted as if they had taken some stimulant, publishing circular telegrams and sending petitions to the Provisional Government demanding to know what was going to happen about their own favourable treatment. The Provisional Government replied that it would continue unchanged. The Ching princes and high officials took a harder line and refused to take part in the meetings of the "Committee for the Readjustment of the Affairs of the Ching House". This committee, which had been formed not long previously, was to make an inventory of the property of the Ching house and divide it into private and public. Shao Ying and the other Ching members of the committee followed up their refusal to attend by announcing publicly to the authorities that they did not recognize it.

More and more former Ching officials came to the Japanese Legation every day to show their integrity, pay their respects, offer money, and secretly explain their "grand strategies for a revival". On Chinese New Year's Day my small drawing room was full of pigtails; I sat facing south in imperial style on a Western-style chair that substituted for a throne and received congratulations.

Many of the old-timers were full of gratitude for my Japanese hosts. They saw grounds for hope in the reception I received from the legation and drew at least a modicum of satisfaction from it. One of them, Wang Kuo-wei, wrote in a memorial: "The Japanese minister . . . does not only take Your Majesty's past glory into account, he sees you as the future ruler of China: how can your subjects and officials fail to be gratified?"

Thirteen days after the Chinese New Year came my twentieth birthday (by Chinese reckoning).[1] As I was in a stranger's house I had not intended to celebrate it, but my host was determined to please me and offered me the main hall of the legation in which to receive congratulations. The hall was furnished for the occasion with magnificent carpets, and behind the arm-chair with a yellow cushion that served as a throne stood a glass screen covered with yellow paper. All the pages wore large Ching hats with red tassels. Over a hundred former Ching officials came from several large cities for the birthday celebrations, which were also attended by members of the Diplomatic Corps as well as princes, high officials, and local Ching veterans, making a total of over 500 people.

I wore a blue patterned silk gown and a black satin jacket, and all the princes, court officials and Ching veterans wore the same. Apart from this the ceremonial usages were much the same as they had been in the palace. Imperial yellow, queues and ninefold kotows combined to give me feelings of anguish and heartbreaking melancholy. After the ceremony I made an impromptu speech. A version of it was printed in the Shanghai press, which, while not entirely accurate, contained the following fairly authentic passage:

---

[1] By Western reckoning my nineteenth birthday.

As I am only a young man of twenty it is not right that I should be celebrating "long life", and I am particularly unenthusiastic about doing so in the present difficulties as a guest under a stranger's roof. But as you have come a great distance I wish to take this opportunity to meet you and talk to you. I am fully aware that in the modern world emperors can exist no longer and I am resolved not to run the risks involved in being one. My life deep in the Great Within was that of a prisoner, and I took no delight in my lack of freedom. I have long nourished the ambition of going abroad and have studied English assiduously to that end, but I was under too many restrictions to be able to realize my hopes.

The continuation or abolition of the Articles of Favourable Treatment seems to me a matter of no importance. Had I ended them voluntarily that would have been acceptable, but it is intolerable for others to do so through compulsion. The Articles were a bilateral agreement and can no more be altered by the decree of one of the parties than an international treaty. The sending of troops to the palace by Feng Yu-hsiang was a violent act devoid of ordinary human feelings when the matter could easily have been settled by negotiation. I have long had a sincere wish not to use that empty title, but being compelled to drop it by armed force has made me feel most unhappy. From the point of view of the Republic such barbarous actions do great damage to the country's name and its reputation for good faith.

Of the motives for my expulsion from the palace I will not speak, and they are probably already known to you. As I was completely powerless it was no martial feat on Feng Yu-hsiang's part to act against me as he did, and it is hard to describe the humiliating intimidation to which I was subjected after leaving the palace. Even if he had been justified in driving me out, why did he impound all the clothes, vessels, calligraphy and books left by my ancestors? Why did he not allow us to take away the rice bowls, tea cups and kitchen utensils that were in daily use? Was this a case of "preserving antiques"? Were they worth anything? I do not think that he would have acted so harshly even in dealing with bandits.

When he says that the restoration of 1917 invalidated the Articles of Favourable Treatment he should remember that I was only a child of twelve[1] at the time and incapable of organizing a restoration myself. But leaving that matter aside, has the so-called "annual subsidy" ever been paid on time since the Articles were signed? Have the grants to

---

[1] Eleven by Western reckoning.

the princes and nobles ever been paid as stipulated in various agreements? Have the living expenses of bannermen ever been met as they should have been according to the articles providing for their favourable treatment? The responsibility for ending the Articles lies with the Republic: to ignore this and give the restoration of 1917 as a pretext is exceedingly biassed.

I do not wish to complain, but I cannot miss this opportunity to reveal the sorrows that lie in my heart, so that if the parliament of the Republic hears of them it will, if it has a whit of human feeling left, feel that this matter must be settled equitably. I would accept such a settlement without demur.

I have another important announcement to make. I will never agree to any proposal that I should seek foreign intervention on my behalf: I could never use foreign power to intervene in domestic Chinese politics.

About the time of my birthday celebration the press was full of attacks on my group, attacks that reflected the indignation of the great majority of people. There were public outcries when the "Committee for the Readjustment of the Affairs of the Ching House" published such things as the postscript to the Articles of Favourable Treatment that Yuan Shih-kai wrote when he was emperor and documentary proof of the way the Household Department had been mortgaging, selling, and removing palace treasures. What caused the most wrath, however, were the connections between the little court and the Japanese and the attempts by Ching fogeys to restore the Articles. A "League Against the Favourable Treatment of the Ching House" appeared in Peking and started to take vigorous action against the little court. Public disapproval expressed itself in the papers in various ways: small satirical items, direct accusations, well-meaning advice and warnings to the Japanese Legation and the Republican authorities. When I look at them today I realize how different my life would have been if I had accepted any of these criticisms. Some of the articles exposed the plots of the Japanese, and I reproduce a part of one of them here. It was carried in the *Peking Daily,* and its account of the plans that the Japanese had for me was so close to what happened later it startles me to read it today:

The darkest part of the plot is to keep him until there is an incident in a particular province, when a certain country will send him there with armed protection and revive the rank and title of his distant ancestors. The province will be separated from the Republic and will receive that country's protection. The second step will be to deal with it in the same way as another country that has already been annexed was dealt with. . . .

Pu Yi's terror and flight were the result of deliberate intimidation by certain people. He has fallen into their trap, which was a part of a prearranged long-term plan. . . . In their present treatment of him they are willing to go to any expense to provide him with everything. The country in question has bought the friendship of each of his followers, who have come under its control without realizing it and will be its tools in future.

These true words seemed to me at the time to be slander and treachery, and I thought that they were intended to trick me into going back to the Northern Mansion and to persecution.

When I was living in the Japanese Legation I went for several bicycle rides at night out of curiosity, taking one or two servants with me; later the main gate of the legation was closed and I was not allowed to go out. On one of these trips I rode as far as the moat outside the Forbidden City and as I looked at the turrets and battlements I thought of the Mind Nurture Palace and the Cloudless Heaven Palace that I had left so recently, and of my throne and of imperial yellow. A desire for revenge and restoration welled up in my heart. My eyes filled with tears as I resolved that I would return here in the future as a conquering king just as the first of my line had done. Muttering an ambiguous goodbye I remounted my bicycle and rode away at a high speed. . . .

Every day of the three months I spent in the legation I received the diligent attentions of my Japanese hosts, oaths of loyalty from old-timers and protests from the public. Under these three influences my ambition and hatred grew unceasingly. I thought that it would not do for me to carry on living there as I ought to be making some preparations for my future. My wish to go abroad and study in Japan came back to me, and one of the legation secretaries was very enthusiastic about the idea.

The struggle between Lo Chen-yu and Cheng Hsiao-hsu with me as the object continued while I was in the legation. This round ended with a victory for Lo when Cheng asked to be relieved of his duties and went back to Shanghai.

Not long after my birthday Lo Chen-yu informed me that he had arranged with one of the legation officials that I should make preparations for going abroad in Tientsin as it was not at all convenient for me to go on staying in the legation. It would be best for me to find a house in the Japanese concession as the one I had already bought was unsuitably situated in the British concession. This all seemed sensible enough to me, particularly as I wanted to see the big city of Tientsin, so I agreed at once. I sent a "Companion of the Southern Study" to find me a house in the Japanese concession in Tientsin, and I finally settled on the Chang Garden. A few days later Lo Chen-yu told me that the house was ready and the National Army was changing its garrisons, so we should take this good opportunity and move at once. I talked it over with Yoshizawa and he agreed to my departure. He also had Tuan Chi-jui informed, and in addition to giving his consent Tuan offered to provide me with a military escort. Yoshizawa had already decided to bring the police chief of the Japanese consulate-general in Tientsin to Peking together with some plainclothes policemen; first I was to go under their protection and then my wives were to follow. All was now settled.

At 7 p.m. on February 23, 1925 I took my leave of the Japanese minister and his wife. We posed for photographs, I thanked them, and they wished me a safe journey. I then left by the back gate of the legation with a Japanese official and some plainclothes policemen and walked to the Chienmen railway station. Here I met Lo Chen-yu and his son. At every station where the train stopped several Japanese policemen and special agents in black civilian clothes would get on, and by the time we reached Tientsin the carriage was almost full of them. As I got out of the train I was met by the Japanese consul-general in Tientsin, Yoshida Shigera, and several dozen officers and men of the Japanese garrison.

Three days later the *Shuntien Times* printed a statement issued by the Japanese Legation stating that my intention of leaving Peking had long been known to the Provisional Government, and that it had never wished to interfere with the plan. My sudden departure had been the result of the unstable situation in Peking.

CHAPTER FOUR

TIENTSIN

The Efforts of Lo Chen-yu

When I reached Tientsin I found that Lo Chen-yu had not told the truth when he told me that my house was ready, and I spent my first day in the Yamato Hotel. The next day Wan Jung, Wen Hsiu and all the others who had been in the Japanese Legation with me arrived, and we all moved into the hastily furnished Chang Garden.

The Chang Garden covered over three acres and included a large house. It belonged to a former Ching general who would not take any rent for it from me, and at first he swept the yard for me himself as a sign of his loyalty. We stayed there for five years, and moved from there to the Quiet Garden after his death when his son asked us for rent.

My aim in coming to Tientsin had been to go abroad, but I ended up by spending seven years there, seven years in which I wavered between different factions and different ideas. The princes, my father included, had far less power over me, and Johnston ceased to be my tutor, although he did visit me in 1926 and canvassed unsuccessfully for support for me from the warlord Wu Pei-fu and others. He later returned to England.

One could divide the people who struggled to win my favour in those seven years into various groups. There were the old ministers" led by Chen Pao-shen who at first hoped for the restoration of the Articles of Favourable Treatment and later just wanted to maintain the status quo. They could be called the "back to the palace faction". Another group round Lo Chen-yu put their hopes in my going abroad and in getting help from foreign countries, principally Japan; they could be considered as the "ally with Japan" or "going abroad" faction, and they included Ching veterans, as well as one or two of the Manchu princes, such as Pu Wei. A third party, in which I was the leading figure, thought that the best method was to contact and buy over warlords. Our "employing military men" group was rather heterogeneous, including Ching veterans and Republican politicians.

When Cheng Hsiao-hsu came back to my service he attached himself to no clique. He seemed both to praise and to attack the proposals that the others put forward; then he would suggest ideas that none of them had brought up, such as the use of foreign advisers and the "open door" (co-operating with any country that was willing to help in a restoration), and his suggestions were opposed by all the other factions. When he later settled on a policy of relying on Japan he overcame all his opponents including his old rival Lo Chen-yu, the leader of the pro-Japanese clique.

Leaving these later developments aside, let us first take a look at Lo Chen-yu. When he came to the Forbidden City he was about fifty. A man of medium height, he wore gold-rimmed spectacles (which he took off when in my presence), and had a yellow-white goatee and a white queue. He spoke slowly in the accent of the part of Chekiang Province from which he came. I first met him after my marriage when he was appointed a "Companion of the Southern Study" and given the job of authenticating the palace's ancient bronzes. In addition to having got himself a reputation as a scholar, he had also caught my attention as a monarchist.

Lo, who had been an official under the Ching, had lived either in Japan or in Japanese concessions in China for nearly all the time since the Revolution of 1911. He had built himself up as an "authority" on antiques through various underhand means, and was a forger of ancient books and seals, willing to "authenticate" fake paintings and pieces of calligraphy for a fee. He ruthlessly plagiarized the scholarship of his associate Wang Kuo-wei. When Wang Kuo-wei committed suicide, possibly because he could tolerate Lo Chen-yu's cruelty no longer, Lo made the most of the occasion. He forged a suicide note from Wang which he used to propagate a myth that Wang had killed himself because of his loyalty to the Ching. Thus Lo improved his standing with me through exploiting the death of his own colleague.

The first thing over which Lo Chen-yu and Cheng Hsiao-hsu quarrelled was the question of whether or not I should go abroad. After I fled from the Japanese Legation to the Japanese concession in Tientsin public opposition to me reached a new peak. An "Anti-Ching League" appeared in Tientsin for the sole purpose of attacking me. Lo Chen-yu and his associates took this opportunity to impress on me that for the sake both of my safety and of my restoration I had no alternative but to go abroad. Their opinion had a considerable amount of support for a time among former Ching officials.

Chen Pao-shen and his clique regarded such ideas as rash. They did not think that I was in any great danger and feared that I might not be welcome in Japan. If it was going to be impossible for me to stay in Japan or China, there was no point in thinking that Tuan Chi-jui, Chang Tso-lin and their like would allow me to return to the Forbidden City and live as I had done before. Although I was not attracted by Chen Pao-shen's advice, the warnings that he gave me made me doubtful about Lo Chen-yu's suggestions.

In 1926 the political situation developed as Chen Pao-shen and his group had hoped. Chang Tso-lin switched to co-operation with Wu Pei-fu and clashed with his former associate Feng Yu-hsiang. Feng Yu-hsiang's National Army was attacked by Chang Tso-lin's Fengtien army, and Feng had to withdraw his men from Tientsin; his units in Peking, meanwhile, were surrounded. When Feng Yu-hsiang uncovered the connections between Tuan Chi-jui and Chang Tso-lin, Tuan escaped from his clutches. After this Feng Yu-hsiang's position in Peking was untenable, and he withdrew from the city. In July the two "Marshals" Chang Tso-lin and Wu Pei-fu met in Peking, an occasion that aroused unbounded optimism among the group that wanted to return to the palace and prompted them to great activity. Chen Pao-shen went up to Peking to see some of his acquaintances and the new prime minister, while Kang Yu-wei, the reformer of 1898, sent telegrams to Chang Tso-lin, Wu Pei-fu, Chang Tsung-chang and others calling on them to restore the Articles of Favourable Treatment. He also wrote Wu Pei-fu a long letter in which he enumerated the "achievements and virtues" of the Ching Dynasty and begged Wu to restore it.

But these were in fact the last days of the Peiyang warlords. Although all the northern warlords suddenly started to co-operate and Chang Tso-lin made himself the commander of the "Army of Pacification", the Northern Expedition, born of the co-operation between the Kuomintang and the Communist Party, began in 1926 to defeat the forces of the northern warlords. With their fronts disintegrating the northern generals had no inclination to worry about articles of favourable treatment. Chen Pao-shen's activities achieved nothing and Wu Pei-fu replied curtly and hypocritically to Kang Yu-wei's letter: "Your loyalty is as unchanging as stone and metal, but if the tune is pitched too high nobody can join in the song." A year after this Kang Yu-wei died of disappointment in Tsingtao.

With all hopes of returning to the palace gone, Chen Pao-shen and his group despaired and Lo Chen-yu became more active. In March 1926, a time when the approach of the Northern Expedition had made me very anxious, the Manchu noble Pu Wei sent a messenger from the Japanese-held city of Lushun with a memorial for me and a letter to Lo Chen-yu. In these he said that he was on the best of terms with the Japanese officials and that he hoped I would move to Lushun, where I would "first be free of danger and then be able to make far-reaching plans. . . . Before travelling abroad one must have a settled residence". I had heard rather too much gossip about Lo Chen-yu to be able to trust him implicitly, but I had a very good impression of Pu Wei. Soon after my arrival in Tientsin he had come down from Lushun to see me and had moved me deeply with one remark: "As long as I am alive the Great Ching shall not perish." So I was naturally stirred by his letter advising me to go to Lushun, and my suspicion of Lo Chen-yu was weakened because Pu Wei chose him as his spokesman.

When the armies of the Northern Expedition captured Wuchang in 1926 and the whole front of the Northern warlords was tottering, Lo Chen-yu told me that the revolutionary armies were "raging floods and wild beasts" and "murderers and arsonists": if I fell into their hands there would be no hope for my life. I resolved to go with him to the Japanese-occupied port of Talien, but then I changed my mind on the advice of Chen Pao-shen. Chen had heard from the Japanese Legation that the situation was not as bad as it looked, a diagnosis that was borne out soon afterwards when the news came through of the Kuomintang purges. Chiang Kai-shek was slaughtering wholesale the Communists who were allegedly "raging floods and wild beasts". About this time we also received reports of British naval vessels bombarding Nanking and of Japanese troop movements in Shantung to block the northward advance of the southern troops. All this news gave me more confidence in the steady attitude of Chen Pao-shen and his group and made me sure that the situation was not as threatening as Lo Chen-yu and the others made out. Chiang Kai-shek was, after all, as frightened of the foreigners as Yuan Shih-kai, Tuan Chi-jui, Chang Tso-lin and their like. I lived in a foreign concession and was as safe as I had been before.

Of course, the advocates of a return to the palace and the advocates of my going abroad did not differ in their ultimate hope of restoration. After seeing their dreams of returning to the palace smashed, Chen Pao-shen and his party reverted to their old theme of advising me to live in obscurity and wait for my chance. On the question of allying with Japan, however, they were not really opposed to Lo Chen-yu's clique. Chen Pao-shen himself conceded that if there was no alternative to my going abroad, the only problem was that of choosing the right people to go with me.

The Ching veterans who stubbornly opposed the idea of my going abroad were, as I remember, very few. There was one of them who said that "Japan is only interested in profit and is incapable of being devoted to the cause of aiding the restoration". Such men as he believed that a restoration could only be achieved by Ching veterans, and they wanted to expel Lo from their ranks.

The quarrel between the two factions was not so much a struggle over proposals and methods as a fight between individuals. Apart from the open memoranda and discussions there was far more bitter secret fighting to win me over. Although the techniques he used were more varied, Lo Chen-yu lost this contest.

Lo came to see me one day in my small audience chamber carrying a long and thin bundle wrapped in cloth.

"Your subject deserves to die ten thousand deaths for disturbing the celestial heart like this; yet if I were to conceal a man's faults because of personal friendship I would be lacking in loyalty and righteousness."

"What are you talking about?" I looked at him in perplexity and watched him open the bundle as slowly and deliberately as an old eunuch washing his face and combing his hair. The bundle contained a pair of scrolls which he unhurriedly unrolled. Before he had finished I recognized them as a couplet that I had written especially for Chen Pao-shen.

"Your subject found these products of the imperial brush in the market. By a great good fortune I have been able to bring them back."

I did not know at the time that Lo Chen-yu and his friends all engaged in such underhand practices as buying over the servants of their rivals, and so I really believed that Chen Pao-shen had been so lacking in respect for the "gracious gift" of the emperor as to allow some of my calligraphy to be sold on a market stall. I was so angry that I did not know what to say. I waved Lo away at once.

Chen Pao-shen was in Peking at the time, and when his friend Hu Sze-yuan heard of the affair he insisted that Chen Pao-shen could not have been guilty of such a fault. Nor did he believe that a servant of Chen's would have dared to steal the scrolls for sale in the market. It was much more likely that he would have stolen them to sell privately to someone. If he did not sell them in the market who could he have sold them to? How did they get into Lo Chen-yu's hands? These were questions that Hu Sze-yuan would not answer. When I pressed him he only told me a story about a minister of one of my imperial ancestors who was unwilling to speak too openly to the emperor about the dangers of making a journey at a time when the emperor was ill and his high officials unreliable. The minister only advised the emperor not to go and did not give his reasons. His advice was shown to have been good when the emperor died on the trip.

I asked, "What do you mean by this story? What has it got to do with Chen Pao-shen?"

"It is Chen Pao-shen to whom your subject refers. He has something to say but he will not say it in so many words."

I lost patience and told him to come to the point, but he would only say that Chen was a loyal subject and that I was of course intelligent enough to get the point of his story myself. Although I did not fathom it I was relieved to hear Hu Sze-yuan speak well of Chen Pao-shen, and the unpleasant impression that had been made by the two scrolls was now removed. After a further series of defeats Lo Chen-yu finally moved to Lushun at the end of 1928 to pursue a different career.

But let us change the subject from the quarrels between the Ching veterans to another reason why I stayed in Tientsin and did not go abroad: the hopes I placed in the warlords.

My Relations with the Commanders of the Fengtien Clique

I was able to associate with as many warlords as I liked during my seven years in Tientsin, and they all gave me illusions of some sort or other. Wu Pei-fu called himself my subject in a letter, Chang Tso-lin kotowed to me, and Tuan Chi-jui asked for an audience with me on his own initiative. The ones in whom I had the fondest hopes were the Fengtien warlords, and it was with them that I associated most closely and for the longest time. This began when Chang Tso-lin kotowed to me.

My father-in-law Jung Yuan came to tell me in great excitement one day in June 1925 that Chang Tso-lin had sent a trusted envoy to give me 100,000 dollars and the message that Chang hoped that he would be able to meet me in the house where he was staying. Chen Pao-shen objected to this as soon as he heard of it; he said that it would be quite impossible for the emperor to go to visit a Republican general, particularly as the place suggested was outside the concessions. I agreed that it would be too humiliating and dangerous and therefore refused. To my surprise Jung Yuan brought Chang Tso-lin's envoy in again the following night, saying that Chang was waiting for me in his quarters and that I would be in no danger in Chinese territory; it was not convenient for him to enter the concession, which was why he was repeating his invitation to me to go to see him. Jung Yuan repeatedly stressed Chang Tso-lin's loyalty, and I remembered the concern he had recently shown for me and what I had been told when I lived in the palace: that Chang Tso-lin's pro-Ching sympathies were second only to those of Chang Hsun. Without telling anyone else I got into a car and set off.

This early summer evening was the first time I had ventured out of the Japanese concession. When I arrived at the Tsao Family Garden where Chang Tso-lin was staying I saw a strange guard of honour, tall soldiers dressed in grey and holding ancient halberds and modern rifles who were lined up by the main gate. The car passed between them and into the garden.

When I got out of the car I was led into a brightly-lit hall, where I saw a short man with a moustache wearing civilian clothes coming towards me. I recognized him at once as Chang Tso-lin. I did not know how I should greet him as this was the first time I had gone out to visit an important Republican figure and Jung Yuan had given me no directions. But to my astonishment he knelt on the floor before me without a moment's hesitation and kotowed, asking, "How is Your Majesty?"

"How are you, Marshal?" I hastened to help him to his feet and we walked into the reception room together. I was in very good spirits and grateful for what he had just done to end my uneasy feeling that I had lowered my dignity by coming to see him. What made me even more pleased, of course, was to discover that this very important man had not forgotten the past.

The room was furnished grandly but inconsistently with Chinese hardwood tables and chairs, a Western-style couch and a glass screen. We sat down at a round table and Chang Tso-lin started talking as he smoked one cigarette after another. No sooner had he opened his mouth than he started to curse Feng Yu-hsiang for forcing me out of the Forbidden City in order to get at the palace treasures. He himself, on the other hand, attached the greatest importance to the preservation of China's ancient culture and riches, had looked after the Ching palace in Fengtien very well, and was planning to get hold of a set of the famous collection *The Complete Books of the Four Libraries*[1] from Peking to preserve in its entirety. He said in a reproachful tone of voice that I should not have fled to the Japanese Legation at a time when he had plenty of troops in Peking with which to ensure my safety. He asked me about my life since my departure and said that I had only to tell him if I wanted anything.

I said that I was well aware of how thoughtful he had been on my behalf, but as Feng Yu-hsiang's men were still in Peking at the time I had been forced to flee to the Japanese Legation. I went on to observe that I had long known how well the imperial palaces and mausolea in Fengtien had been looked after and that I understood his feelings.

"If Your Majesty would like to come up to Fengtien and live in the palace there, it would be quite possible for me to arrange it."

"Marshal Chang, you are too kind."

But Marshal Chang changed the subject to my daily life. "If you need anything in future just write to me."

The only thing I lacked was a throne, but I could scarcely say so in as many words.

During our conversation we were alone in the room except for some flies. It occurred to me that there were never flies in the middle of the night in the concession.

A junior officer came in after a while and said, "The chief of staff wants to see you, sir." Chang Tso-lin waved his hand and said,

---

[1] A huge collection of books made at the orders of the emperor Chien Lung.

181

"There is no hurry, tell him to wait for a moment." I got up at once and said that I would be going as he must be very busy. He replied at once, "No hurry, no hurry." I caught a glimpse of a woman's face behind the screen (later I heard that this was his fifth concubine) and I felt that he must really be in a hurry. I took my leave of him again and this time he did not try to keep me.

Every time I went out I was accompanied by one of the plain-clothes Japanese policemen who were stationed at the Chang Garden, and this evening was no exception. I did not realize that Chang Tso-lin had not noticed him standing beside my car, and as he was seeing me off he said in a loud voice:

"If those Japanese put the finger on you let me know and I'll sort them out."

The car drove out of the grounds past the strange guard of honour and back to the concession. The next day the Japanese consul-general came to give me a warning:

"If Your Majesty makes another secret trip to Chinese territory the Japanese government will no longer be able to guarantee your safety."

Despite Chang Tso-lin's claim that he knew how to deal with the Japanese and the protest of the consul it was common knowledge at the time that there were links between the Japanese and Chang Tso-lin, and that without the munitions supplied by Japan Chang would have been unable to maintain so large an army as he did. So the hopes this meeting had given me were not damped by this protest or by the objections of Chen Pao-shen and his group.

When the Tanaka cabinet came to power in Japan in 1927 my hopes of restoration grew even stronger. The prime minister of this government was Tanaka Giichi who became notorious for the memorial in which he outlined the plans for Japanese expansion in East Asia and elsewhere. His cabinet made it quite clear that they had a special interest in the Northeast of China, which they regarded as being quite different from other parts of the country and where they were prepared to intervene militarily to protect Japan's interests.

After Chang Tso-lin gained the support of the Tanaka cabinet he became the leader of all the warlords of north China and the commander of the Army of Pacification. When the troops under Chiang Kai-shek advanced northwards the Japanese soldiers who were "protecting" Japan's "legitimate interests" in the Northeast and Inner Mongolia came as far south as Tsinan, hundreds of miles from either, where they perpetrated the Tsinan massacre. The Japanese commander Okamura issued a warning to Chiang Kai-shek (and the chief staff officer of the Japanese garrison in Tientsin sent me a copy of it as a token of the concern he felt for me). Eager to win favour with imperialism, Chiang Kai-shek, whose hands were still dripping with the blood of the Communists, workers and students he had been slaughtering since his betrayal of the revolution on April 12, 1927, respectfully withdrew from Tsinan on receiving this warning and banned all anti-Japanese activities by the people.

At this time my relations with the Fengtien warlords were growing closer than ever, and they became open after my meeting with Chang Tso-lin. My father's chief steward, who had many sworn brothers among the Fengtien commanders, was one of the people who introduced Fengtien generals to me. When they came to the Chang Garden the etiquette observed was no longer that of the Forbidden City: they did not kotow to me and I did not confer upon them the right to ride a horse or be carried in a litter at court. They would bow to me or shake hands, and from then on we would behave as equals; and I did not affect the style of an emperor when writing to them. The closeness of the relationship between me and any Fengtien general would be decided by his attitude to my restoration.

One of the Fengtien generals in whom I had the highest hopes was Chang Tsung-chang. When I saw him in Tientsin he was a hefty fellow of over forty, and his bloated face was tinged with the livid hue induced by opium smoking. He had drifted to Yingkow at the age of fifteen or sixteen and had worked in a gambling shack where he spent his time with local crooks, vagabonds and gamblers. After a spell as a petty bandit chief in the Northeast he went to the Russian port of Vladivostok and became the chief private detective of the Chinese chamber of commerce. As he threw his money around generously and was good at building up his connections he became a leading figure in the Vladivostok underworld by co-operating closely with the tsarist civil and military police. He ran brothels, gaming houses and opium dens. After the Wuchang Rising of 1911 the southern revolutionaries sent emissaries to the Sino-Russian frontier who managed to persuade a local bandit chief called Bullet Liu to join their side with his men, whom they turned into a cavalry regiment under Liu's command. As Chang Tsung-chang had been the middleman he accompanied them to Shanghai where, by some piece of cunning, he became a regimental commander in the revolutionary army with Bullet Liu under him as one of his battalion commanders. With the outbreak of the "Second Revolution" (the attempt to overthrow Yuan Shih-kai in 1913) he switched to the side of the counter-revolution and won the admiration of the Peiyang warlord Feng Kuo-chang for his achievements in slaughtering revolutionaries. He was put at the head of Feng Kuo-chang's guard battalion, and later rose through various means to the command of the 11th Division.

After being defeated in Kiangsu and Anhwei he fled to the Northeast where he sided with Chang Tso-lin and was given a brigade. As the fortunes of the Fengtien army prospered he rose to head first a division and then an army, and to be Commissioner for Military Affairs in Shantung and Head of Bandit Extermination for Kiangsu, Anhwei and Shantung. He went on to become Commander of the Combined Armies of Chihli and Shantung, a position in which he was virtually a local emperor. Because of his disreputable origins the southern press gave him the nickname of "the Dog-meat General". Later he was rechristened "the Long-legged General" because he always ran away the moment he lost a battle.

In April 1928 he fled to Japan after his army collapsed under a pincer attack on the Luan River in Hopei Province by Chiang Kai-shek and Chang Tso-lin's son Chang Hsueh-liang. He returned to Shantung in 1932 on the pretext of sweeping his family tombs and secretly persuaded a local officer to rebel in the hope that he would be able to use his troops to restore his rule in Shantung. In September his murder was arranged by the provincial chairman of Shantung, and such was the odium in which he was held that his body was left to lie in the open: the head of his secretariat could find nobody willing to move it away at any price, and the local undertakers refused to provide the wood for his coffin. Finally his corpse had to be removed by the very provincial authorities who had organized his killing.

This universally detested monster was a welcome visitor to the Chang Garden and a man in whom I placed the greatest hopes. When I lived in the Northern Mansion in Peking Chang Tsung-chang had come in disguise to visit me and show his concern for me. After I moved to Tientsin he would come and see me whenever he was in the city. His visits were always in the middle of the night as he slept by day and smoked opium in the evening, after which he was in very good spirits and would talk for hours about anything.

In 1926 Chang Tso-lin and Wu Pei-fu joined forces to attack Feng Yu-hsiang and challenged him to battle at Nankou to the northwest of Peking. The first units to occupy Nankou after Feng Yu-hsiang's retreat were those of Chang Tsung-chang. On hearing of Chang Tsung-chang's success I sent him a letter-cum-edict of congratulation on his victory against the "reds" and salvation of China from "communism".

I did not have to wait for the newspaper reports to hear of Chang Tsung-chang's victory as I had my own intelligence service. There were people who gathered information for me and others who translated foreign papers. When I learnt from the Chinese and foreign press and from my own intelligence reports of Chang Tsung-chang's victory and his increasing influence I went almost wild with joy. I hoped that Chang Tsung-chang's victory would be complete and that he would thus lay the foundations for my restoration. During his giddy rise the "Dog-meat General" would not commit himself definitely on this, and it was only after he became the "Long-legged General" that he seemed to think about it.

In 1928 Chiang Kai-shek, Feng Yu-hsiang, Yen Hsi-shan (the warlord ruler of Shansi Province) and others announced their co-operation and made a co-ordinated attack in north China. Skirting round the Japanese troops who were helping Chang Tsung-chang along the Tientsin-Pukow Railway they swallowed up Chang Tsung-chang's Shantung base and forced him to flee towards the Northeast. Chang Tso-lin had been killed by the Japanese in an explosion and his son and successor, the "Young Marshal" Chang Hsueh-liang, refused to allow Chang Tsung-chang through the passes leading to the Northeast.

Chang Tsung-chang's troops were in a desperate position on the Lutai-Luanchou sector as they were under attack from two directions, and disaster was imminent. Just at this moment a staff officer of Chang's came to see me with a letter in which he boasted how many troops and how much artillery he had left and claimed that he would have no difficulty in recovering Peking and Tientsin. He went on to say that he was in the process of training new armies which cost 2,500,000 dollars a month to maintain. "I humbly beg that in your wisdom you will grant me something and thus enable your humble soldier to know that he has something on which he can rely." The officer who had brought this message repeatedly stressed that Chang Tsung-chang was in sight of victory and that all he needed was some support from me.

When Chen Pao-shen and Hu Sze-yuan heard that I was thinking of throwing away some more money they came and talked me out of it, and I ended up by sending Chang nothing more substantial than a hortatory edict. Soon after this came Chang Tsung-chang's complete collapse and his flight to Japan. The further he got from me the more people there were who carried messages and letters between us. Chang Tsung-chang's letters, which became fuller and fuller of expressions of loyalty to the Ching house, all asked me for money. I heeded the pleas of Chen Pao-shen and stopped giving him money or writing to him. All the same, I still felt grateful to the Fengtien clique, although Chang Tso-lin was already dead.

It is common knowledge that Chang Tso-lin was murdered by the Japanese. I later heard that the reason why they killed him was because he was becoming less and less obedient; this was because he was under the influence of his son the "Young Marshal" Chang Hsueh-liang who wanted to break with Japan and make friends with

America. Because of this the Japanese said that he was "ungrateful and unfriendly".

I later heard an account of Chang's murder from the Japanese war criminal Colonel Kawamoto who participated in the plot. He said that he directed the personnel of the Japanese Kwantung Army staff who first arranged that the place where Chang would meet his end would be Huangkutun Railway Station at the junction of the Peking-Fengtien and the South Manchuria lines. "We buried thirty sacks of high explosive at the junction, and installed electric equipment in a watch-tower some 500 metres away to set off the explosion. We placed a derailing device north of the junction and had a platoon of shock troops hidden nearby. At 5.30 on June 4, 1928 Chang Tso-lin's blue armoured train arrived. The button was pressed and Chang and the train were destroyed together." To cover up the truth the Kwantung Army sent soldiers and workmen to repair the damaged track, and killed two Chinese whose bodies they placed at the scene of the murder. They stuffed their pockets with forged letters and documents from the Kuomintang's Northern Expedition and also arrested ten innocent local inhabitants, saying that the whole business had been planned by the Northern Expedition. "We had all the pro-Japanese warlords under very tight control," said Kawamoto. "When they could be useful to us we helped them; and when we had no use for them we found ways to eliminate them."

Although Chang Tso-lin's murder startled me and some of the former Ching officials tried to make me see a warning in it, I ignored their advice as I regarded myself as not in the same class as Chang Tso-lin. He, after all, was only a military chief and they could find others to replace him; I was the emperor, and the Japanese could not find another one in the whole of China. The members of my entourage advanced the argument that "the people of the Northeast loathe the Japanese from the bottom of their hearts and the Japanese try to prohibit Chang Hsueh-liang from co-operating with the Kuomintang. The Japanese are strong enough to take the Northeast by force, but if they did so it would not be capable of running itself; without Your Majesty on the throne they will find it very difficult to achieve anything". I was completely convinced that Japan recognized this, and built my policy on this assumption. If I wanted to rely on the strength of Japan I had first to win the hearts of the people of the Northeast. I therefore looked for former military chieftains of Chang Tso-lin whom I could use in my restoration activities. The man who acted on my behalf among the commanders of the Fengtien clique was Shang Yen-ying, a Ching veteran who came from a Manchu family that had been stationed in Kwangtung and was a former Hanlin academician; he was now a member of the Red Swastika Society of the Northeast. As Chang Hsueh-liang had made it quite clear that he wanted to co-operate with Chiang Kai-shek, Shang Yen-ying had to operate in the greatest secrecy. To put it briefly, his activities achieved nothing.

Semionov and the "Second Chukeh Liang"

I cannot remember how much money I spent or how much jade, pearls and jewellery I gave away in trying to win the friendship of military men and buy them over, but I do know that the one who got the most was the White Russian Semionov.

Semionov was a tsarist general who led the remnants of his troops into the Chinese frontier regions of the Northeast and Inner Mongolia after his defeat by the Soviet Red Army. There they looted, raped and burnt and engaged in every other kind of evil-doing. They once tried to invade the Mongolian People's Republic, and after being put to rout they tried to establish a base on the Sino-Mongolian frontier, where they were driven away by the local Chinese forces. By 1927 they had been reduced to being a small bandit group. At this time Semionov was very active in Peking, Tientsin, Shanghai, Lushun, Hongkong, Japan and other places looking for a backer among Chinese warlords and foreign politicians. When he found that there was no market for what he was trying to sell he became a swindler pure and simple. He was captured by Soviet troops after the Second World War and while I was a prisoner in the

Soviet Union I heard that he was hanged. Throughout my seven years in Tientsin I was constantly in contact with this murderer of the Chinese, Soviet and Mongol peoples. He received huge sums of money from me, and in him I placed unbounded hopes

Semionov was first recommended to me by the Mongol noble Sheng Yun and Lo Chen-yu, but when Chen Pao-shen objected I refused to see him. Later Cheng Hsiao-hsu met Semionov through an introduction from Lo Chen-yu and thought that he had the makings of a most useful foreign official. He sang Semionov's praises to me and recommended that we should first get him and Chang Tsung-chang (the "Dog-meat General") to co-operate. As I happened at the time to be very hopeful about Chang Tsung-chang I agreed to Cheng's suggestion. Cheng Hsiao-hsu's activities enabled Chang Tsung-chang to receive foreign mercenaries from Semionov and also brought about an increase in the numbers of the White Russian troops. Chang and Semionov later signed a "Sino-Russian Anti-Bolshevik Military Convention".

After much encouragement from Cheng Hsiao-hsu I met Semionov at the Chang Garden in October 1925. I was very pleased with the interview and thought that he was bound to "accomplish great deeds in the face of difficulties, overthrow communism and restore the dynasty". I gave him 50,000 dollars on the spot to help him in his activities. Later Cheng Hsiao-hsu, Semionov, Liu Feng-chih and others had their photograph taken together and became sworn brothers, showing their great loyalty to the Ching house.

At that time a new wave of anti-Soviet and anti-communist activities was sweeping the world after the defeat of the fourteen-nation intervention against the Soviet Union. I remember Cheng Hsiao-hsu and Semionov telling me that Britain, America and Japan had decided that his men were to be the anti-Soviet shock troops and that he was to be supported with munitions and money. The "Russian imperial family" was also supposed to have the highest hopes in him. Tsarist representatives were in contact with Cheng Hsiao-hsu but I cannot remember the details. What I do recall is that Semionov had a plan which involved me very closely: he was going to use his supporters and troops in the Northeast and Inner

Mongolia to set up an "anti-communist" base there with me as ruler. I opened a bank account for Semionov to help him meet his operating expenses; this account was managed by Cheng Hsiao-hsu and provided Semionov with money whenever he wanted it. I think that the first deposit in it was 10,000 dollars.

Semionov once explained to me that he did not really need this money from me as he was going to raise contributions of 180,000,000 roubles from White Russian émigrés (later he pushed the figure up to 300,000,000); later he would receive financial support from the finance ministries of America, Britain and Japan. It was only because the money was not yet in his hands that he needed a little from me for the moment.

After this he often asked Cheng Hsiao-hsu to provide him with more funds, always on the grounds that the astronomical sums of money were not yet to hand, and he never failed to outline some astounding project in which they would be used. He once said that the Japanese military commander in Tientsin had arranged with Chang Tso-lin that he should go forthwith to Fengtien to discuss the "great plan"; but unfortunately he had no way of meeting his travel expenses. Another time he said that the Soviet consul in Shanghai had seen him on instructions from his superiors in order to come to an agreement with him by which the Soviet government would grant him a certain part of the Far East in which to set up a self-governing region. He asked for money to pay for a trip to Tokyo to investigate the matter. I have no way of calculating how much money he had from me, but I do recall that in the three months before the "September 18th Incident"[1] alone he relieved me of 800 dollars.

One of the numerous intermediaries between Semionov and myself was a Wang Shih, who claimed that he enjoyed the implicit confidence of Semionov and also had the closest connections with important Japanese and with Chinese warlords. I was always hearing from him such phrases as: "This is the most critical stage"; "this is

---

[1] On September 18, 1931 the Japanese imperialists launched a large-scale invasion of China's Northeast.

the last chance"; "now is the decisive moment when the course of the next thousand years will be settled: this chance must not be missed"; "do not lose this opportunity — it will never come again"; and so on. He had the knack of talking me into a state of high excitement.

He was also capable of writing memorials filled with such heady statements as a claim that the Japanese had decided to enlist 8,000 Koreans to serve under Semionov and provide all the pay and supplies, and were also going to muster another 10,000 White Russians on the same terms. The British were going to break off relations with Soviet Russia and give him the 80,000,000 dollars that were deposited in the Hongkong and Shanghai Banking Corporation. "They are only waiting to confirm the truth of the report before handing the money over. . . . France and Italy also sympathize and both want to contribute; America wants to offer a preliminary grant of 5,000,000 dollars and will give further assistance for the organization of an international anti-communist army of volunteers in Manchuria and Mongolia with him [Semionov] as its leader, an army that will co-operate in the destruction of Soviet Russia."

As Cheng Hsiao-hsu was not at the Chang Garden at the time Wang Shih's request for a personal interview with me to discuss this wild scheme of his was blocked by Chen Pao-shen and Hu Sze-yuan and he never got through the main gate.

Hu Sze-yuan was in charge of my office in Tientsin and was the person who sieved out the people and memorials I would see from those I would not. I had given him this job as I thought that he was honest. He pointed out to me that the memorials of Wang Shih were a tissue of lies. I accepted his advice and that of Chen Pao-shen and decided to have nothing to do with this Wang Shih or any other representatives of Semionov.

But as soon as Cheng Hsiao-hsu came back to Tientsin he talked me into paying out more money for his "foreign officials", including an Austrian and an Englishman. The Austrian was a former nobleman who had held office in the department of works of the Austrian concession in Tientsin. He said that he was a very important man in Europe, where he could build up support for my restoration. I appointed him as an adviser and sent him to Europe to act on my behalf, giving him 1,800 dollars as six months' salary. The English-man was a journalist called Ross who said that it was essential to have a newspaper to achieve a restoration and asked me for 20,000 dollars with which to run one. I gave him 3,000, but the paper folded after a few days.

In spite of Hu Sze-yuan's attempts to keep them out, many people managed to get into the Chang Garden on the strength of having links with military men or supporting the restoration. From 1926 onwards batch upon batch of defeated generals and failed politicians flocked to the concessions, and the number of my protégés increased faster than ever.

Liu Feng-chih, the "second Chukeh Liang",[1] was the one of the more noteworthy of these. He was recommended by a former subordinate of Chang Hsun's as "a modern Chukeh Liang. He is a first-rate strategist, and with him on your side the great enterprise of the restoration is almost bound to succeed." Liu Feng-chih was then about forty, and when I met him he first boasted that he was a man of fantastic ability, and then went straight on to suggest that I give him some antiques, paintings and calligraphy with which he could make contact with the men in power.

"Scrolls in Your Majesty's handwriting get nowhere with people like that." This was the first time I had heard such a thing said, and although it made me feel uncomfortable I admired him for his frankness. I felt that as he dared to say things that others would not, his words were bound to be true. I was most liberal with him, allowing him to take large quantities of some of the most valuable objects in my possession. Later he specified precisely what he wanted. For one of Chang Tso-lin's subordinates he requested jewellery to the value of ten thousand dollars. To win over three other Fengtien generals he indicated that they should each be given ten court pearls, and for someone else he demanded the pearl that

---

[1] The name of Chukeh Liang (181-234), a statesman of the Three Kingdoms period, was a byword for political and military skill.

First he posted notices announcing that he was going to carry out military manoeuvres and cut all communications. Then he set his troops to digging, and after three days and nights they cleared out all the treasure that had been buried with Chien Lung and Tzu Hsi.

Chien Lung and Tzu Hsi were the most extravagant of the rulers of the Ching. I have read a description of the tombs, though it may not be too accurate.

The tunnel to the tomb was lined with white marble and led through four marble gates. The vault was octagonal with a domed ceiling on which were carved nine gleaming golden dragons. It was about the same size as the Palace of Central Harmony in the former palace. Chien Lung's inner and outer coffins were made of hard wood that had been seasoned by long burial and were placed on top of an eight-sided well. Apart from ingots and funerary vessels of gold and silver everything in the tombs was made of rare jewels. The funerary objects of Tzu Hsi mostly comprised pearls, gems, emeralds and diamonds, and her phoenix crown was made of enormous pearls and gold wire. On her coverlet was a peony consisting entirely of jewels, and on her arm was a bracelet of dazzling brilliance in the form of a large chrysanthemum and six small plum blossoms all set with diamonds of various sizes. In her hand was a demon-quelling wand over three inches long made of emerald, and on her feet she wore a pair of pearl shoes. Apart from all this the coffin contained seventeen strings of pearls and gems strung together as prayer beads and several pairs of emerald bracelets. The things buried with Chien Lung were calligraphy, paintings, books, swords, ornaments fashioned from jade, ivory and coral, golden statues of the Buddha and so on; of these the articles made of silk had already perished and could not be distinguished.

The report of Sun Tien-ying's grave-robbery from the official responsible for the protection of the Eastern Mausolea gave me a shock worse than the one I had received when I was expelled from the palace. The royal clan and the former Ching officials were all roused by it. Men of every faction, whether they had been lying low or not, all flocked to my house and expressed their hatred for the troops of Chiang Kai-shek, and Ching veterans from all over the country sent funds pouring in for the restoration of the mausolea.

They had spirit tablets for Chien Lung and Tzu Hsi set up in the Chang Garden with tables for incense and mats for people to kneel on. The veterans came in an unending stream to bow, kotow and weep as if it were a funeral. The Ching house and the veterans published telegrams to Chiang Kai-shek and to Yen Hsi-shan, the commander of the garrison of the Peking-Tientsin region, demanding the punishment of Sun Tien-ying and insisting that the authorities repair the tombs. It was decided that the funeral services at the Chang Garden would continue until the job of reconstruction was completed.

The initial reaction of the Chiang Kai-shek government was satisfactory. Yen Hsi-shan was ordered to carry out an investigation and a divisional commander whom Sun Tien-ying had sent to Peking was arrested by Yen. But it was not long before the news came through that the officer had been released, and Chiang Kai-shek decided not to follow the matter up. It was said that Sun Tien-ying sent some of the booty to Chiang Kai-shek's new bride Soong Mei-ling: the pearls from Tzu Hsi's phoenix crown became decorations for Madame Chiang Kai-shek's shoes. My heart smouldered with a hatred I had never known before, and standing before the dark and gloomy funerary hall I made an oath before my weeping clansmen:

"If I do not avenge this wrong I am not an Aisin-Gioro."

I remembered what Pu Wei had said to me the first time he saw me in Tientsin.

"As long as I am alive the Great Ching shall not perish," I announced.

My longing for restoration and revenge reached a new intensity.

In those days Cheng Hsiao-hsu and Lo Chen-yu were the people closest to me, and every historical anecdote or piece of news they told me served to move me to indignation and strengthen my determination to achieve restoration and revenge. To fight the National Government of the Kuomintang to the end and continue the funeral until the mausolea were repaired were both ideas they suggested to me.

The situation grew more and more unfavourable for us. The investigation into the grave-robbery was dropped and the new authorities in the Peking-Tientsin area included no old friends like Tuan Chi-jui. My father moved his whole family from Peking to Tientsin as he was afraid to live there any longer. My mood changed from indignation to depression. The inmates of the Chang Garden understood that the wedding between Soong Mei-ling, the daughter of a family of compradors in the service of Britain and the U.S.A., and Chiang Kai-shek, a stockbroker who was also connected with the underworld, showed that Chiang Kai-shek had more powerful backing than Tuan Chi-jui, Chang Tso-lin, Sun Chuan-fang or Wu Pei-fu had ever had. By the end of the year Chiang Kai-shek's National Government in Nanking had been recognized by all countries including Japan, and his power was greater than that of any previous warlord. I felt that my prospects were very gloomy and thought that under the rule of so ambitious a man there was no question of a restoration; even maintaining my foothold in his sphere of influence would be a big problem. I used to resort to divination to try and find out what the fate of the Chiang Kai-shek government and myself would be.

Nobody burning with ambition and longing for revenge as I was could have left everything to the will of heaven and not tried to do something himself. My experience of the past few years and the story of Chiang's rise to power combined to make me believe that if one wanted to achieve anything it was necessary to have military power, for the foreigners would support the man with an army as a matter of course. If a full-blooded "Great Ching Emperor" like myself had troops the foreigners would be bound to take me more seriously than some marshal who had started as nothing more than a bandit chief or a gangster. I decided to send some of the most trusted members of my family to military school in Japan, and regarded this as more important than going abroad myself.

I chose my brother Pu Chieh and my brother-in-law Jun Chi and asked the Japanese consul in Tientsin to recommend a private tutor to teach them Japanese. The man he selected, Toyama Takeo, turned out to be a member of the Japanese Black Dragon Society who knew quite a few Japanese politicians. He later went to Japan to work for my dream of restoration, but after I went to the Northeast he was squeezed out as he did not belong to the army clique. When he had taught Pu Chieh and Jun Chi Japanese for some time he went back to Japan to try and make arrangements for them to study there. He reported that although they would not be able to enter the Japanese Army Cadet School for the moment, they could first go to a special school for the sons of the Japanese nobility. My two future generals left for Japan with Toyama in March 1929, seven months after the affair of the Eastern Mausolea.

Consulate, Garrison and Black Dragon Society

By 1928 most of my advisers thought that the only hope of a restoration lay with Japan, to whom I could be very useful in the Northeast. They consequently advised discreet negotiations with the Japanese, and I found myself more and more in agreement with them.

I have already told how I began to trust the Japanese after being an object of their "concern" from the time I entered the Northern Mansion. After staying in the Japanese Legation and moving to Tientsin I grew increasingly confident that Japan would be the main source of foreign support for my future restoration.

The Japanese consul-general had invited me to visit a primary school for Japanese children during my first year in Tientsin. The Japanese children lined the road with paper flags in their hands and welcomed me with shouts of "banzai" ("ten thousand years"). This scene made my eyes fill with tears and my chest heave with sighs. When the fighting in one civil war between warlords was approaching Tientsin all the foreign garrisons in the city were organized into an allied army, and when they announced that they would deal with the National Army if it came too close to the concessions the Japanese garrison commander paid a visit to the Chang Garden especially to say to me: "Please do not worry, Your Majesty. We are determined not to allow the Chinese soldiers to put one foot inside the concessions." I was very gratified to hear this.

At New Year and my birthday the Japanese consul and the senior officers of the garrison used to come to congratulate me. They would also invite me to watch the military parade on the Japanese emperor's birthday. I remember that the Japanese commander invited a number of high-ranking refugees to one of these reviews. When I arrived at the parade ground the commander rode over especially to salute me, and when the review was over all we Chinese guests joined the Japanese in shouting "Tenno banzai" ("Long live the Japanese Emperor").

Colonels on the staff of the Japanese garrison used to come and tell me about current affairs, and they did this job most conscientiously for many years: sometimes they brought along diagrams and tables that they had specially prepared. One of these was Yoshioka, who was later "Attaché to the Imperial Household". He was with me for ten years during the "Manchukuo" period, and I shall have more to say about him in Chapter Six.

The main subjects of these talks by the Japanese staff officers were the civil wars, and they would often put forward their analysis as "The root cause of China's disorders is that she lacks a leader and has no emperor." They would go on to discuss the superiority of the Japanese imperial system and say that the hearts of the people of China could be won only by the "Hsuan Tung Emperor". The feebleness and degeneracy of the Chinese armed forces was a favourite topic of theirs: they compared them, of course, with the Imperial Japanese Army. The combination of these talks and the military reviews gave me a strong belief in the might of the Japanese armed forces and great confidence in the support it was giving me.

Once when I was taking a stroll beside the Pai River I saw a Japanese naval vessel moored in the river. I do not know how the captain realized who I was, but he suddenly appeared on the riverbank and respectfully invited me to come on board his boat for a visit. When I went aboard the boat, the *Fuji*, I was saluted by the Japanese naval officers. As this was an impromptu occasion there were no interpreters on either side and we had to converse in writing.[1] The captain later paid me a return visit with a number of officers. I gave him a signed photograph when he asked me for one, and he indicated that he regarded this as a very great honour. This incident made me feel that the Japanese respected me from the depths of their hearts. After the total failure of my efforts to win over warlords and buy up politicians and foreign advisers the Japanese occupied an even more important place in my thoughts.

At first I considered the Japanese as a single entity, which did not, of course, include the common people, and consisted of the Japanese of the Peking Legation and the Tientsin consulate and garrison, as well as the *ronin* friends of Lo Chen-yu and Sheng Yun who held neither military nor civil office. The reason why I had this view of them was that they all "protected" me and treated me as an "emperor", all shared the same contempt for the Republic, all praised the Great Ching, and all expressed their willingness to help me when I first brought up the question of my going to Japan.

I had decided that I wanted to go to Japan under the persuasion of Lo Chen-yu when I was frightened by the approach of the Northern Expedition in 1927. After discussions with the consul-general the matter was referred to Japan. The Tanaka cabinet had indicated that it would welcome me and decided that I would be received in the manner appropriate to a foreign sovereign. Lo Chen-yu told me that the Japanese military authorities had made preparations to give me a military escort for my journey. But after the crisis cooled down Chen Pao-shen and Cheng Hsiao-hsu persuaded me not to go. When "Down with imperialism" and "Abolish the unequal treaties" ceased to be official slogans after the founding of the National Government in Nanking I began to realize that while the Japanese were as "respectful" as ever and they still "protected" me, they were divided in their attitudes as to whether I should go abroad. This split aroused my strongest indignation, and this was how I found out about it.

---

[1] Chinese and Japanese can communicate to a certain extent by writing the Chinese characters that are used in the scripts of both languages.

Lo Chen-yu said to me one day in the latter part of 1927: "Although the Japanese concession is fairly safe there are all sorts of people around here. According to the Japanese command a number of plainclothes agents (he referred to men doing underground work who, in the understanding of the Chang Garden, carried weapons) of the revolutionary party (a term used in the Chang Garden to refer to both the Communist Party and the Kuomintang) have slipped in and Your Majesty's safety is consequently a matter of concern. In your subject's opinion it would be advisable to stay in Japan for the time being; there would be no objection to going to Lushun first. Prince Kung (Pu Wei) has arranged everything there and the Japanese military authorities are willing to help and be responsible for Your Majesty's protection." I was already nervous of the "plainclothes agents of the revolutionary party", and after hearing these suggestions from Lo Chen-yu and receiving a letter from Pu Wei I resolved once more to go abroad. Ignoring Chen Pao-shen and Cheng Hsiao-hsu's protests I ordered Cheng to go to the Japanese consul-general Kato at once and ask him to see me personally.

Cheng Hsiao-hsu hesitated for a moment and then asked, "If Your Majesty invites Kato to come and see you, who will interpret? Hsieh Chieh-shih?"

I saw what he meant. Hsieh Chieh-shih was very close to Lo Chen-yu, and Cheng Hsiao-hsu was clearly displeased at having one of Lo's men interpret for me, and I was aware that Lo would not be pleased at having Cheng's son or Chen Pao-shen's nephew do the job either. I thought it over and announced my decision: "I'll have an English interpreter. Kato knows English."

Kato arrived with the two assistant consuls. After listening to my request Kato replied:

"I cannot give an immediate reply to Your Majesty's question, which I must refer to Tokyo."

I wondered why it was necessary to refer the matter to Tokyo when the military headquarters had told Lo Chen-yu that there would be no problem about it. Some of the wealthy refugees in Tientsin used to go to Lushun to avoid the heat of summer without even having to inform the consulate-general, so why was there so much fuss about me? Before I had finished saying all this Kato asked an awkward question: "May I ask whether this was Your Majesty's own idea?"

"Yes, it was," I answered irritably. I also said that recently I had heard that I would be in danger if I stayed in Tientsin. According to the Japanese garrison the revolutionaries had sent in a number of secret agents recently: surely the consulate was aware of this.

"Those are all rumours. Your Majesty need not believe them." Kato was visibly distressed. I found it most odd that he should dismiss military intelligence reports as rumours. On the basis of those reports I had previously asked him to increase the strength of my guards, and he had complied with my request. Did he believe the reports or not?

"How could the military intelligence reports be rumours?"

Kato was silent for a long time while his two assistants fidgeted uncomfortably on the sofa.

"Your Majesty can be quite confident that there is no danger whatever," Kato said at last. "Naturally I shall refer the question of going to Lushun that Your Majesty raised to my government."

This conversation gave me my first intimation of the discord between the consulate and the garrison, and I regarded it as both strange and annoying. I sent for Lo Chen-yu and Hsieh Chieh-shih and questioned them about it, and they told me that what they heard from Japanese in or associated with the garrison all confirmed that things were so. They also said:

"The military intelligence reports are thoroughly reliable. They have always given a very clear picture of every move of the revolutionaries. Anyhow, even if the reports of a planned assassination are only a rumour we must still take precautions."

A few days later my father-in-law Jung Yuan told me that some friends of his who lived outside had told him that assassins in the service of Feng Yu-hsiang had been arriving in the British and French concessions recently, so that the situation was very alarming. A member of the household told me that he had noticed suspicious people near the main gate peering into the grounds. I hastily summoned the head of my general affairs office and the commander of my guard and told them to ask the Japanese police to tighten the precautions at the gate. I also gave instructions that the guards keep a careful watch on strangers outside the gate and allow nobody in or out at night.

I was woken up one night by a gunshot outside the window which was soon followed by another one. I jumped up from my bed and ordered the guard to muster, convinced that Feng Yu-hsiang's plain-clothes agents were here at last. The whole household got up and guards were posted everywhere. The policemen on the main gate were put on the alert and the Japanese detectives stationed in the house went out to investigate. When they captured the man who had fired the shots he turned out, to my astonishment, to be a Japanese.

Tung Chi-hsu, the head of my general affairs office, told me the next day that he was a member of the Black Dragon Society called Kishida and that when he was taken to the Japanese police headquarters the Japanese military authorities had removed him at once. I now had a good idea of how things really stood.

I had had some previous contact with members of the Black Dragon Society. In 1925 I had met Tsukuda Nobuo, an important figure in the society, as the result of Lo Chen-yu's urgings. Lo had told me that many powerful people in Japan, including some in the army, were planning to help me achieve my restoration, and had sent their representative Tsukuda to have a private talk with me. He said that as this was a chance that should not be missed I should send for the man at once. I had never heard of this Tsukuda before, but some of the Household Department officials who knew him said that he had been a frequent visitor at the various princely mansions since the 1911 Revolution and was on quite good terms with a number of the princes of the royal clan. Although I was stirred by what Lo Chen-yu told me I felt that as the Japanese consul-general was the formal representative of his country and my protector he should be invited to be present at the conversation. I therefore sent someone to inform him and invite him to be present at the occasion. As soon as Tsukuda saw the consul he turned and fled, to the astonishment of Chen Pao-shen, Cheng Hsiao-hsu and everyone else present. As I look at it today it is clear that this move of Lo Chen-yu's and the attempt by Kishida to frighten me with gunshots in the night were all connected with Tsukuda's activities, which were in turn undoubtedly backed by the Japanese garrison.

I sent for Chen Pao-shen and Cheng Hsiao-hsu to ask them their views on the affair of the gunshots. "It looks," said Cheng, "as though both the Japanese army and government want to have Your Majesty living under their protection in areas under their control. Although they are not co-operating with each other this does us no harm. But Lo Chen-yu's way of doing things is too reckless and can only lead to disaster; he must on no account be given important work to do."

"Both the Japanese garrison and the Black Dragon Society act completely irresponsibly," was Chen Pao-shen's opinion. "You should ignore everyone except the Japanese minister and consul-general." After thinking the matter over I felt that they were right and decided not to ask the consul-general to be allowed to leave Tientsin. I lost interest in Lo Chen-yu and the next year he sold his house in Tientsin and went to Talien.

Strange to relate, as soon as Lo Chen-yu had gone there were fewer rumours, and Jung Yuan and Chi Chi-chung brought no more alarming intelligence reports. It was only a long time later that I began to understand why.

It was my English interpreter who explained things to me. Because he was related by marriage to my father-in-law Jung Yuan, and because he had been in contact with the Japanese garrison in the course of his work he knew something of what had been going on behind the scenes, and later he told me about it. The Japanese garrison had set up a special secret organization to deal with the Chang Garden, and Lo Chen-yu, Jung Yuan and Hsieh Chieh-shih at least were connected with it. This network had a base in a house known to the public as the Mino Residence.

After translating for my interview with Kato my interpreter had been kept by Lo, Jung and Hsieh who wanted to hear about the conversation. They had started shouting when they heard that Kato had not been at all keen to let me go abroad, and the interpreter gathered from their discussion that a member of the military staff had said to Lo that they wanted to take me to Lushun. Lo and the others took the interpreter to the Mino Residence to find the staff officer, and although they did not find him the interpreter discovered the secret establishment. He later heard from Jung Yuan and others that they got opium, girls and money there.

Mino Tomoyoshi who owned the place was a staff major who often came to the Chang Garden with the Japanese commanding officer. I never dreamed at the time that this man had established secret links with members of my household, that he knew everything that went on there, and that he had used Jung Yuan and others to pass the rumours on to me which had made me want to flee to Lushun. When I heard something of the truth about the Mino Residence I realized that the reason why the Japanese army was going to such lengths to win control over Jung Yuan and his like was because they were struggling with the consulate-general over me. This quarrel, as Cheng Hsiao-hsu had pointed out, could only benefit me.

Later on Cheng Hsiao-hsu told me something about the Black Dragon Society. This society, the biggest of the *ronin* organizations, had previously been called the "Black Ocean Association". It had been founded by the *ronin* Hiraoka Kotaro after the Sino-French War (1883-85) and was the first organization of agents to carry out espionage activities in China. It started out with bases in Foochow, Yentai (Chefoo) and Shanghai and operated under such covers as consulates, schools and photographers. The name of the Black Dragon Society implied "beyond the Amur River" (the Chinese name for the Amur is Black Dragon River) and was first used in 1901. The society played an important role in the Russo-Japanese War of 1904-05 and its membership was said to have reached several hundred thousand with correspondingly huge funds. Toyama Mitsuru was the most famous of its leaders and under his direction its members had penetrated every stratum of Chinese society. They operated everywhere: at the side of Ching nobles and high officials and among pedlars and servants, including the attendants in the Chang Garden. Many Japanese personalities (such as Doihara, Hirota Koki, Hiranuma Kiichiro, Arita Hachiro and Kazuki Seiji) were disciples of Toyama's. Cheng Hsiao-hsu said that Toyama was a Buddhist with a long silver-grey beard and a "kindly" face who was passionately fond of roses and hated to leave his garden. Yet he was the man who planned such appalling conspiracies and murders.

Lo Chen-yu should be given the credit for Cheng Hsiao-hsu's recognition of the power of the Black Dragon Society and the Japanese army. Cheng, Lo and Chen Pao-shen originally represented three different schools of thought. Lo regarded anything that military men or Black Dragon figures said as completely reliable, and the main reason why he trusted Semionov was because of his connections with the society. Chen Pao-shen on the other hand thought that no Japanese were trustworthy except those in the consulate-general who represented the Japanese government. Cheng Hsiao-hsu sided openly with Chen Pao-shen at first, but later Lo's boastings and the infamous conduct of the Black Dragon Society enabled him to see the way some forces in Tokyo were heading and to divine the real intentions of the Japanese authorities. He saw that Japan was a force on which he could rely and finally decided to modify his plan of working for the joint administration of China by all the foreign powers. He went to Japan to see the Black Dragon Society and the Japanese general staff.

Cheng Hsiao-hsu had begun to hope for increased intervention by Japan in Chinese politics when he despaired of getting international support for the White Russian brigand Semionov. When he changed his line he took a much longer view than Lo Chen-yu and had no time for the Mino Residence or the garrison in Tientsin: his objective was Tokyo. At the time, however, he did not regard Japan as our only potential foreign helper; he thought of her rather as our first.

He went to Japan with my permission and the consent of the Japanese minister Yoshizawa. In Japan he made contact with the army and the Black Dragon Society, and he reported with great satisfaction to me on his return that the majority of influential people expressed "concern" and "sympathy" for me and my restoration and showed an interest in my plans for the future. He said that we only had to wait for the moment to come in order to ask for assistance.

While in Japan he met all kinds of people who were interested in my restoration. They included military and civil officials who had been connected with me in Peking and Tientsin, the important Black Dragon figure Tsukuda who had fled at the sight of the consul-general, and Kishida, the member of the society who had fired the shots in the night. He also met some important men who had previously stayed in the background and who would later be prime ministers or war ministers or hold other important posts.[1] Cheng Hsiao-hsu was probably too excited by the way they reacted to his "policy of opening up the whole country". When the first batch of Japanese "guests" came rushing through the open door after the foundation of "Manchukuo" he was still clinging to his dream of joint administration and proclaiming to the outside world the "open door and equal opportunity". He was like a servant who helped a gang of robbers and opened the gate of his master's house to let them in and then wanted to send invitations to all the other gangs. The first gang naturally kicked him aside in a fury.

Life in the Temporary Palace

After I had been living in the Chang Garden for a while I felt that this would be the best place for me to stay until the time was ripe for my restoration or I was forced to leave. This was one of the reasons why my enthusiasm for going abroad faded.

It seemed to me that the Chang Garden (and later the Quiet Garden) was free of all the things I disliked about the Forbidden City while preserving all the essentials. The things I most loathed in the Forbidden City were the rules which did not even allow me to ride in a car or go for a walk in the streets, and what came next

---

[1] They included Konoe Fumimaro, Ugaki Kazushige, Yonai Mitsumasa, Hiranuma Kiichiro, Suzuki Kantaro, Minami Jiro and Yoshida Shigeru.

on my hate list was the infuriating Household Department. I now had the freedom to do as I liked, and while others could remonstrate they could not interfere.

The one essential element of my life in the Forbidden City, my authority, was preserved. Although I now wore an ordinary Chinese jacket and gown or, more often, Western clothes instead of the cumbersome imperial robes, people still kotowed and bowed to me. The place where I now lived had been built as an amusement park and had no glazed tiles or carved and painted beams, but it was still called a "temporary palace". I found a foreign-style house with flush lavatories and central heating far more comfortable than the Mind Nurture Palace, and nobles would come from Peking in rotation to stand in attendance. What had been the ticket office in the days when it was a pleasure ground was now a substitute "Guard Office of the Cloudless Heaven Gate". Although there was no longer a Southern Study, a Great Diligence Hall or a Household Department, people saw the "Office in Charge of the Affairs of the Ching House During Its Stay in Tientsin" as their combined reincarnation. I was still addressed in exactly the same way as before and dates were still given in terms of the reign period of Hsuan Tung. All this seemed to me both natural and essential.

The only former senior official of the Household Department still with me was Jung Yuan. The others were either looking after my property in Peking or had retired on grounds of old age. The first batch of edicts I issued after my arrival in Tientsin included the following two. One was, "Cheng Hsiao-hsu, Hu Sze-yuan, Yang Chung-hsi, Wen Su, Ching Fang-chang, Hsiao Ping-yen, Chen Tseng-shou, Wan Sheng-shih and Liu Hsiang-yeh shall be advisers in Tientsin". The other read, "An Administrative Office shall be established under Cheng Hsiao-hsu and Hu Sze-yuan and a General Affairs Office shall be set up under Tung Chi-hsu. The Finance Office shall be headed by Ching Fang-chang and the Office for External Relations shall be headed by Liu Hsiang-yeh". Chen Pao-shen, Lo Chen-yu and Cheng Hsiao-hsu were the "privy ministers" whom I saw daily. They and the other advisers had to come every morning and wait in a row of single-storeyed buildings to the west of the main building to be "summoned to audience". People who had asked for an "audience" would wait to be called in a small lodge by the main gate, and their numbers included soldiers, politicians, former Ching officials, all kinds of "modern" figures, poets, writers, doctors, soothsayers, astrologers, physiognomists, the head of the reactionary Youth Party, a tennis star, journalists and a member of the Control Commission of the Kuomintang. The Japanese police stationed at the Chang Garden lived in a house opposite and used to note down all the comings and goings. Whenever I went out a Japanese plainclothes policeman would follow me.

The economics of the Chang Garden were naturally on a far smaller scale than those of the Forbidden City, but I still had a considerable fortune. Of the large quantities of valuables I had brought with me from the Forbidden City, some had been converted into money which was now earning interest in foreign banks and some had been turned into real estate to bring in rent. I still owned a lot of land in the Northeast and north China. The Ching house and the Republican authorities set up a special office to deal with the renting and sale of these lands which were the "private property of the emperor". The two sides split the loot, and our share from the sale of some of this property was one of our sources of income. In addition we still had the great quantities of art treasures that Pu Chieh and I had moved out of the palace over a period of six months, as I described in Chapter Three.

After I moved to Tientsin there were many places to which money had to be sent every month and a number of offices were set up for this purpose: the "Peking Office", the "Office of Mausolea and Temples", the "Liaoning Office", the "Imperial Clan Bureau" and the "Office for the Administration of (the Emperor's) Private Property" (this was the joint Ching-Republican office mentioned in the previous paragraph). There were also officials appointed to look after the imperial tombs of the Ching house. According to a document I have found, the monthly expenditure for Peking and the mausolea alone was 15,837 dollars 84 cents; and the Tientsin figure must have been over ten thousand. The biggest item on the budget was the money spent on trying to buy over or influence warlords, and this was not included in the sum mentioned. Purchases, excluding such items as cars or diamonds, probably accounted for two-thirds of an average month's expenses. I spent far more money on buying things when in Tientsin than I had done in Peking, and the amount increased every month. I never tired of buying pianos, watches, clocks, radios, Western clothes, leather shoes and spectacles.

Wan Jung had been a young lady of Tientsin, and so she knew even more ways of wasting money on useless objects than I did. Whatever she bought for herself Wen Hsiu would want too, and, when I bought it for Wen Hsiu, Wang Jung would want more, as if a failure to do so would have detracted from her status as empress. This in turn would make Wen Hsiu complain and ask for more. This competitive buying eventually compelled me to set a limit to their monthly expenditure; Wan Jung's allowance was naturally somewhat higher and was at first a thousand dollars with Wen Hsiu's about eight hundred. When we ran into financial difficulties the allowances were cut to three hundred and two hundred respectively. There was of course no limit to my personal spending.

As a result of our astounding extravagance the Chang Garden was reduced to desperate financial straits just as the Forbidden City had been, and sometimes we were unable to pay our bills, our rent, and even the salaries of the "privy ministers" and the "advisers".

While spending incalculable sums of money on buying enormous quantities of useless objects I became far more convinced than I ever had been in the days when Johnston was with me that everything foreign was good and everything Chinese, except the imperial system, was bad.

A stick of Spearmint chewing-gum or a Bayer aspirin would be enough to make me sigh at the utter doltishness of the Chinese, though I did not include myself as I saw myself as superior to all my subjects, and even thought that the brilliant foreigners shared my own estimate of myself.

The treatment I received in the foreign concessions was quite unlike that accorded to any other Chinese. In addition to the Japanese, the consuls and senior military officers of America, Britain, France and Italy and the heads of foreign firms were all extremely respectful to me and addressed me as "Your Imperial Majesty". On their national days they would invite me to review their troops, visit their barracks and see their newly-arrived aircraft and warships; and they would all come to congratulate me at New Year and on my birthday.

Before Johnston left me, which was not long after my arrival in Tientsin, he introduced me to the British consul and the commander of the British garrison. They introduced me to their successors, who in turn introduced me to theirs, so that my social contacts with the British military commanders continued unbroken. When the Duke of Gloucester, the third son of King George V of England, came to Tientsin he visited me and accepted a photograph of me to take to his father, and George V later wrote a letter thanking me for it, and also sent his own photograph for the British consul-general to present to me. I also exchanged photos with the king of Italy through the Italian consul-general.

I visited a number of barracks and watched many parades of foreign troops. When these soldiers — whose presence in China had been conceded by my ancestress Tzu Hsi in 1901 — marched before me in their martial splendour I was very pleased as I felt that the way the foreigners were treating me proved that they still regarded me as emperor.

There was a "Country Club" in Tientsin run by the English, a very grand establishment where only the foreign bosses were allowed to set foot, Chinese being absolutely forbidden to pass the main entrance. I was the only exception to this rule.[1] I was allowed to enter freely and even to take members of my household, and we all enjoyed the delights of being "special Chinese".

I made the most of the clothes and diamonds of the foreign stores such as Whiteway, Laidlaw & Co. to dress myself up like a foreign gentleman from the pages of *Esquire*. Whenever I went out I used to wear the very latest in Western clothes tailored from English cloth. I would have a diamond pin in my tie, diamond cuff-links

---

[1] In its last days a few Chinese of the comprador-capitalist type were allowed in if accompanied by foreign members. This place was taken over after liberation and turned into a people's club.

in my sleeves, diamond rings on my fingers, a "civilization stick" in my hand, and German Zeiss spectacles on my nose. My body would be fragrant with the combined odours of Max Factor lotions, eau-de-Cologne and mothballs, and I would be accompanied by two or three Alsatian dogs and a strangely dressed wife and concubine.

This way of living drew many criticisms from Chen Pao-shen and Hu Sze-yuan. They never opposed my spending habits or my relations with foreigners, but when I went to the Chung Yuan Company for a haircut, or happened to go to the theatre or the cinema wearing Western clothes they would always come to remonstrate about the loss of imperial dignity. When repeated protests had no effect Hu Sze-yuan submitted a memorial in which he took the blame on himself and asked my permission to retire.

He had previously asked leave to retire when he had reckoned that I had lost something of my imperial dignity by going to the theatre with my wife Wan Jung to see the famous Peking opera actor Mei Lan-fang. When I repeatedly begged him to stay, rewarded him with two fox-fur coat linings, and stressed my determination to accept his criticisms his sorrow had turned to joy. He had praised me as an "illustrious ruler" because I accepted the remonstration, and both sides were happy. I dealt with his new resignation over my visit to the barber's shop in much the same way.

Wan Jung's twentieth[1] birthday occurred in our first year in Tientsin and her father arranged for a foreign orchestra to come and play for the occasion. As soon as one old former Ching official heard this news he hastened to remonstrate with me, protesting that "foreign music has a mournful sound" and could not possibly be played on the birthday of an empress. The old fellow was given two hundred dollars and the foreign orchestra cancelled. This must have been the time when I started to give rewards to ministers who criticized me.

From then until my imprisonment I never went out to a theatre or a barber's saloon again. The reason why I followed Hu's advice was not because I was worried that he might go on complaining but

---

[1] Nineteenth by Western reckoning.

because I thought he was right in saying that it was undignified for me to go to a theatre. I can give an example to show the "progress" I made. When a Swedish prince visited Tientsin and wanted to meet me I refused because I had seen a picture of him with the actor Mei Lan-fang in the papers and thought that I should show my disapproval of his degrading behaviour.

Hu Sze-yuan and other members of Chen Pao-shen's party differed from Cheng Hsiao-hsu, Lo Chen-yu and their associates in that they seemed to have despaired of a restoration and were opposed to trying out anything dangerous. They attached more importance than Cheng and the others to my royal dignity, which was another reason why I obediently did as they told me. Although I found many of their suggestions bigoted I always accepted ones in which they showed their loyalty. Although I was living a strange life in a foreign settlement I never forgot my position and remembered that an "emperor" had to abide by precedent.

When my consort Wen Hsiu suddenly asked for and obtained a divorce in 1931 the old-timers did not neglect to ask me to issue an edict demoting her from the rank of consort to that of commoner, and I naturally complied.

Wen Hsiu's divorce reminds me of my irregular relationship with her. The reason she left me was not so much a matter of emotions as of the emptiness of our life in the Chang Garden. Even if I had only had one wife she would not have found life with me at all pleasant as my only interest in life was in restoration. Frankly speaking, I did not know what love was, and where husband and wife were equal in other marriages, to me wife and concubine were both the slaves and tools of their master.

Wen Hsiu had been brought up from her earliest years to accept the inferior role of a woman in feudal society and she began the life of a "palace consort" before she reached the age of fourteen, so that the ideas of her duty to her sovereign and her husband were very deeply embedded in her. That she dared to ask for a divorce in spite of this was a sign of great courage. She overcame all kinds of obstacles to obtain it, and was badly treated afterwards. It has been said that she was egged on to ask for it by her family for the sake of a considerable alimony, but in fact the difficulties her family created for her caused her great distress. She had very little of the 50,000 dollars alimony left after she had paid her lawyers and the middlemen and when her family had taken what they wanted; and her psychological losses were even worse. A brother of hers actually published an open letter to her in a Tientsin paper in which he attacked her and accused her of ingratitude to the Ching house.

It appeared on the surface that Wen Hsiu was forced out by the "empress" Wan Jung, and while this was not the whole truth it was certainly one of the reasons for Wen Hsiu's departure.

I do not know much about what happened to Wen Hsiu after her divorce except that she became a primary-school teacher and died in 1950. She did not remarry.

CHAPTER FIVE

TO THE NORTHEAST

The Unquiet Quiet Garden

In July 1929 I moved from the Chang Garden to the Quiet Garden. This house had previously had a different name, and the change to "Quiet Garden" was not without significance.

After the Northern Expedition the power of the Kuomintang extended to the north of China. The warlords with whom I was on good terms were collapsing, and the Northeast, in which I had placed such high hopes, had proclaimed its allegiance to the National Government in Nanking. Everyone in the Chang Garden had despaired. Some of the Ching veterans in my entourage had scattered, and of the ministers who stayed with me, only Cheng Hsiao-hsu, Lo Chen-yu and a few others still talked about restoration. The only question that the others considered was how the new dynasty of Chiang Kai-shek was going to treat me. I too was very worried about this.

Our anxiety did not, however, last long. We soon saw that under the Nanking Kuomintang government civil wars continued just as they had under the Peking warlord regime. The unification achieved by Chiang Kai-shek became more and more illusory, and hopes revived in the Chang Garden when all had seemed lost. It seemed to us that the great enterprise of unification could be accomplished only by me, a view that was expressed not only by the Ching veterans in my service but also by the Japanese staff officers who came to give me my talk about current developments every week. The name I chose for my new house — Quiet Garden — did not mean that I wanted peace and quiet: it implied that I intended to wait quietly for my opportunity.

After two years of waiting in the Quiet Garden we got some news in the summer of 1931.

Two months before the "September 18th Incident" my younger brother Pu Chieh, who was studying in Tokyo, was about to come back to China on holiday when he received an invitation from a battalion commander named Yoshioka Yasunori to stay with him for a few days before going back to China. Yoshioka had previously been a staff officer with the Japanese forces in Tientsin and had frequently come to the Chang Garden to give me weekly summaries of current events. Pu Chieh was treated with great hospitality by Major Yoshioka and his wife. When he was saying goodbye to them Yoshioka took him aside and said gravely, "When you get to Tientsin you can tell your elder brother that Chang Hsueh-liang has been behaving disgracefully recently and that something may be happening soon in Manchuria. Please ask Emperor Hsuan Tung to look after himself: his situation is by no means hopeless." Pu Chieh told me about this when he arrived in Tientsin on July 10. On July 29 the Japanese viscount Mizuno Katsukuni came to visit me and I received him in the presence of Cheng Hsiao-hsu and Pu Chieh. In the course of this ordinary meeting my visitor gave me an extraordinary present: a Japanese fan on which was written a couplet, "Heaven will not let Kou Chien fail. The age does not lack a Fan Li".[1]

Viscount Mizuno had gone to see Pu Chieh before his return to China and had explained to him the significance of the couplet. Pu Chieh wrote to me to tell me about it. It referred to a story of the civil war in Japan between the northern and southern dynasties. The emperor Godaigo, who was under the control of the Kamakura shogunate, brought about his own fall, was captured by the shogunate, and was exiled to Oki. During his exile a warrior carved this couplet on the trunk of a cherry tree as a hint to him. Later this Japanese "Kou Chien" overthrew the shogunate with a crowd of "Fan Li's" and returned to Kyoto. This was the beginning of the "Kemmu Restoration". What Viscount Mizuno omitted to mention

---

[1] Kou Chien was a king of the state of Yueh in the Spring and Autumn Period who had been badly defeated by the neighbouring state of Wu. Fan Li was an able minister who enabled King Kou Chien to avenge his defeat and destroy the state of Wu.

was that less than three years after his return to Kyoto Emperor Godaigo was driven out by a new military leader, Ashikaga Takauji. But I was interested not in the history but in receiving this hint from a Japanese. The crisis in the Northeast was building up, and I had been dreaming of reascending the throne for several nights running. This hint seemed to me to be a call to action, irrespective of whether it sprang from the concern of an individual or was the result of prompting from some official quarter.

The attack launched by Japanese troops in Shenyang on September 18 and the retreat of the Chinese troops galvanized the Quiet Garden. As soon as I heard the news I longed to go to the Northeast, but I knew that this was impossible without the consent of the Japanese. Cheng Hsiao-hsu told me that the situation in Shenyang was still confused and advised me not to be too impatient: sooner or later the Japanese were bound to invite me to go and the best thing at the moment was to get in touch with as many people as possible. I therefore decided to send Liu Hsiang-yeh to see the senior Japanese officers in the Northeast, including Uchida Yasuda (the head of the South Manchuria Railway) and Honjo Shigeru (the commander of the Kwantung Army). I also sent my chief steward Tung Chi-hsu to the Northeast to see the Ching veterans there. Another member of my entourage, Shang Yen-ying, thought of going to visit the Northeastern military commanders with whom he was acquainted. Soon after these three had gone Cheng Hsiao-hsu's prediction was fulfilled and an emissary of the Japanese Kwantung Army came to see me.

On the afternoon of September 30 an interpreter named Yoshida from the Japanese Tientsin garrison came to the Quiet Garden to tell me that the Japanese commander, Lieutenant-General Kashii Kohei, wanted me to come alone and see him about an important matter. I went to the Japanese barracks full of happy anticipation, and when I arrived General Kashii was waiting for me outside the front door of his house. In the drawing room two people were standing respectfully: Lo Chen-yu wearing a Chinese jacket and gown and a stranger in Western clothes. From his bow I guessed that the stranger was a Japanese, and then General Kashii introduced him to me. His name was Kaeisumi Toshiichi and he had been sent by Colonel Itagaki of the Kwantung Army staff. After introducing him General Kashii left.

There were only three of us in the room. Lo Chen-yu greeted me and produced a large envelope containing a letter from a distant relation of mine, Hsi Hsia, who was chief of staff to Chang Tso-hsiang, the deputy head of public security in the Northeast. Hsi Hsia had taken advantage of the absence of Chang Tso-hsiang, who was also chairman of Kirin Province, to order that the gates of Kirin city be opened to welcome the Japanese troops, who were thus able to take Kirin without firing a shot. He said in his letter that the chance for which he waited for twenty years (since the 1911 Revolution) had at last arrived. He begged me not to miss this opportunity and to come at once to the "land where our ancestors arose" to take charge of the plan. He also said that I could win the Northeast with Japanese support and then go on to think about the rest of the country. As soon as I reached Shenyang, Kirin would proclaim my restoration.

After I had finished reading the letter Lo Chen-yu repeated its main theme and told me at length about his activities and "the unselfish assistance" of the Kwantung Army. According to him, "restoration" could be expected throughout the Northeast in a matter of days, my "subjects" were longing for my return, and the Kwantung Army had agreed to my restoration and sent Kaeisumi to contact me. Everything was settled: I only had to set out and a Japanese naval vessel would take me to Talien. He was so excited as he spoke that his face went red, his whole body quivered, and his eyes all but popped out of their sockets.

I looked at Lo Chen-yu and Kaeisumi feeling unsettled. It was clear that this meeting with Lo was unlike any previous one. We were now talking in the Japanese garrison and he had with him a representative of the Kwantung Army. In the second place he had the letter from Hsi Hsia. Moreover, I had read in the Talien press the previous day that "all walks of life in Shenyang are ready to greet the former Ching emperor", and the Tientsin papers were full of reports of the retreats of the Chinese troops in the Northeast and of the way that Britain was covering up for Japan at the League of Nations.

I told Lo and Kaeisumi that I would give them an answer when I had thought the matter over. General Kashii then reappeared and said that I would be in danger if I stayed in Tientsin and that he hoped I would take the advice of Colonel Itagaki and go to the Northeast. These words of his seemed truer and truer as I drove home in my car. My suspicions had been swept away, but my excitement was doused with cold water when I got back to the Quiet Garden.

The first to come out against the idea was Chen Pao-shen, followed by Hu Sze-yuan and Wan Jung's tutor, Chen Tseng-shou. Their reaction was that Lo Chen-yu was being reckless as usual and that one should not put one's trust too lightly in the representative of a mere colonel. They said that the situation in the Northeast, the real attitude of the powers and the state of public opinion were not yet clear. I should at least wait until Liu Hsiang-yeh returned from his mission of investigation before taking any decisions. I shook my head impatiently at this disappointing advice.

"Hsi Hsia's letter cannot be nonsense."

The eighty-four-year-old Chen Pao-shen was visibly embarrassed, and he hesitated for a while before saying very sadly: "It has always been the hope of your humble subject that the old order would be restored, as it is only natural that heaven will comply with the wishes of the people. But to act rashly in the present confusion might lead us into inextricable difficulties."

Seeing that these old fellows could not be convinced I had Cheng Hsiao-hsu sent for at once. I imagined that Cheng, who was full of vigour for all his seventy-one years, would be delighted by the invitation from the Kwantung Army and Hsi Hsia's letter. His reactions, however, were not what I had hoped for.

"After the ups and downs of the past a new dawn is breaking. The restoration will undoubtedly begin in Manchuria, and could not be prevented even if the Japanese did not welcome Your Majesty." After a moment's thought he added, "It would be safer, however, to wait until Tung Chi-hsu returns before Your Majesty moves."

221

Differences Among the Japanese

With the factions in the Quiet Garden still at odds the Japanese deputy consul in Tientsin came to see me the following day. The consulate knew all about my visit to the Japanese garrison. They understood my feelings and my circumstances, but felt that I would do best to act with caution and stay in Tientsin for the moment. As they were responsible for my protection they were obliged to give me this warning.

From that day onwards the deputy consul advised restraint either in person or through Chen Pao-shen and his nephew or Cheng Hsiao-hsu and his son. At the same time Yoshida, the interpreter attached to the Japanese garrison, was constantly telling me that the Japanese military were determined to help me reascend the throne as he tried to persuade me to go to the Northeast at once.

My new view of the Japanese army and government differed from that of Chen Pao-shen. He believed that according to the natural order civilians should rule, and stoutly maintained that I should not do what I was told by military men in the absence of any indication from Tokyo. My view was different. I thought that my fate was in the hands of soldiers, not politicians. I saw that while the Japanese were announcing to the world that they were ready to adopt peaceful methods to solve the "Sino-Japanese differences", the Kwantung Army was continuing to advance and attack the retreating Chinese troops. Although I did not understand that the shouts of protest of Chiang Kai-shek and Wang Ching-wei as they yielded national territory to the enemy were nothing but deceptions, I could see that the decisive element in the situation were the Japanese soldiers. Where Chen Pao-shen felt that the lukewarm attitude of the foreign powers was worrying, I thought that Britain at least supported me. Soon after my visit to the Japanese barracks, Brigadier F. H. Burnell-Nugent, the commander of the British troops in Tientsin, had come to see me, and had offered his personal congratulations on the opportunity that the "September 18th Incident" had created for me and even said that he would be proud to serve as a soldier under my dragon flag if I came to the throne in Manchuria. Soon after this I met Johnston again. He was in China on British Foreign Office business and he took the opportunity to come and see me. He was excited about my prospects, and he asked me to write a preface for his book *Twilight in the Forbidden City*. He said that he was going to add an epilogue called "The Dragon Goes Home".

The news that Liu Hsiang-yeh and Tung Chi-hsu brought back with them when they returned from the Northeast was fairly encouraging. Tung Chi-hsu came back first and said that the opinion of the Ching veterans he had met in Shenyang was that the time was ripe and I should not delay. When Liu Hsiang-yeh returned his news was that although he had been unable to see Uchida or Honjo he had met the Kwantung staff officer Colonel Itagaki and the Ching veteran Chin Liang and was able to confirm that what I had been told by Lo Chen-yu and Kaeisumi was quite true. Chin Liang had been extremely optimistic: "Everything in Fengtien is ready and we are only waiting for the arrival of Your Majesty." He had also been to Kirin and found out that it was true that the Japanese army controlled the whole of the province, and that Hsi Hsia and others were ready to support a restoration at any time.

In addition to this there were rumours circulating at the time that made me impatient to move. Tientsin journalists were very fast news gatherers, and my visit to the Japanese barracks was soon common knowledge. Some papers were even saying that I had already gone to the Northeast by boat. At the same time rumours were being spread from an unknown source that the Chinese were planning to take some action against me. I was more convinced than ever that I could not stay in Tientsin any longer.

I sent Cheng Hsiao-hsu's son Cheng Chui to say to the Japanese consul-general that even if the time had not yet come for me to go to Shenyang there could surely be no harm in my going to stay in Lushun first, where I would be safer. The consul replied at once that there was no need for me to go to Lushun, and he asked Cheng Chui to tell me that Uchida Yasuda could not agree to my moving at present. As Uchida was a veteran politician greatly respected by the army it would be best to act cautiously; as for my safety, he was prepared to take full responsibility for it. The consul ended up by saying that he intended to have an exchange of views with the garrison commander, General Kashii. The next day his deputy came to tell Cheng Chui that he and the general had agreed that neither of them was in favour of my leaving Tientsin at once.

This information left me feeling confused, and I invited the garrison interpreter to come and see me to clarify the situation. To my surprise he told me that the meeting between the consul-general and the garrison commander had never taken place and that General Kashii wanted me to leave with Kaeisumi at once. He suggested to me that I write a letter to the garrison command stating clearly that I wanted to go. I wrote the letter. Somehow the consul-general heard of it and hurried over to see Chen Pao-shen and Cheng Hsiao-hsu to find out whether I had really written it or whether it was a forgery.

I was very annoyed about the friction between the Japanese civil and military authorities, but I did not know what to do about it. Then a letter came from Liu Hsiang-yeh who had gone to the North-east again in which he said that he had found out the real feelings of Honjo, the commander of the Kwantung Army: as the three provinces of the Northeast were not yet entirely under control, it would be better to wait until they were unified and stable. As this was the opinion of the supreme arbiter of my destiny I had no choice but to obey him and wait. I now realized that in addition to the difference of opinion between the consulate-general in Tientsin and the garrison there was even discord within the Kwantung Army.

Having told Lo Chen-yu and Kaeisumi that I would not be leaving for the time being I waited for news as the days dragged past like years. I issued numbers of "imperial edicts" and sent my two nephews Hsien Yuan and Hsien Chi to the Northeast to win over some Mongol princes and give jade to Chang Hai-peng and Kuei Fu who had been among the first to submit to the Japanese occupation forces. At the request of a Japanese officer I wrote letters to the resistance fighter Ma Chan-shan and some patriotic Mongol princes advising them to surrender. I distributed a large batch of appointments and prepared a plentiful reserve of edicts of appointment to official posts with blank spaces for the names.

I should mention that at this time I acted on a suggestion from Cheng Hsiao-hsu, who was becoming less cautious now, and sent my brother's Japanese teacher to Japan to make contact with the new Army Minister, Minami Jiro, and the Black Dragon Society leader Toyama Mitsuru. I wrote each of them a letter (copied from drafts by Cheng Hsiao-hsu) whose authenticity I later denied at the International Military Tribunal for the Far East. Three weeks later I met the Kwantung Army staff officer Doihara and it was decided that I would go to the Northeast.

Meeting Doihara

Of the twenty-five war criminals tried by the International Military Tribunal for the Far East the two found guilty of the most offences were Doihara and Itagaki. The charges against them were roughly similar and covered seven "crimes against peace" as well as the most important of the "conventional war crimes and crimes against humanity", namely "ordering and permitting the violation of treaties". They were hanged in 1948.

Doihara was a Japanese soldier who built his career out of aggression against China. He first came to China in 1913 and was adjutant to a Kwantung Army adviser to the Northeastern warlords for over ten years. He was closely associated with Chang Tso-lin, but when the Kwantung Army decided to eliminate Chang in 1928 Doihara took part in the plot to blow him up. Soon after this he was promoted to the rank of colonel and was in charge of a secret service organization in Shenyang. From 1931 to 1935 he was involved in many Japanese plots against China, planning riots, setting up local puppet authorities, and engineering outbreaks of fighting.

After a short spell as a brigade commander Doihara was put in command of the secret service network of the Kwantung Army.

After the "July 7th Incident" of 1937 Doihara reverted from undercover work to an open military role as a divisional commander, later
rising to command Japanese armies in China and Southeast Asia.

Because of the mysterious stories that were told about him the
Western press described him as the "Lawrence of the East" and the
Chinese papers said that he usually wore Chinese clothes and was
fluent in several Chinese dialects. But it seems to me that if all
his activities were like persuading me to go to the Northeast he
would have had no need for the cunning and ingenuity of a Lawrence:
the gambler's ability to keep a straight face while lying would have
been enough. When I met him he wore not Chinese clothes but
Japanese-style Western ones, and his spoken Chinese was nothing
marvellous, as he had to use the services of the Tientsin garrison
interpreter Yoshida to be sure that there would be no misunder-
standings.

He was forty-eight, and the flesh round his eyes was going flabby.
He had a little moustache on his upper lip, and throughout our
interview his face wore a kindly and respectful smile. This smile
was enough to make one feel that every word he spoke was completely reliable.

After politely inquiring about my health he got down to business.
First he explained the Japanese action to me. He said it was aimed
solely at dealing with the "Young Marshal" Chang Hsueh-liang,
under whose rule "the people of Manchuria were reduced to destitution and the Japanese had no guarantees for their rights and safety,
so that Japan had no alternative but to take military action". He
claimed that the Kwantung Army had no territorial ambitions in
Manchuria and "sincerely wants to help the Manchurian people to
set up their own independent state". He hoped that I would not
miss this opportunity and would soon return to the land from which
my ancestors had arisen to undertake the leadership of the new
state. Japan would sign a treaty of mutual defence with this country
and its sovereignty and territorial integrity would be protected by
Japan with all the might at her disposal. As head of this state I
would be able to take charge of everything.

His sincere tone, his respectful smile, his reputation and his position all prevented me from taking the same attitude to him as I had to Lo Chen-yu and Kaeisumi. Chen Pao-shen's fears that Kaeisumi did not represent the Kwantung Army and that the Kwantung Army did not represent the Japanese government now seemed unfounded. Doihara was an important figure in the Kwantung Army and he had stated unambiguously that "His Majesty the Emperor (of Japan) trusts the Kwantung Army".

There was still one big problem that worried me. I asked what form the new state would take.

"As I have already said, it will be independent and autonomous, and it will be entirely under Your Majesty's control."

"That is not what I asked. I want to know whether it will be a republic or a monarchy."

"This problem will be solved after you come to Shenyang."

"No," I insisted. "I will only go if there is to be a restoration."

He smiled slightly and without changing the tone of his voice replied: "Of course it will be a monarchy; there's no question of that."

"Very well. If it is to be a monarchy I will go."

"In that case I must ask Your Majesty to leave as soon as possible, and to be in Manchuria by the sixteenth without fail. We can discuss the details in Shenyang. Yoshida can arrange your journey."

He wished me a safe voyage and bowed to me as politely as before. Our interview was over. After he had gone I met Chin Liang, who had come with him. He brought me news from some of the Ching veterans in the Northeast and said that they could obtain the submission of the former Northeastern army. I now felt that there were no more obstacles in my way.

After Doihara's departure the army interpreter Yoshida told me that I should not tell the consulate-general about the interview and that he would arrange my journey to Talien. I decided that I would discuss the matter with nobody but Cheng Hsiao-hsu, but as the news of my interview with Doihara was in the press the next day I had to answer advice and criticism from many quarters. Chen Pao-shen was horrified about it, as were several others of my close advisers.

Three days or so after Doihara's visit I agreed to see an emissary from the Chiang Kai-shek government in Nanking, which was offering to revive the Articles of Favourable Treatment and pay me either a yearly grant or else a single lump sum provided that I lived anywhere except in Japan or the Northeast. But I remembered the desecration of the Eastern Mausolea by Kuomintang troops and distrusted Chiang, suspecting that he was only interested in getting me away from the Japanese to save his face, and that once he had me in his power I would be helpless. Besides, what was the imperial title he was offering me worth compared with the imperial throne that Doihara had promised, and how could a sum of money be a greater attraction than the whole Northeast? I gave the emissary a noncommittal answer, and by the time he came to see me again I had left Tientsin.

In addition to the many visitors who tried to see me in those crowded days I also had a heavy mail. In some letters the writers offered me advice and warnings. There was one from a member of my own Aisin-Gioro clan who begged me not to "acknowledge a bandit as my father" and advised me to value my reputation in Chinese eyes. But I was too far carried away by my dream of restoration to heed any warnings. Naturally, I did not make my true feelings public. In an interview with a Tientsin journalist I vigorously denied that I had any intention of going to the Northeast; but by the time this was printed in his paper I was already on the boat.

There was another incident that took place two days before my departure from Tientsin that I should mention. A personal assistant called Chi Chi-chung came running into the room shouting, "Bombs, two bombs".

I was sitting in an armchair, and this news gave me such a fright that I was incapable of standing up. In the ensuing confusion I found out a stranger had delivered a present with the card of a former adviser to the pacification headquarters of the Northeast. The stranger had deposited the parcel and disappeared. When it was inspected two bombs were found inside a basket of fruit.

Before the excitement had died down Japanese police and army officers arrived and took the bombs away. The next day the interpreter Yoshida told me that investigation had proved that the two bombs had been produced in the arsenal of Chang Hsueh-liang. "Your Majesty must receive no more strangers, and the sooner you leave the better."

"Very well. Please make the arrangements as quickly as possible."

"Yes, sire. I hope that Your Majesty will not talk about this to anybody who is not directly concerned."

"I won't. I'll only take Cheng Hsiao-hsu and his son and a couple of assistants."

In those two days I received a number of threatening letters and a phone call that was taken by my personal assistant Chi Chi-chung. According to Chi, the call had come from a waiter in the Victoria Café who warned me that I should not go and eat there for the time being as some "suspicious people" had been making inquiries about me. This considerate waiter had apparently gone on to say that these suspicious characters looked as if they had weapons concealed in their clothing. More surprisingly still, he had been able to see that they had been sent by Chang Hsueh-liang.

I do not know who that waiter was, if he ever existed, but the servant Chi Chi-chung, who was also the man who reported the delivery of the bombs, had accompanied me to Tientsin from Peking as a trusted page. He was a favourite of mine, one of the three personal assistants who accompanied me to the Northeast, and he undoubtedly helped Cheng Hsiao-hsu and the Japanese to get remarkably accurate information about my actions and moods. I sent him to a military academy in Japan, and he became a major-general in the puppet army of North China before being suppressed after liberation for counter-revolutionary activities.

After the bombs, the threatening letters and the telephone call came the "Tientsin Incident". This was one of Doihara's masterpieces. The Japanese arranged for a crowd of Chinese agents of theirs to make trouble in the Chinese-administered part of the city. A state of emergency was then announced in the Japanese concession and communications with the Chinese city cut. Armoured cars drove up to "protect" the Quiet Garden, which was now isolated from the outside. The only people allowed in and out were Cheng Hsiao-hsu and his son Cheng Chui.

As I look back now I think that the reason why Doihara was in such a hurry to get me to the Northeast may have been because the young officers in the Kwantung Army were impatient to force the hands of a rival faction.

If it was simply because he was frightened that I would change my mind, he overestimated the influence that the people around me had on me. I had decided to go, and even some of my advisers who were supporters of Chen Pao-shen were starting to advocate active co-operation with Japan, though they still did not have much trust in the Japanese army and thought that it would be better to deal with the government. All the same, they did not want to miss this chance any more than I did; but they were worried that serving Japan might bring only dishonour without any compensating rewards. The condition on which they suggested I should collaborate with Japan was that I should have the right of making appointments. They were concerned that they might not be able to become high officials, and were fully prepared to trade the honour and the economic interests of the nation in exchange for positions for themselves.

The Secret Crossing of the Pai River

I was to leave for the Northeast on November 10, 1931. According to the plan I was to slip out of the main gate of the Quiet Garden that evening without anyone noticing. This gave me a lot of worry. My first idea was not to go out of the main gate but to tell my driver at the last moment to leave by the garage gate. When I sent my most trusted personal assistant, Big Li, to go and see whether the garage door could be opened he reported that it had not been used for so long that the outside was pasted over with advertisements. The method I finally used was one suggested by Chi Chi-chung. I hid in the luggage compartment of a convertible while one of my servants acted as a driver with Chi Chi-chung sitting beside him, and thus we left the Quiet Garden.

Not far from the main gate the interpreter Yoshida was waiting for us in a car, and when he saw our car come out of the gate he followed us at a discreet distance.

This was the third day of the Tientsin disturbances and there was a state of martial law in the Japanese concession and the neighbouring Chinese-administered district. Whether the disturbances and the martial law were deliberately arranged or simply a coincidence I cannot say for sure, but they created most suitable circumstances for my flight. When my convertible was stopped by Japanese troops at a roadblock, past which no other Chinese vehicles were allowed to go, a wave of the hand from the interpreter was enough to let us through. Although my substitute driver was terrible (the first thing he did after coming out of the Quiet Garden was to hit a telegraph post and make me bump my head badly) we managed to reach our destination, a Japanese restaurant.

After the car stopped Chi Chi-chung sent the driver away and the interpreter opened the compartment in the back of the vehicle, helped me out, and went into the restaurant with me. Here another Japanese officer was waiting and he produced a Japanese army greatcoat and cap which he put on me. He then accompanied me and the interpreter in a Japanese military car which drove straight to a dock on the bank of the Pai River without obstruction. They helped me out of the car, and when I saw that we were no longer in the Japanese concession I was alarmed. The interpreter Yoshida told me in a low voice that it did not matter as we were in the British concession.

I hurried along the concrete wharf supported on both sides by the two officers until a tiny and unlit motor launch appeared before us. In the cabin I saw Cheng Hsiao-hsu and his son Cheng Chui and was relieved to see that they were there as had been arranged. There were also three other Japanese, of whom one was the Kaeisu-mi I had met at the garrison headquarters and another was a *ronin* called Kudo Tetsusaburo who had previously worked for the Mongol noble Sheng Yun. The captain of the vessel told me that there were ten soldiers on board to protect it. The boat belonged to the transport section of the garrison, and it had been specially fitted with sandbags and armour plating for this "transport" mission. About twenty years later I read some reminiscences by Kudo in the Japanese magazine *Bungei Shunju* in which he recalled that there was a large drum of petrol hidden in the boat, and that if we had been discovered by Chinese troops and been unable to escape, the Japanese soldiers would have set light to it and destroyed the boat and us along with it. While I sat only a few feet from this petrol drum I thought that I was getting closer and closer to "happiness".

The interpreter and the other officer who had brought me to the dock went ashore and the boat left the wharf. I gazed at the shore as our lights came on and was overcome with emotion as I gazed at the river. I had been to the Pai River before in daytime and had even begun to dream about it as my future route to the other side of the ocean and to restoration. Now that I was actually sailing down it I was overcome with emotion and searched for words with which to express my excitement.

My happiness was a little premature, as I discovered when Cheng Chui told me that once we were outside the foreign concessions we would be within the power of the Chinese and might encounter Chinese troops there.

My heart jumped into my mouth. The faces of everyone I could see were set and nobody spoke. After two hours of total silence there suddenly came a shout from the riverbank: "Halt!"

I lay on the floor paralysed as if all my nerves had been cut. The Japanese soldiers in the cabin went up on deck, and from the deck I heard orders given in low voices and footsteps.

I saw through the window that there were soldiers behind each of the sandbags ready to fire. The boat seemed to be slowing down and heading for the bank. The lights went out and there was a sound of rifle-fire from the shore. Almost at once the motor roared into life and the boat leapt forward and away from the bank. The shots and shouting on the shore sounded fainter and fainter. The

Japanese plan had succeeded. First they had gone towards the bank as if they were obeying instructions and then they had bounded away, taking the soldiers on the bank by surprise.

A moment later our lights came on again and the atmosphere in the cabin became lively. In the middle of the night we reached the mouth of the river at Taku, and while we waited for the merchant-man *Awaji Maru* to meet us outside the river the Japanese troops produced *miso* soup, pickled cabbage and Japanese *sake*. Cheng Hsiao-hsu grew very lively and started talking about the racial and cultural links between China and Japan, reciting impromptu poems and describing the episode as a part of a "heroic enterprise".

Cheng Hsiao-hsu had another reason that he did not mention for being happy that evening. He had realized before any other of my advisers that underneath the friction between the Japanese government and army there lay unity. He wrote in his diary on the day after I was visited by Doihara that his son Cheng Chui had been told by the Japanese consul-general that the purpose of Doihara's visit was to invite me to go to Shenyang and that the consulate would pretend to know nothing about it.

Isolated

Aboard the *Awaji Maru* Cheng Hsiao-hsu talked all day about his ambition to govern the country, and on the morning of the 13th we put in at the South Manchuria Railway dock at Yingkow in Liaoning Province.

I never thought about why it was necessary to land at Yingkow in order to go to Shenyang, as all that I had wondered about was how the people of the Northeast would greet me at the harbour. I had imagined that there would be a crowd to give me the sort of welcome I had received when I went to the Japanese primary school in Tientsin — people waving flags and cheering. But the nearer the boat drew to the dock the less sign there was of such a welcome.

There were no crowds, no flags. When I went ashore I found out that the handful of people there to meet me were all Japanese.

When I was introduced to them I learnt that they had all been sent by Colonel Itagaki and that they were led by one Amakasu Masahiko. This fellow had not got much of a name in China but was notorious in Japan. At the time of the great earthquake of 1923 he had killed the progressive Osugi Sakae, his wife and nephew on behalf of the army which wished to take advantage of the confusion caused by the disaster to put pressure on the Left. Public opinion forced the army to make him a scapegoat and sentence him to life imprisonment through a court martial, but he was soon released and sent to study in France. The subjects Amakasu chose were art and music, and a few years later he returned to Japan and was posted to work in an undercover organization of the Kwantung Army. According to a book published in Japan after the Second World War the explosion on the railway line at Liutiaokou that was the signal for the "September 18th Incident" of 1931 was Amakasu's work. But when I met him on the Yingkow wharf I never would have dreamed that this polite bespectacled man had such an unusual past, or that without his handiwork I might never have gone to the Northeast.

Amakasu showed Cheng Hsiao-hsu, Cheng Chui and myself into a waiting carriage and took us to the station. After about an hour in a train we changed into another carriage. Without having been given a word of explanation on the journey I arrived at the warm springs sanatorium district of Tangkangtzu, and full of suspicion I entered the Tuitsuike Hotel.

This hotel was run by the Japanese South Manchuria Railway Company and was a luxuriously furnished Western building in the Japanese manner. It was reserved for Japanese army officers, high officials of the South Manchuria Railway and Chinese bureaucrats. I was taken to a grand drawing room on the first floor where Lo Chen-yu, Shang Yen-ying and Tung Chi-hsu were waiting. After greeting me Lo Chen-yu told me that he was in the middle of discussing my restoration and the founding of the new state with the Kwantung Army and explained that it would not do for the news of my arrival to leak out before the conclusion of the discussions;

it would also be wrong if any of us but him were to be seen outside. I did not understand the real significance of this and simply thought that I had now found out why nobody had come to welcome me. I thought that the talks with the Kwantung Army would present no problem and that soon the secrecy would be over and it would be announced that I, the Great Ching Emperor, had returned to the throne in the palace of my ancestors in Shenyang. The thought made me so excited that I paid no attention to the worried expressions of Cheng Hsiao-hsu and Cheng Chui. I happily ate an exotic Japanese supper and gazed out of the window at the beautiful sunset then went to bed, at peace with the world.

The next morning I discovered that my joy had been too early. After washing I called for my assistant Chi Chi-chung and said that I wanted to go out for a stroll to look at the scenery.

"It's not possible. They won't let anyone out," said Chi Chi-chung with a worried expression on his face.

"Why not?" I asked in surprise. "Who said so? Go downstairs and ask."

"They won't even let us downstairs."

I found out that I was isolated in the Tuitsuike Hotel: that strangers were forbidden to come near the hotel and that the people staying downstairs could not come up to the first floor, which was only being used by my little party. What most perplexed me was why we were not allowed downstairs. I sent for Lo Chen-yu but nobody knew where he had gone. Cheng Hsiao-hsu and his son were both furious and wanted me to demand an explanation from the Japanese. The senior of the Japanese who were staying with us were Kaeisumi and Amakasu, and when Chi Chi-chung brought the former to see me his face was covered with smiles.

"This is a safety precaution, a safety precaution for Your Majesty," he said in Chinese with a Japanese accent.

"How long are we going to stay here?" asked Cheng Hsiao-hsu.

"That depends on Colonel Itagaki."

"What about Hsi Hsia and the others? Didn't Lo Chen-yu say that Hsi Hsia was going to take me to Fengtien?"

"That too depends on Colonel Itagaki."

"What about Lo Chen-yu?" asked Cheng Chui.

"He's gone to Fengtien to see Colonel Itagaki. They are still discussing the new state, and when they have reached agreement Lo will come to take His Majesty to Fengtien."

"This is terrible." Cheng Chui walked away with an angry gesture. I was taken aback by this breach of court etiquette, but what really caught my attention was Kaeisumi's remark that the nature of the "new state" was still under discussion. This was very odd. Had not Doihara and Hsi Hsia both said that there were no problems and that all that was necessary was for me to come and ascend the throne? What did Kaeisumi mean when he said that it was still under discussion? When I asked this question Kaeisumi's reply was vague:

"To carry out so great an undertaking is easier said than done. Be patient, Your Majesty. When the time is ripe you will be invited to go."

"To go where?" cut in Cheng Chui. "To Fengtien?"

"That will be decided by Colonel Itagaki."

I left them in a bad temper and called Tung Chi-hsu to come and see me in another room. I asked him why he had sent me a telegram from Shenyang saying "everything ready". Tung replied that he had been told to send it by Yuan Chin-kai and did not know anything about it. I asked Shang Yen-ying what he thought of the matter, but he was incapable of a sensible reply; he wished he had his planchette, and then he would have been able to seek an explanation from the gods.

I did not know at the time that the Japanese were in a state of desperate confusion. Japan was internationally isolated, and within the country there were still differences of opinion over what form their rule over this new colony should take, so that the Kwantung Army could not yet allow me to take the stage. My only reaction was that the Japanese were not being as respectful towards me as they had been in Tientsin and that Kaeisumi was behaving quite differently from the way he had when I had met him there. After a week of uneasy waiting I received a telephone call from Itagaki asking me to move to Lushun.

Why was I not going to Shenyang? Kaeisumi explained with a smile that this would be settled after I talked to Itagaki. Why go to Lushun? Kaeisumi answered that in Tangkangtzu I was in great danger from "bandits" and that I would be much better off in Lushun as it was a big city and far more convenient. This sounded reasonable to me and so I caught a train which arrived in Lushun the following morning.

In Lushun I stayed in the Japanese Yamato Hotel. Here, as before, the whole of the upper part of the building was reserved for the use of my little party. I was told that I was not to go downstairs, and the people downstairs were not allowed up. Kaeisumi and Amakasu also told me that talks about the new state were continuing and that there was no need for me to be impatient as someone would come and invite me to Shenyang in due course. After a few days here Cheng Hsiao-hsu and his son were given the same treatment as Lo Chen-yu and allowed out freely; they were even able to go to Talien. The gloomy expression disappeared from Cheng Hsiao-hsu's face and he started to talk in the same way as Lo Chen-yu: "It would injure Your Majesty's celestial dignity were you to show your face. If you wait until your ministers have arranged everything then Your Majesty can ascend the throne at the appropriate time and receive homage with decorum and propriety." He also said that I should not meet anybody as it would not be right to publicize my presence before everything was settled. The Kwantung Army were my hosts for the time being, and until I ascended the throne I should regard myself as their guest. Meanwhile it was only right that I should do as my hosts thought fit. So although I was still feeling impatient I had no choice but to force myself to wait.

But these people who were always addressing me as "Your Majesty" and serving me with such apparent diligence thought of me not as a real monarch but as a king in a pack of cards. The Japanese, who were under pressure from the Western powers and domestic opinion, had me up their sleeves, and they wanted to keep me secret until the time came to play me. Cheng, Lo and the others also each wanted to have me to himself in order to beat their opponents and be the only one to get rewards from the Japanese. This was why I was isolated. When I was in Tangkangtzu Lo Chen-yu took advantage of restrictions imposed by the Japanese to prevent me from making any contacts, cutting Cheng Hsiao-hsu and myself off from the Kwantung Army. Once we reached Lushun Cheng Hsiao-hsu was able to establish his own links with the Japanese in competition with Lo. Then the two of them combined to keep out any third rival while they fought for favour with the Japanese.

I did not understand all this at the time. All I could see was that Lo and the two Chengs were hand in glove with the Japanese and isolating me from everyone else. They were not worried by Tung Chi-hsu or by Shang Yen-ying, who only knew how to consult the oracles and beg for help from the gods, but they took the strictest measures against people who came from Tientsin to see me and were even rude to my wife Wan Jung.

Before my departure from Tientsin I had left an edict with a servant to be given to Hu Sze-yuan. In it I had told him to follow me to the Northeast and had instructed Chen Tseng-shou (Chen Pao-shen's nephew) to bring Wan Jung. When they heard that I was in Lushun they went to nearby Talien. Lo Chen-yu told them that the Kwantung Army had given orders that they were not to be allowed to go to Lushun. Wan Jung was suspicious of this order and thought that something must have happened to me, so she started to weep and shout. In this way she managed to get permission to come to Lushun to see me just once. After about a month the Kwantung Army moved me to the house of the son of the former Prince Su, and only then were Wan Jung and my second and third sisters allowed to live in the same place as me.

I had wanted Chen Tseng-shou and Hu Sze-yuan to move in with me, but Cheng Hsiao-hsu told me that the Kwantung Army had laid it down that nobody was to see me except himself, his son, Lo Chen-yu and Wan Sheng-shih. I asked him to try and arrange something with Amakasu and Kaeisumi; the only result was that Hu Sze-yuan was allowed to see me once, on condition that he returned to Talien the same day.

As soon as he saw me Hu Sze-yuan started to cry and say that he would never have thought that after so many years in my service he would be prevented even from seeing me. Although this frightened me, I tried to console him by telling him that when I was free to do so I would send an edict calling him and Chen Tseng-shou to my side. Hu stopped crying and told me in detail how Cheng Hsiao-hsu and Lo Chen-yu were making difficulties for them and accusing them of nourishing private ambitions and trying to squeeze out "good and loyal people".

Hu and his friends never succeeded in defeating Lo Chen-yu and Cheng Hsiao-hsu. Chen Pao-shen came to Lushun when I had been there for about two months, but Cheng Hsiao-hsu, who had all but defeated Lo Chen-yu in the battle for the favour of the Kwantung Army and did not want another rival on the scene, managed to get Chen Pao-shen sent away after only two days.

During my first few weeks in the Northeast Lo Chen-yu and Cheng Hsiao-hsu fought out their last battle. Lo Chen-yu held the initiative at first, but was foolish enough to insist on a Ching restoration in his negotiations with the Japanese although it would have been politically embarrassing for them. When Cheng Hsiao-hsu and I moved to Lushun Lo found to his surprise that the Kwantung Army had invited Cheng to join the talks. He did not know about Cheng's links with the Japanese military in Tokyo or with Kaeisumi in Tientsin. Just as he had previously taken over Lo Chen-yu's connections with Colonel Takemoto in the year I left the Forbidden City, Cheng had now made Lo's Kaeisumi into his own friend. Amakasu realized after a few conversations with Cheng Hsiao-hsu and his son Cheng Chui that they were far more "flexible" than Lo Chen-yu, who craved for all the ritual and ceremony of the old Ching empire. Although Cheng Hsiao-hsu was shocked when he first heard that the Kwantung Army wanted me to be "President of the Republic of Manchuria and Mongolia" he soon adapted himself to the idea that the Japanese did not want an emperor and made it clear that provided he was premier of the new regime he would persuade me to agree to become head of state.

After the foundation of "Manchukuo" Lo Chen-yu was not satisfied with the post he was offered and went back to his antique business, while Cheng Hsiao-hsu became puppet premier.

Disappointment

I felt very frightened while I was in Lushun. The reason for this was not my isolation but being told by Kaeisumi and other Japanese that the Kwantung Army had not yet settled the form of the new state. This was even more vexing than having nobody to greet me at the harbour had been; then I had believed that "preparations were incomplete" or my arrival had "not yet been announced". But what did they mean when they said that the form of the state had not been settled? Why had Doihara asked me to come to the Northeast if it had not been decided?

Cheng Hsiao-hsu and Kaeisumi told me that Doihara had not been lying and that it was quite true that the Kwantung Army supported my restoration. But as this was a Manchurian affair it had to be discussed with the Manchurians, and naturally the matter was "undecided" until the consultations were over.

On February 19, 1932 came the news that the "Administrative Committee for the Northeast" had passed a resolution to set up a republic in the Northeast. This committee was composed of a number of high officials who had submitted to the Japanese and was chaired by Chang Ching-hui. This body also issued a "declaration of independence" on the same day. Everyone in my entourage except Cheng Hsiao-hsu and his son was terrified and indignant.

I was seething with hatred of Doihara and Itagaki as I paced up and down like a madman, breaking cigarettes in half. I threw a book of divination that I had been using to the floor. I remembered my Quiet Garden and thought that if I could not be a real emperor I would be much better off leading a comfortable life as an exile. I could sell some of my treasures and have a good time abroad. I decided to let the Kwantung Army know that if they would not agree to my demands I was going back to Tientsin. Neither Lo Chen-yu nor Cheng Hsiao-hsu opposed this idea when I told them about it. I agreed to a suggestion of Lo's that I should send a present to Itagaki, and I gave Lo some of the valuables I had brought with me to take to him. Just then Itagaki telephoned asking Lo and Cheng to go for talks with him. I asked Chen Tseng-shou to write out for me the reasons why the "right system" (the restoration of the Ching monarchy) was necessary and gave the document to Cheng and Lo to hand to Itagaki, instructing them to stand firm and make my views clear to him.

There were twelve reasons, of which the last four were added by Chen Tseng-shou:

1. The right system is essential if we are to follow the moral code of East Asia that dates back five millennia.

2. The right system is essential to the carrying out of the Kingly Way[1] and moral principles.

3. To rule the state one must have the trust and respect of the people, and for this the right system is essential.

4. China and Japan are fraternal countries, and for their joint survival and welfare they must respect the time-honoured morality and ensure that both peoples have an identical spirit. For this the right system is essential.

5. China has suffered from the disasters of democracy for over two decades, and, apart from a selfish minority, the great majority of the people loathe the Republic and long for the Ching Dynasty. For this reason the right system is essential.

6. The Manchu and Mongol peoples have always preserved their ancient customs, and the right system is essential if we are to win their allegiance.

7. The Republican system is very widespread while the numbers of the unemployed daily increase. This constitutes a

---

[1] A political philosophy of the Confucianists of ancient China. They wanted the feudal rulers to rule the country with "benevolence" and "righteousness", and they called this the "Kingly Way".

most serious threat to the Japanese Empire, but if the imperial order is revived in China this will do a great deal to preserve the intellectual and spiritual qualities of the peoples of our two countries. For this reason the right system is essential.

8. The Great Ching has a history of over two hundred years in China and of over a century in Manchuria before that. To observe the way of life of the people, calm their minds, maintain the peace of all parts of the country, preserve the oriental spirit, carry out the revival of Kingly government and consolidate the imperial order in our two countries, it is essential to have the right system.

9. The rise of Japan dates from the Kingly rule of Emperor Meiji. His edicts to his ministers all propagate morality and give instruction in loyalty and righteousness. While science was learnt from Europe and America, morality was based on Confucius and Mencius. As the ancient spirit of the Orient was preserved and the people were saved from the contagion of disgusting European practices, they love and esteem their elders, and protect their country as readily as one's hand protects one's head. That is why I respect him. The right system is essential if we are to follow in the steps of the great Emperor Meiji.

10. The Mongol princes continue to use their old titles, and if they are abolished under a republic they will be disappointed and disaffected, and there will be no way of ruling them. For this reason the right system is essential.

11. Japan deserves our deepest admiration for the way in which she has assisted the Three Eastern Provinces (the Northeast) and taken thought for the welfare of their thirty million people. My wish is that we should not restrict ourselves to thirty million people but should take the Three Eastern Provinces as a base from which to arouse the whole nation and save the people from the disasters that have befallen them. This would lead to the common survival and prosperity of East Asia, a matter which closely involves all of the ninety

million people of Japan. There should therefore be no divergence between the political systems of our two countries. To bring about the prosperity of both countries the right system is indispensable.

12. Since I retired from office in 1911, I have lived among the people for twenty years. I have had no thought for my personal glory and have been guided only by a wish to save the people. If someone else would undertake the responsibility for the country and bring disasters to an end with the True Way, I would be happy to remain a commoner. If I am forced to assume this burden, it is my personal opinion that without the correct title and real power to appoint officials and administer the country, I will be unable to bring twenty years of misgovernment to an end. If I am ruler only in name and am hedged in by restrictions I will be of no help to the people and will only make their plight worse. This would not be my original intention, and would increase my guilt, and I absolutely refuse to bear the responsibility for this. If I were only concerned about my personal glory, I would be only too pleased to be given the land and the people after two decades of living in obscurity. What would I care whether I become president or monarch? It is purely for the sake of the people, of the state, of our two countries of China and Japan, and of East Asia as a whole, and not because of the slightest self-interest, that I maintain that the right system is indispensable.

But although Cheng Hsiao-hsu agreed to present my demands for a restoration of the Ching Dynasty to Itagaki he never did so. Instead he agreed to the Japanese proposal that the new state be a republic, and he undertook to persuade me to become its "chief executive". I was told much later that he said to Itagaki, "His Majesty is like a blank sheet of paper on which your army can paint whatever it likes." While I did not know at the time that he had said this, I was furious with him and the others for having allowed themselves to be tricked by the Japanese. Cheng Hsiao-hsu tried to pacify me by citing historical precedents and telling me that my hopes of restoration would be finished if I did not go along with the Japanese now. When this did not work he said that as Itagaki wanted to see me that afternoon I could talk to him then.

"Let him come," I angrily replied.

Meeting Itagaki

I met Itagaki Seishiro[1] on the afternoon of February 23, 1932, in the presence of an interpreter from the Kwantung Army. Itagaki was a short man with a shaven head and the pallor of his clean-shaven face was in contrast to the blackness of his eyebrows and his small moustache. He was the most neatly-dressed Japanese officer I had ever seen: his shirt cuffs were of dazzling whiteness and the creases in his trousers razor-sharp. This elegance and his habit of gently rubbing his hands made one feel that he was cultured and debonair.

First he thanked me for the presents I had sent him and then he went on to say that he had come on the orders of General Honjo, the commander of the Kwantung Army, to report to me on the "foundation of the new state of Manchukuo". Starting with "the failure of the tyrannical government of the Chang family to gain the people's allegiance and the total absence of guarantees for Japan's interests in the Northeast" he went on to elaborate slowly and at length on the "justice" of the actions of the Japanese army and its "sincerity in helping the Manchurian people to establish a paradise of the Kingly Way". As he spoke I nodded in approval and hoped that he would hurry up and answer the question in which I was really interested. At last he came to the point:

---

[1] Itagaki Seishiro had been on the staff of the Kwantung Army since 1929 and was one of the chief plotters behind the September 18th Incident and the consequent setting up of a Japanese puppet state in the Northeast. He later played a leading and disreputable role in other events, such as the Japanese invasion of the rest of China, the setting up of other Chinese puppet regimes, and the attack on the Soviet Union at the Khasan Lake.

"The new state will be called Manchukuo ('Manchuland'). Its capital will be Changchun, which will be renamed Hsinking ('New Capital'), and it will be composed of five races: Manchus, Hans, Mongols, Japanese and Koreans. In view of their efforts in Manchuria over many decades the legal and political position of the Japanese will naturally be the same as that of the other nationalities: they will, for example, have the same right as the others to hold office in the new state."

Without waiting for the interpreter to finish translating he produced the "Declaration of Independence of the Manchu and Mongol People" and the five-coloured "Manchukuo flag" from his briefcase and put them on the table in front of us. I was almost bursting with indignation. Pushing these objects aside with a trembling hand I asked:

"What sort of state is this? It certainly isn't the Great Ching Empire!"

"Of course, this will not be a restoration of the Great Ching Empire," answered Itagaki, unflustered as always. "This will be a new state. The Administrative Committee for the Northeast has passed a unanimous resolution acclaiming Your Excellency head of state. You will be the 'Chief Executive'."

"Your Excellency" sent the blood rushing up to my face. Never before had I been thus addressed by the Japanese, and I was not prepared to tolerate the abolition of my imperial title, not even in exchange for the two million square *li* and thirty million people of the Northeast. I was so worked up I could scarcely sit still.

"If names are not right then speech will not be in order, and if speech is not in order then nothing will be accomplished. The people of Manchuria are longing not for me as an individual but for the Great Ching Emperor. If you abolish the title their loyalty will be lost. I must ask the Kwantung Army to reconsider this."

Itagaki gently rubbed his hands and said, his face wreathed in smiles:

"The Manchurian people have expressed their wishes by acclaiming Your Excellency as the head of the new state, and the Kwantung Army is in full agreement with them."

"Japan has an imperial system, so how can the Kwantung Army agree to the founding of a republic?"

"If Your Excellency does not like the word 'republic', then we will not use it. This will be a state built on the chief executive system."

"I am very grateful for all the enthusiastic help your country has given, but I cannot accept a 'chief executive system'. The imperial title has been handed down to me by my ancestors, and were I to abandon it I would be lacking in loyalty and filial piety."

Itagaki seemed to be most understanding. "The office of chief executive will only be temporary. It is perfectly well known that Your Majesty is the twelfth emperor of the Great Ching Dynasty, and I am sure that after the formation of a national assembly a constitution will be adopted restoring the imperial system."

The words "national assembly" enraged me once more, and shaking my head for emphasis I said, "There are no good national assemblies, and the first Great Ching Emperor was never given his title by any assembly."

The argument continued for over three hours without our reaching agreement. Finally Itagaki, who had smiled throughout the discussion, picked up his case as a sign that he did not want to go on any longer. The smile vanished from his face, which was now paler than ever, and when he addressed me he reverted from "Your Majesty" to "Your Excellency": "Your Excellency should think it over carefully. We will continue our discussions tomorrow." With that frosty remark he left me.

That evening I gave a banquet for Itagaki as Cheng Hsiao-hsu had warned me that it would be dangerous to get on bad terms with the Japanese, reminding me of the fate of Chang Tso-lin. The occasion passed off smoothly, and the subject of the day's talks was carefully avoided.

The next morning Itagaki summoned Cheng Hsiao-hsu, Lo Chen-yu and other advisers of mine to the Yamato Hotel and asked them to give me his final decision:

"The demands of the Army cannot be altered in the least. We will regard their rejection as evidence of a hostile attitude and act accordingly. This is our last word."

This reply stunned me. My legs turned to jelly and I collapsed speechless into an armchair.

While Lo Chen-yu and the others were silent Cheng Chui urged me to accept the Japanese proposals. His father backed him up, speaking in an excited voice:

"The Japanese always do what they say they will, and we must not walk straight into trouble. Besides, they are well-disposed towards you and will allow Your Majesty to be head of state, which is the same as being emperor. Is today's opportunity not the reason why I have been serving Your Majesty all these years? If Your Majesty insists on refusing, I am afraid that I must pack my belongings and return home." This threat made me feel desperate.

"If Your Majesty agrees to the Japanese army's demands," added Cheng Chui, "you will be able to strengthen your position in the future and we will be able to do things the way we want to."

"Although one may regret the present situation there is nothing we can do about it," was Lo Chen-yu's dejected view. "Our only course is to set a time limit of one year, and if the imperial system is not restored by then Your Majesty can resign. Let us see how Itagaki reacts to that." Seeing no other way out I sighed and sent Cheng Hsiao-hsu to see if Itagaki would agree.

Cheng soon returned, his face beaming, to say that Itagaki had agreed and was going to give "a little banquet for the future Chief Executive" that evening.

Thus it was that both trembling with fear and dreaming of my future restoration I shamelessly became a leading traitor, and the cover for a sanguinary regime which turned a large part of my country into a colony and inflicted great sufferings on thirty million of my compatriots. I also laid the foundations for the rise of Honjo, Itagaki and the rest of them; as Cheng Hsiao-hsu observed in his diary, all of their careers would have been finished had I refused to co-operate.

The Pedigree of the Ching House

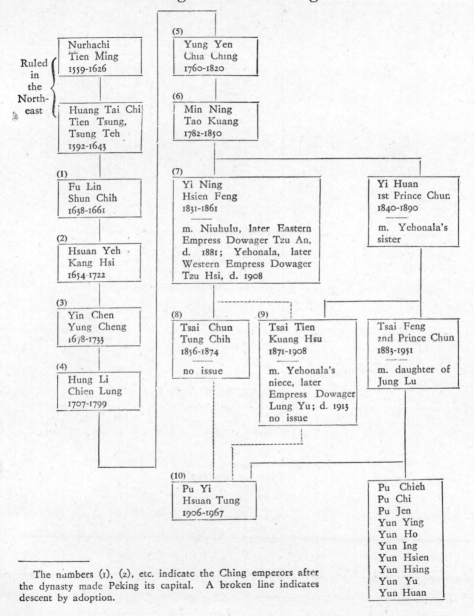

Ruled in the Northeast:
- Nurhachi Tien Ming 1559-1626
- Huang Tai Chi Tien Tsung, Tsung Teh 1592-1643

(1) Fu Lin Shun Chih 1638-1661
(2) Hsuan Yeh Kang Hsi 1654-1722
(3) Yin Chen Yung Cheng 1678-1733
(4) Hung Li Chien Lung 1707-1799

(5) Yung Yen Chia Ching 1760-1820
(6) Min Ning Tao Kuang 1782-1850

(7) Yi Ning Hsien Feng 1831-1861
m. Niuhulu, later Eastern Empress Dowager Tzu An, d. 1881; Yehonala, later Western Empress Dowager Tzu Hsi, d. 1908

Yi Huan 1st Prince Chun 1840-1890
m. Yehonala's sister

(8) Tsai Chun Tung Chih 1856-1874
no issue

(9) Tsai Tien Kuang Hsu 1871-1908
m. Yehonala's niece, later Empress Dowager Lung Yu; d. 1913 no issue

Tsai Feng 2nd Prince Chun 1883-1951
m. daughter of Jung Lu

(10) Pu Yi Hsuan Tung 1906-1967

Pu Chieh
Pu Chi
Pu Jen
Yun Ying
Yun Ho
Yun Ing
Yun Hsien
Yun Hsing
Yun Yu
Yun Huan

The numbers (1), (2), etc. indicate the Ching emperors after the dynasty made Peking its capital. A broken line indicates descent by adoption.

从皇帝到公民

——我的前半生——

上册

爱新觉罗·溥仪著

詹纳尔译

★

外文出版社出版

（中国北京百万庄路24号）

外文印刷厂印刷

中国国际书店发行

（北京399信箱）

1964年（大32开）第一版

1983年第二版第二次印刷

编号：（英）11050—31

00280

11—E—619DA